BOYS ADRIFT

BOYS ADRIFT

The Five Factors Driving the Growing Epidemic of
Unmotivated Boys and Underachieving Young Men

LEONARD SAX, M.D., Ph.D.

BASIC
BOOKS

A Member of the Perseus Books Group
New York

Basic Books are available at special discounts for bulk purchases in the United
States by corporations, institutions, and other organizations. For more
information, please contact the Special Markets Department at the Perseus
Books Group, 2300 Chestnut Street, Suite 200, Philadelphia, PA 19103, or call
(800) 255-1514, or e-mail special.markets@perseusbooks.com.

Designed by Timm Bryson

Library of Congress Cataloging-in-Publication Data
Sax, Leonard.
   Boys adrift : five factors driving the growing epidemic of unmotivated boys
   and underachieving young men / Leonard Sax.
      p. cm.
   Includes bibliographical references.
   ISBN-13: 978-0-465-07209-5
   ISBN-10: 0-465-07209-7
   1. Boys—Education. 2. Young men—Education. 3. Motivation in education.
   4. Sex differences in education. I. Title.
LC1390.S29 2007
371.823—dc22

                                                                    2007012761

10 9 8 7 6 5 4 3 2 1

For my daughter,
Sarah Emma

CONTENTS

A WORD OF CAUTION

In this book, I discuss psychiatric conditions such as Attention Deficit Hyperactivity Disorder (ADHD), as well as some of the medications used to treat such conditions. The discussion here is intended to provide general guidance and background information. Nothing stated here should be taken as a guide to specific treatment of any individual. In particular, you should never change a medication or discontinue any medication without consulting your physician.

LEONARD SAX, M.D., PH.D.

BOYS ADRIFT

1

THE RIDDLE

I didn't know what to say.

I'd just finished speaking to a parents' group in Calgary, Alberta, in March 2004. The talk—about the subtleties of difference between how girls and boys learn, how they play, and how they are motivated—had gone well. I began doing these talks for parents' groups, and for schools, in 2001. By March 2004 I was pretty comfortable with the format.

The presentation is the easy part. The questions afterward are more difficult.

"Dr. Sax, my son Billy[1] is very bright," one father said. "We've had him tested, twice, and both times his overall IQ has been in the 130 range. But he just has no motivation to learn."

"What do you mean?" I asked.

"I mean that he doesn't do his homework and he won't study for tests. He doesn't seem to care whether he gets an A or a C or an F."

"How old is he?" I asked.

"Sixth grade."

"Umm. What does he like to do in his spare time?" I asked.

"Actually Billy loves to read. Science fiction mostly. He just refuses to read the books the school assigns. I don't know why he seems to hate school so much. It's a good school."

"Which school does he attend?" I asked.

Dad named a local private school that I knew to be very prestigious. Class sizes at that school are small. The teachers are well trained and highly regarded. Tuition is more than twenty thousand dollars a year.

Stall for time. "Have you spoken with anyone at the school?" I asked.

He nodded. "The school counselor thinks Billy might have ADD, but I just don't buy that. How could he have ADD? He's read Isaac Asimov's entire *Foundation* trilogy twice. He can quote whole passages from *The Lord of the Rings,* he's even memorized some of the poems in Elvish. That just doesn't sound to me like a boy who has ADD. Billy loves to read. He just doesn't like school."

I paused. I wanted to say that I couldn't give any specific advice without meeting Billy myself and doing my own evaluation, an evaluation that would take a minimum of two hours. That was the truth—but I knew it would sound like a cop-out, since I was flying out early the next morning to return to my home in the suburbs of Washington, DC. There would be no time to meet with Billy on this trip.

While I hesitated, a woman spoke up: "My son's in a similar predicament, but he's younger. Second grade. Outside of school my Jason is as sweet as an angel. But he's been sent to the principal's office several times now for hitting other kids. He says he was just playing. He's never actually hurt anybody, but the teachers say they have to refer any child who hits another child. Referral to a specialist is mandatory after three episodes. So now they're saying that I have to have Jason evaluated."

I wanted to point out that Jason's predicament wasn't in any way similar to Billy's situation. Billy hasn't been hitting anybody, but he seems to lack the motivation to succeed at school. Jason's problems seem to be not motivational but behavioral. But I knew better than to say that.

I just didn't know what to say. So I turned the tables. I asked the parents a question of my own: "How many of you are in a similar situation: You have a son who's having school problems of some kind, but it's not clear why?"

About half the parents raised their hands.

"I'd like to hear from you, then. What do you think is going on? Do you have any thoughts as to why your son is having a problem?"

"School has become too academic," one father said immediately. "Kindergarten isn't kindergarten anymore. My son, and my daughter last year, came home with homework their first week of kindergarten. Can you imagine assigning homework to kids in kindergarten? Five-year-old kids with an hour of homework to do. It's absurd. No wonder kids hate school."

Several parents nodded. But why would that affect boys more than girls, I wanted to ask. Another father said, "The schools have become feminized. The only adult male at my son's elementary school is the janitor. The teachers all want the students to sit still and be quiet. For some boys, that's not easy."

"It's not the teachers who are to blame," a woman said softly but firmly. "It's the kids. I'm sorry, I don't mean to give offense, but kids today are lazy. The boys especially. They'd rather just sit at home and play video games. They wouldn't go to school at all if it were up to them. I know a boy across the street who doesn't do anything except play with his PlayStation. He doesn't do homework, he doesn't help around the house, he doesn't play sports. It's just video games, video games, video games."

More nods.

"When I was their age, we had to walk to school, three miles each way, no matter the weather," an older man said. "We didn't have any of these school buses you see nowadays. We had to walk. Even in the snow. And I'll tell you one thing. When you've walked three miles in the snow to get to school, you make darn sure you learn something. You don't want that long walk to be for nothing. I think it motivates you. Nowadays the kids get chauffeured everywhere. No wonder they don't have any motivation. They don't have to work for anything."

No one made any reply. After a moment, a young woman said, "I read somewhere that plastic might have something to do with it."

"How do you mean?" I asked.

"Something about plastic. It's like hormones in beef. It messes up children's brains. That's why so many boys are having problems."

That sounds a little far-fetched, I wanted to say. But I've learned that it's best to humor the people with the wackiest ideas—while still expressing courteous skepticism, so that the sane people won't think you've completely lost your marbles. "But why would plastic affect boys differently from girls?" I asked politely. "Aren't girls and boys equally exposed?"

"I don't know. It just does," the woman said.

The pace of my speaking engagements, both for parents and for teachers, picked up substantially after the publication in 2005 of my book *Why Gender Matters: What Parents and Teachers Need to Know About the Emerging Science of Sex Differences.* I've now spoken at more than 230 venues around the United States, Canada, Australia, and Mexico. The scene described above has been repeated dozens of times. I've engaged in ongoing correspondence with parents and teachers who are struggling to encourage boys to work up to their potential. And of course I've seen many such boys in my own medical practice in Maryland.

I've heard any number of explanations for why so many boys are having trouble connecting with school. Some parents blame the school. In some cases, Mom believes it's because the boy's father walked out when her son was little, so he's never had a strong male role model. Others blame video games or "society" or plastics or Hollywood. One parent even blamed Hillary Clinton, and several have blamed George W. Bush.

"What's the connection between President Bush and your son's problems in school?" I asked that parent.

"Our country is spending so much money on that stupid war, when we ought to be spending money on the schools," she replied.

But how would spending more money on public schools help your son, I wondered. Your son attends a private school.

But I didn't ask that question. I wasn't interested in having an argument. I was interested in finding some answers.

I'm a family physician. I've lived and worked in the same suburb of Washington, DC, for the past seventeen years. We have more than seven thousand patients in our practice. I've seen hundreds of families where the girls are the smart, driven ones, while their brothers are laid-back and unmotivated. The opposite pattern—with the boy being the intense, successful child while his sister is relaxed and unconcerned about her future—is rare.

It's not just my suburb, either. As you and I review what's known about this problem, we will see that the problem of boys disengaging from school and from the American dream is widespread. It affects every variety of community: urban, suburban, and rural; white, black, Asian, and Hispanic; affluent, middle-income, and low-income.

The end result of this spreading malaise is becoming increasingly familiar. Emily (or Maria or Shaniqua) goes to college, she earns her degree, she gets a job. She has a life. Justin (or Carlos or Damian) may go to college for a year, or two, or six, and he may or may not get a degree, but he doesn't get very far. He may have a great time at college, in part because there are now three girls at college for every two boys. At some large universities, there are now two young women for every young man. But the young women at college are more likely to be studying while the young men are goofing off.[2] That boy just doesn't seem to have the drive that his sister has. He ends up working part-time at the mall or at Starbucks. Eventually he's back home living with his parents, or with his girlfriend's parents or another relative.

But here's what's really strange, and new, about this picture: That young man isn't bothered by his situation. His parents are. His girlfriend, if she hasn't left him yet, is at least having second thoughts about him. But he's oblivious to their concerns as he surfs the Net on the computer they've provided, or plays video games on the flat-screen television they bought for him.

But haven't boys always been that way?

During the question-and-answer section of another one of my talks focusing specifically on boys, one father objected: "Dr. Sax, I'm not hearing anything new here. Haven't boys always regarded school as a boring waste of time? Wasn't that pretty much Tom Sawyer's attitude? What's changed?"

He's got a point. There's a long tradition of iconic American boys who disdain school, from Tom Sawyer to Ferris Bueller. But while those boys weren't heavily invested in school, they were still highly motivated to succeed—on their own terms, pursuing their own schemes. Tom Sawyer is determined to outwit Injun Joe, to go exploring with Huck

6

Finn, and to win the affection of Becky Thatcher. Ferris Bueller disdains school because he has other more important and engaging missions to accomplish in the real world—which for him is any world outside of school.

What's troubling about so many of the boys I see in my practice, or the boys I hear about from parents and teachers, is that they don't have much passion for any real-world activity. Some of the boys are seriously engaged in video games, but as we'll see in chapter 3, most of the video games these boys play seldom connect with the real world—unless you want to shoot people or fly combat aircraft. The boys I'm most concerned about don't disdain school because they have other real-world activities they care about more. They disdain school because they disdain everything. Nothing really excites them.

Even more disturbing is the fact that so many of these boys seem to regard their laid-back, couldn't-care-less attitude as being somehow quintessentially male. "You need to care about what grade you get. It's important," one mother told her son.

"Girls care about getting good grades. Geeks care about grades. Normal guys do not care about grades," her fourteen-year-old son informed her in a matter-of-fact tone, the same tone he might use to show her how to program the TiVo. That's just the way it is—for that boy. For many boys, not caring about anything has become the mark of true guy-dom. This attitude is something new, as we'll see in more substantive detail beginning in the next chapter.

The hostility I'm seeing toward school among so many boys—no longer confined to black and Latino boys in low-income neighborhoods, but now including white and Asian boys in affluent suburbs—is also new. If you're my age, or older, you can remember forty years ago when the Beach Boys had a major hit with their song "Be True to Your School": "Be true to your school . . . just like you would to your girl." That song describes a boy who is proud to wear a sweater emblazoned with the school's initials, a boy who insists that allegiance to one's school should be on a par with the enthusiasm a boy has for his girlfriend. There is no trace of irony in the song. If you're my age or older, you remember Sam Cooke singing "Don't know much about history . . . but maybe by being an A-student, baby / I could win your love for me" in his song "Wonderful World." It's hard to imagine any popular male vocalist singing such a line today, except as a joke. Can you imagine Akon or 50 Cent or Snoop Dogg or even Taylor Hicks singing, without irony and in all seriousness, about wanting to earn an A at school to impress a girl? I can't.

These changes may be insignificant by themselves, but I believe they are symptomatic of something deeper. As we'll see in the next chapter, a growing proportion of boys are disengaging from school. More and more of them will tell you that school is a bore, a waste of time, a tedium they endure each day until the final bell rings. As far as the boy is concerned, his real life—the life he cares about—only begins each day when the final bell rings, allowing him finally to leave school and do something he really cares about. "What he really cares about" may be playing video games, hanging out with his friends, or doing drugs and alcohol. It may be anything at all—except for school or anything connected with school.

"But you need to care about your schoolwork, or you won't get into a good college," his mom says.

"I hate school," her son answers. "It's like prison. I'm just doing my time till they let me out. Then I'm done. Why would I want to sign up for four more years?"

A smaller and smaller proportion of boys are going on to college. Right now, the student body at the average university in the United States is 58 percent female, 42 percent male (with similar numbers in Canada and Australia).[3] And going to college doesn't guarantee any positive result, particularly for boys. In fact, college is where the gender gap in motivation really shows up. Most girls who enroll in a four-year college will eventually earn a degree. Most boys won't.[4]

Over the past fifty years, college campuses have undergone a sex change: they've changed from majority male to majority female. Here are the numbers for the male proportion of students enrolled in four-year colleges and universities in the United States, 1949–2006:

1949: 70 percent of undergraduate students were male
1959: 64 percent were male
1969: 59 percent were male

1979: 49 percent were male
1989: 46 percent were male
1999: 44 percent were male
2006: 42 percent were male[5]

Colleges and universities now are scrambling to recruit qualified males. One mother told me that when it was time for her son to apply to college, she had some worries that turned out to be misplaced. Her recollection of her own college experiences thirty years ago led her to be concerned that admission offices would discriminate against her son, because, after all, he is a white male. "Instead," she said in her e-mail to me, "I found that males today are on the receiving end of a kind of affirmative action for any boys who test well. This gets them into college, but doesn't teach them how to cope with the bigger choices they will eventually have to face."

Male students attending four-year colleges and universities today are now significantly less likely than their female peers to earn high honors or to graduate. Just thirty years ago, the opposite was true: in that era, young men were more likely than young women to graduate.[6] Today, Justin is significantly less likely than his sister Emily to go to college, less likely to do well at college, and less likely to graduate from college. This is not an issue of race or class. We're talking about brothers and sisters from the same family. They have the same parents, the same resources.

Certainly, not all boys have been infected by this weird new virus of apathy. Some are still as driven and intense as their sisters. They still want the same independence, financial and otherwise, for which we expect young people to strive. Because we still see some of these successful young men around us, it's easy to miss the reality that more young men than ever before are falling by the wayside on the road to the American dream. The end result, then, are frantic parents wondering why their son can't, or won't, get a life. He's adrift, floating wherever the currents in the sea of his life may carry him—which may be no place at all.

Why does one young man succeed, while another young man from the same neighborhood—or even the same household—drifts along, unconcerned?

Where is he headed?

Is there anything you can do about it?

Those will be the central questions that you and I will explore together.

For the past seven years, I've spent every available moment studying these questions. In 2001, I wrote an academic paper on this topic for a journal published by the American Psychological Association.[7] In 2005, as I mentioned, I published my first book, *Why Gender Matters.* That book was in part a progress report on my research on this question, although I also addressed some of the ways in which American society has become toxic to girls.

In addition to being a board-certified family physician, I have the advantage of being a PhD psychologist with a background in scholarly research. So I've been able to investigate what I'm seeing, quantitatively and systematically. I've talked with parents and with their sons in large cities like New York, Chicago, Toronto, and Los Angeles, as well as in smaller cities like Daytona Beach and San Antonio and Cleveland and Calgary and Memphis. I've visited schools in affluent suburbs like Chappaqua, New York and Shaker Heights, Ohio and Potomac, Maryland and in the "nicest" areas of San Francisco and Tampa, as well as the "bad" areas of North Philadelphia and Dallas and Columbus (Ohio); and also in diverse rural communities. After seven years, I think I'm finally getting a handle on what's going on. I've identified five factors that are driving this phenomenon. I'm also finally in a position to share some tested strategies to decrease the likelihood that your son will succumb to this epidemic of apathy—as well as practical tips for helping your son find his way back if he's already disengaged.

More Than Just School

This book begins with a careful evaluation of how the theory and practice of education have changed over the past forty years, and how those changes have disengaged a growing proportion of boys from school.

That's the first factor, which I take up in chapter 2. But this book is about much more than boys disengaging from school. In chapter 5, for example, we will consider evidence that some characteristics of modern life—factors found literally in the food we eat and the water we drink— may have the net effect of emasculating boys. We will see that the average young man today has a sperm count less than half what his grandfather had at the same age.[8] Likewise, a young boy today has bones that are significantly more brittle than a boy of the same age thirty years ago. The explanations for the drop in sperm counts and for the decline in bone density are complex, as we will see. We will find that the parent who said something about "plastics" may not be so wacky, after all.

In chapter 3, we will explore in detail the controversy surrounding video games. We will hear from respected scholars who insist that video games are good and useful for children, both girls and boys. We will hear from other scholars who have found that video games disengage kids from the real world, scholars who believe that the harm video games do in terms of motivation and violent behavior far outweigh any cognitive benefit. You'll see that I tend to side with those researchers who give thumbs-down to video games, but I will make every effort to let you decide for yourself who's right.

In chapter 4, I talk at length about the growing tendency to prescribe medications such as Adderall, Ritalin, Concerta, Metadate, Focalin, Dexedrine, and other stimulants to American children, particularly boys. We will explore research suggesting that these medications may have adverse consequences that your doctor may not know about—adverse consequences not for cognitive function, but for motivation. The most serious cost of taking these medications may be a loss of drive.

In chapter 6, we will begin to calculate the consequences of these four factors—not only in terms of academic achievement, but also in parameters that are harder to quantify: parameters such as pursuing a real-world goal or sustaining a romantic relationship. Chapter 7 introduces a fifth factor specific to the culture of North America in the twenty-first century—and contrasts modern North American culture with the culture of other continents and other times. In the closing chapter, chapter 8, I try to pull all five factors together and consider specific strategies that parents, educators, counselors, and others involved in the lives of boys and young men might usefully deploy. I will also recommend some relevant strategies at various points throughout each chapter.

Please don't misunderstand me. When I talk about the problems I'm seeing in the boys whom I encounter in my practice, I'm not saying that girls don't have problems. Girls have problems too. I know just as many parents who are concerned about their daughters as I know parents who are concerned about their sons. But the problems are different.

- "I told my eleven-year-old daughter that under no circumstances would her father and I allow her to buy those low-rise jeans. I just couldn't believe that any store would even have such an item on sale for girls her age. But she said we were totally clueless. When her father and I held our ground, she started shouting 'You're ruining my life! Why do you hate me?!' How are we supposed to handle that?"[9]
- "My Samantha has never had any problems making friends. But something happened at the start of eighth grade. She says that her best friend—or the girl she thought was her best friend—totally betrayed her and started saying things about her that aren't true. Cruel things. And now she's the odd girl out. I hear her crying at night into her pillow and it breaks my heart, it really does. But I don't know what to do. She doesn't want me to interfere."
- "Caitlyn is always talking about how she wants to be a size two or a size zero. She looks beautiful just the way she is: five feet four, 120 pounds, size four or size six depending on the label. Everybody says what a pretty girl she is. Still she's always talking about how fat she is and how she needs to lose weight. I'm worried she's at risk for an eating disorder."

These are serious problems, every bit as difficult and as consequential as the boys' issues I will address throughout the book. But the problems the girls face are different from the boys'. The girls' problems are no less important. Just different.

This book is about the boys—and the five factors driving their growing apathy and lack of motivation.

2

THE FIRST FACTOR
Changes at School

Your son is five years old. He's smart. He's friendly. But at your first confer-ence with his kindergarten teacher, the teacher tells you that your son is fidgety and has trouble sitting still. "He's not doing as well as he could be. And it's very distracting to the other children," she says. She suggests that you may want to have him tested for ADHD.* "There was a boy in my class just like your son, last year," she says reassuringly. "He was bright, just like your son, but he had trouble doing what was expected of him. We all knew he could do better. He was such a smart boy. Just like your son. The pedia-trician suggested Adderall. I'll tell you something, going on Adderall made a world of difference for that boy. It was like night and day. He became a really excellent student."

"But I don't think my son needs to be on medication," you say. "And—he's only five years old."

"Well, we could just put him in the play group," the teacher says. "Those are the kids who aren't ready to learn to read and write. Every child is dif-ferent, we understand that. In the play group, he could run around, jump up and down, play with blocks, without distracting the other children."

"The play group?" you say. "But I thought the play group was for slow learners. My son is not a slow learner."

---

*ADHD = attention-deficit hyperactivity disorder.

"I agree," the teacher says. "That's why I think you should have him tested."

Two decades ago, a pastor named Robert Fulghum published a slim book of essays entitled *All I Really Need to Know I Learned in Kindergarten.* Pastor Fulghum's book stayed on the *New York Times* best-seller list for nearly two years, selling over fifteen million copies. The title essay emphasized the key lesson he himself had learned in kindergarten, namely, to "live a balanced life," by which he meant that every day one should

> Learn some and think some and draw and paint and sing and dance and play and work every day some.

Sounds nice.

Pastor Fulghum was drawing on recollections of his own kindergarten experience in 1942–43 along with the kindergarten experiences of his four children in the 1960s and early 1970s. But even while the pastor's book was selling millions, celebrating the kindergarten he and his children had known, kindergarten was changing. Pastor Fulghum had written about how children in kindergarten actually could ". . . draw and paint and sing and dance and play. . . . " But that's no longer true. Today, most kids don't "draw and paint and sing and dance and play" in kindergarten. They learn to read and write. As the superintendent of my own school district wrote six years ago, the twenty-first-century kindergarten needs to be "rigorous" and "academic."[1] Traditional kindergarten activities such as finger painting and duck-duck-goose have been largely eliminated, replaced by a relentless focus on learning to read and write. "Kindergarten" isn't kindergarten anymore, as that parent in Calgary correctly observed in the opening of chapter 1. Kindergarten has become first grade. In 2007, the kindergarten curriculum at most North American schools, both public and private, looks very much like the first-grade curriculum of 1977. Nowadays it's all about learning to read and write.

Why Is That a Problem?

In 2006, a distinguished team of fifteen neuroscientists, based primarily at the National Institute of Mental Health (NIMH) in Bethesda, Maryland, published a remarkable account of the development of the human brain. Since the early 1990s, these investigators have been doing MRI scans on the brains of young children. These scientists are watching the brain develop. The same children return to the laboratory every year or two to be scanned. This remarkable study is the only major ongoing project to document how the brain develops in a particular child over a period of many years.[2]

The team's 2006 report was their most definitive account yet: detailed information on the brain development of roughly two thousand children and young people, four through twenty-two years of age. Some of the participants have been in the study for as long as twelve years. Among the most striking findings in the report are the differences in the developmental trajectories of girls compared with boys. The researchers found that the various regions of the brain develop in a different sequence and tempo in girls compared with boys. In some regions of the brain, such as the parietal gray matter—the region of the brain most involved with integrating information from different sensory modalities—girls and boys develop along similar trajectories, but the pace of the girls' development is roughly two years ahead of the boys'. In other regions, such as temporal gray matter—the region of the brain most involved with spatial perception and object recognition—girls and boys develop along similar trajectories, but the pace of the boys' development is slightly faster than the girls'. In yet other regions, such as occipital gray matter—visual cortex—the trajectories of brain development are remarkably different, with no overlap between girls and boys. In this region of the brain, girls between six and ten years of age show rapid development, while boys in the same age group do not. After fourteen years of age, this area begins to diminish slightly in girls—the amount of brain tissue in this region actually shrinks in girls over fourteen—while in boys over fourteen this area is growing at a rapid pace.[3]

It's important to remember that brain maturation is often associated with a pruning, or reduction, in the size of brain regions. The fact that one region of the brain is shrinking in teenage girls while the same region is growing in teenage boys doesn't mean that boys are smarter than girls, or that girls are smarter than boys. It just means that girls and boys are different. Differences do not imply an order of rank. Oranges and apples are different, but that doesn't mean oranges are better than apples. Ovaries and testicles are different, but that doesn't mean that ovaries are better than testicles.

The findings of the group at NIMH were not completely unexpected. Previous studies had already shown that the various regions of the brain develop in a different sequence and tempo in girls compared with boys. Indeed, studies using functional rather than anatomical parameters have suggested that sex differences in the pace of brain development may be even greater than those suggested by the NIMH study.[4]

It now appears that the language areas of the brain in many five-year-old boys look like the language areas of the brain of the average three-and-a-half-year-old girl.[5] Have you ever tried to teach a three-and-a-half-year-old girl to read? It's frustrating, both for the teacher and for the girl. It's simply not developmentally appropriate, to use the jargon of early childhood educators. You're asking her to do something that her brain is just not yet ready to do.

Trying to teach five-year-old boys to learn to read and write may be just as inappropriate as it would be to try to teach three-year-old girls to read and write. Timing is everything, in education as in many other fields. It's not enough to teach well. You have to teach well to kids who are ready to learn, kids who are developmentally "ripe" for learning. Asking five-year-old boys to learn to read—when they'd rather be running around or playing games—may be the worst possible introduction to school, at least for some boys. Here's why.

Imagine visiting a twenty-first-century kindergarten—which is to say, a kindergarten where children are expected to do what first-graders were expected to do thirty years ago, a kindergarten where children are expected to sit for hours doing paper-and-pencil exercises. In the typical kindergarten you will often find that the teacher has divided the children into two groups. Over here, with the teacher, are the kids who are ready to learn to read and write: mostly girls, one or two boys. Over there, on the other side of the room, are the other kids: the kids whom the teacher has (correctly) recognized are not ready to learn to read and write. That group is mostly boys, with one or two girls.

There's one thing five-year-old girls and boys are equally good at: figuring out who's in Dumb Group. By November, the kids in Dumb Group are aware of their inferior status, and they don't like it.

"I hate school," Brett tells Mom.

"Why, honey?" Mom asks.

"I just hate it. It's stupid."

After further questioning and coaxing, Mom finally extracts what sounds like the real explanation. "That teacher doesn't like me. That teacher hates me," Brett tells Mom.

Mom gets on the job. She's going to figure out whether the teacher really doesn't like Brett, and if so, why. She gets permission to visit the kindergarten. But after two visits, she can't find a shred of evidence to support Brett's accusation. The teacher is friendly and encouraging to all the students. In fact she seems genuinely fond of Brett. "Brett isn't ready to sit still for hours at a stretch, so we don't ask him to," the teacher explains to Mom. "The reading drills can be awfully dull for some of the kids. We understand that. So we let Brett play in the play corner with the other boys."

The teacher's intentions are good. But most five-year-olds are keenly aware of their status in the eyes of the adults. A boy whom the teacher has relegated to Dumb Group may conclude that the teacher doesn't like him. After all, the teacher spends most of her time with the kids who are in the accelerated reading curriculum. Because the teacher doesn't spend much time with Brett, Brett has decided she doesn't like him. That's unfair and illogical, but Brett is not a grown-up. He's a five-year-old child. And most five-year-old children, whether girls or boys, are likely to conclude that if the teacher is spending most of her time with the kids in Smart Group, then the teacher must like the kids in Smart Group better.

Professor Deborah Stipek, dean of the school of education at Stanford University, has found that kids form opinions about school early. Imagine asking a boy who has just finished kindergarten two questions: "Do you like school? Do you think the teacher likes you?" I asked Brett those questions. He answered: "I don't like school. I hate school. And that teacher hates me."

Once that young boy has decided that the teacher doesn't like him, Stipek and others have found, he's likely to generalize that belief to other teachers and other classrooms.[6] He is likely to go to school next year with a negative attitude. When he's put in Dumb Group again (which is almost inevitable, because the kids in Smart Group now have a year's head start on him), he may decide that school just isn't for him. "School is dumb," he may say. And he means it. Return four years later and ask him the same questions. Brett is now nine years old. Ask him: "Do you like school? Do you think the teacher likes you?" The answers you get will be the same: "I hate school. And all the teachers hate me. Except for Mr. Kitzmiller, the gym teacher."

Critics of American education often point out, quite accurately, that the United States spends more money per pupil than most other developed countries and yet accomplishes less. On the international test most widely administered around the world, the United States ranks at #25, well below countries whose per-pupil spending on education is much lower, such as Hungary (#23), Poland (#21), the Czech Republic (#15) and Finland (#1).[7] Finland, incidentally, consistently scores at or near the very top of all of these international rankings. What's the most distinctive characteristic of public education in Finland? Very simple: Children in Finland don't begin any formal school until they are seven years old.[8]

Nevertheless, by the time they're teenagers, Finnish children are beating American children by large margins on the same test. In the latest round of testing, for example, the average fifteen-year-old in Finland scored 545 in reading; fifteen-year-old American students taking the same examination scored 490. In problem solving, the average Finnish teenager scored 547, while the average American teenager scored a dismal 480.[9]

How could starting kids in school two years later lead to superior performance when those children become teenagers? Simple. If kids start school two years later and are taught material when they are developmentally prepared to learn, kids are less likely to hate school. If kids don't hate school, it's easier to get them to learn. If kids do hate school, as many American boys do, then the teacher is starting out with a major handicap before even stepping into the classroom.

Waiting until seven years of age to begin the formal, "rigorous," reading and writing curriculum of today's kindergarten might reduce or ameliorate a significant fraction of the problems we see with boys and school. For many boys, there's a huge difference in readiness to learn between age five and age seven—just as there's a huge difference in readiness for a girl between three and five.

Hold Him Back So He'll Get Ahead

Many parents have figured out that the accelerated pace of today's kindergarten is not a good match for their five-year-old son. Particularly in affluent neighborhoods, it's become common for parents to enroll their son in kindergarten one year later than the district would normally enroll that child; it's not unusual to find that half the boys, or more, are enrolled in kindergarten at age six rather than at age five. In low-income neighborhoods—where many working parents simply can't afford to keep their children home another year—typically fewer than 3 percent of boys will be held back.[10] One reason that boys from low-income neighborhoods are doing so much worse in school than boys from more affluent neighborhoods, beginning in early elementary education, may be that the boys from more affluent neighborhoods are starting school at a later age, on average, than the boys from the poor neighborhoods.

Addressing the issue of holding boys back, Dana Haddad, director of admissions for an exclusive private elementary school in Manhattan, says, "It's become a huge epidemic." All the parents at Ms. Haddad's school are waiting a year to start their boys in kindergarten; some are even holding their girls back, just to be on the safe side. "The gift of a year, that's what I always say to my parents," says Betsy Newell, director of another prestigious private elementary school in Manhattan. "The gift of a year is the best gift you can give a child."[11]

I published a paper six years ago suggesting that simply starting boys in kindergarten one year later than girls might prevent many boys from deciding, very early, that school isn't for them.[12] Doing something earlier doesn't necessarily mean that you will do it any better. In fact, it may mean that you do it less well in the long run.

The pace of education has accelerated, but boys' brains don't grow any faster now than they did thirty years ago. That's one part of the first factor leading boys to disengage from school. But schools have changed in other ways as well. To understand how these other changes might affect boys differently from girls, you need to understand how girls' motivation to succeed in school so often differs from that of boys.

What Are Little Girls Made Of?

The first question we will try to answer is why the acceleration of the early elementary curriculum might affect boys differently from the way it affects most girls. As we've seen, Reason #1 is: different regions of the brain develop in a different sequence and tempo in girls compared with boys. As a result, most five-year-old girls are better able to adapt to the rigorous academic character of kindergarten than five-year-old boys are. Even for those girls, I don't think that the accelerated curriculum of today's kindergarten is best—I believe it leads ultimately to a narrowing of girls' educational horizons—but it is less likely to alienate them from school altogether. Many five-year-old girls are able to do what the kindergarten teacher wants them to do. They can sit still. They can be quiet for a few whole minutes without interrupting or jumping up and down. They are more likely to possess the fine motor skills required to write the letters of the alphabet legibly and neatly.

Reason #2 has to do directly with the question of motivation, the huge blind spot of contemporary educational psychology—about which I'll have more to say in just a moment. Girls and boys differ in terms of their desire to please the teacher. Most girls are at least somewhat motivated to please the teacher. Many boys don't share that motivation.

Before we consider the research on this gender difference, let me share with you a story that a middle school teacher told me. It was the first day of school. She was greeting her homeroom students for the first time. "Good morning, everybody. My name is Ms. Jackson," she said. "I'd like to welcome all of you to eighth grade. I'll be your homeroom teacher." She turned to write some information on the whiteboard at the front of the room.

One of the boys, Jonathan, took the small stack of textbooks from his desk and dumped them on the linoleum floor, making a loud noise. Some of the boys giggled.

Ms. Jackson turned, startled. She saw the books scattered on the floor next to Jonathan's desk.

"Aw geez, I'm sorry, Ms. Jackson," Jonathan said, slowly and insolently. "I had no idea whatsoever that those books would make such a racket."

Three boys at the back of the room laughed. Ms. Jackson wasn't sure what to say. But Emily, the girl sitting next to Jonathan, was not amused.

"Jonathan, you are such a dweeb," Emily said. "Can't you at least wait a day or two to show us what a total loser you are?"

When I heard this story, it brought to mind a recent study of chimpanzees living in the jungles of Tanzania. Three anthropologists—Elizabeth Lonsdorf, Lynn Eberly, and Anne Pusey—spent four years watching chimpanzees in their natural habitat in the wild. These chimpanzees have their own particular way of doing things. For example, they like to "fish" for termites. Adult chimps break a branch off a tree, cut the branch to the desired length, strip the leaves off the branch, stick the branch down into a termite mound, wait a minute or two, and then carefully pull the stick back out for a yummy snack of fresh termites.

Lonsdorf, Eberly, and Pusey found consistent sex differences in how young female and young male chimps learn from their elders. Girl chimps pay close attention to the adult (usually a parent) who is showing them the procedure. Girl chimps then do just what the adult showed them: she breaks off a branch, cuts it to the same length as the adult had done, strips the leaves as the adult had done, and so forth. But the young males ignore the grown-ups; they prefer to run off and wrestle with other young male chimps, or to swing from trees.[13]

Are gender differences primarily hardwired—by which I mean that gender differences derive primarily from genetically programmed differences between girls and boys—or are they learned primarily from social cues? I still encounter people who insist that most of the sex differences we observe between girls and boys are not hardwired. Instead, they insist that girls and boys behave differently because our society expects them to. We expect boys to be noisy and to throw things, while we expect girls to behave like little ladies. Or so the story goes.

One reason I think it's important to study our close primate relatives such as chimpanzees, gorillas, bonobos, and orangutans is because it gives us a more complete context in which to consider such questions. If sex differences were primarily socially constructed—if girls typically behave better than boys do because girls are taught to play with Barbies while boys are encouraged to play with guns—then we wouldn't expect to see dramatic sex differences in the behavior of juvenile female chimpanzees compared with juvenile male chimpanzees. But we do. Juvenile female chimps and juvenile male chimps learn and play in dramatically different ways, despite the fact that the girl chimps have never played with a Barbie, and the boy chimps have never played with toy guns.

As a human male, I share many genes with a male chimpanzee that I do not share with any human female.[14] Recent work comparing the human genome with the chimpanzee genome suggests that I share 99.4 percent of my genes with a male chimpanzee—slightly more than I share with a human female.[15] That does not mean that I am in general more like a male chimpanzee than I am like a female human. But in certain specific ways—for example, in the way I see, hear, and smell—I may actually have more in common with a male chimpanzee than I have with a human female.[16] And those areas of commonality are important to understand.

The entire order of primates is characterized by profound sex differences, and those sex differences are fairly well conserved across the order.[17] Young male monkeys, like young male gorillas and young male humans, are significantly more likely to engage in aggressive rough-and-tumble play than are young females from any of those species.[18] Likewise, young female primates are far more likely to babysit a younger sibling than a young male primate would be.* That's true in our species as well: girls are far more likely to babysit a younger sibling than their brothers are.

Girls are more likely to affiliate with the adults. They are more likely to share common aims and values with the grown-ups. Boys and young men, on the other hand, are less likely to be sympathetic to adult aims and values and are more inclined to engage in delinquent behaviors such as smashing mailboxes, street racing, mooning police officers, among others, than girls are. A boy who smashes mailboxes "just for the fun of it" will raise his status in the eyes of at least some other boys. A girl who smashes mailboxes just for the fun of it is unlikely to raise her status in the eyes of most of the other girls. Girls are more likely to listen to what the grown-ups are saying, and to do what the grown-ups ask, particularly if there are no boys around. (If boys are around, some girls become more likely to misbehave, perhaps because they perceive that disrespecting the adults will raise your status in the eyes of at least some of the boys.[19])

Girls are more likely to see the situation from the perspective of the grown-ups. In one study, investigators examined twenty cases where students were plotting a school shooting but the plan was detected and stopped before any violence occurred. In eighteen of those twenty incidents, girls—not boys—alerted school officials or other adults to the plot. All the potential shooters were boys. "Boys feel like snitches if they tell on a friend, [while] girls [can] more openly seek out adults with their concerns," said James McGee, author of the study. Boys' first allegiance is to other boys. Girls are more likely to see the situation from the parents' perspective.[20]

---

*Primatologists don't use the word *babysitting*; they prefer the term *alloparenting*. When Mom needs to forage, she leaves her baby with her daughter, never her son. Our primate cousins commonly engage in alloparenting, but it's always the daughter, not the son, who watches baby. See David Watts and Anne Pusey, "Behavior of juvenile and adolescent great apes," pp. 148–167 in Michael Pereira and Lynn Fairbanks, *Juvenile Primates: Life History, Development, and Behavior,* New York: Oxford University Press, 2002.

Some of these differences diminish as children grow up. Some don't. Women are more likely to take their medication the way the doctor prescribed; men are less likely to comply, and men are less likely to go to the doctor in the first place. Most girls and most women are comfortable asking for directions if they get lost; many boys, and many men, would rather wander for hours than stop and ask for directions.[21]

Why might it be the case that among most primates—including humans—juvenile females are more likely to affiliate with the grown-ups than the juvenile males are? Here's one possible explanation. Among primates generally, females are more likely to live near their parents after they are fully grown up, while the males are more likely to move away. In the great majority of primate species, "females reside in their natal groups for life, whereas males disperse around puberty and transfer to other groups," say primatologists Michael Pereira and Lynn Fairbanks.[22] There are some exceptions. Among the muriqui—also known as the woolly spider monkey—many young females leave the troop at puberty, while most of the young males stay with the troop into which they were born, for life. But the muriqui today are found only in a few isolated forest tracts along the Atlantic coast of southeastern Brazil. The latest estimate of the total number of living muriqui is less than five hundred, and the number is dwindling rapidly as coastal Brazil is deforested.[23]

If you expect to live near Mom for the rest of your life, you might make more of an effort to get along with her. Most girls seem to grow up with a desire to get along with the grown-ups—and that's true not just for human females, but also for females from most primate species. Primate females appear to have some built-in tendency to do what the grown-ups ask them to do, to try to please the grown-ups, to adapt to the grown-up culture. That's also true among humans, or so the evidence seems to show. Young girls are more likely than young boys are to pay attention to what the grown-ups say, to follow the rules, to care about what the grown-ups think. Likewise, researchers have found that little girls are significantly more likely than little boys to stay close to Mommy and to do what Mommy says.[24]

It's easy to see how these sex differences are relevant to education. Girls will do the homework because the teacher asked them to. Boys are more likely to do the homework only if it interests them. If it bores them, or if they think it's "stupid," they are more likely to ignore it. Researchers have consistently found that girls are significantly more likely than boys to do the assigned homework,[25] in every subject.[26] Even the highest-achieving boys are significantly less likely to do the homework than the comparably achieving girls.[27] Girls at every age get better grades in school than boys do, in every subject—not because girls are smarter, researchers have found, but because girls try harder.[28] Most girls would like to please the teacher, if possible. Most boys don't care much about pleasing the teacher or about getting straight A's—and boys who do try to please the teacher and who do care about their grades will lower their status in the eyes of the other boys.[29] Girls are more likely to assess their work as their teachers do. Boys are less likely to care what the teacher thinks of their work. That divergence leads to an enduring paradox: at every age, girls do better in school, but are less satisfied with their achievements, compared with the boys.[30] In 2006, researchers at the University of Pennsylvania reported that girls' greater self-discipline and self-control—perhaps deriving from their greater motivation to please the teacher—appears to be a key distinguishing factor that has enabled girls to survive and thrive in the accelerated world of twenty-first-century education.[31]

The acceleration of the early elementary curriculum, with its emphasis on phonics and reading drills, by itself might well have created a minor gender crisis in education. But unfortunately this acceleration is not the only major change in education over the past thirty years. Education has changed in two other substantial ways that have exacerbated gender differences.

The Tree of the Knowledge of Good and Evil

In English, the verb to know can have two very different meanings, reflecting two different kinds of knowledge. Consider these two sentences:

I know Sarah.
I know pediatrics.

We English speakers use the same word, *know*, in both sentences. As a result, English speakers may not fully appreciate just how different these two meanings are. My knowledge of my daughter Sarah is very different from my knowledge of pediatrics, even though Sarah is a little girl. My knowledge of Sarah is experiential knowledge. I know that Sarah likes to be rocked side-to-side but not front-to-back. I know that Sarah likes to be bounced on my knee like she's riding a horsie, but she generally doesn't like to be held close against the chest.

In biblical Hebrew, the word *know* refers primarily to experiential learning. When we read that "Cain knew his wife," it meant that he had "carnal knowledge" of her: they had sex. In English, we read about "the tree of the knowledge of good and evil," but the Hebrew might be better translated as "the tree of the *experience* of good and evil." Adam and Eve are forbidden to eat from that tree. They are forbidden the experience of evil.

Most European languages use two different words for these two kinds of knowledge. In French, *to know* in the sense of knowing a person is *connaître*; *to know* in the sense of knowing a subject in school is *savoir*. In Spanish, *to know* as in knowing a person is *conocer*; *to know* in the sense of book learning is *saber*. In German, knowledge about a person or a place that you've actually experienced is *Kenntnis*, from *kennen*, "to know by experience"; knowledge learned from books is *Wissenschaft*, from *wissen*, "to know about something."

ENGLISH	GERMAN	SPANISH
I know Sarah.	*Ich **kenne** Sarah.*	***Conozco** a Sara.*
I know chemistry.	*Ich **weiss** um Chimie.*	*Sé química.*

There is a fundamental belief running through all European pedagogy that both *Wissenschaft* and *Kenntnis* are valuable, and that the two ways of knowing must be balanced.

Seven years ago, I accompanied a class of Swiss third-graders on a field trip through the Dolder forest, high above Zürich. The teacher divided the children into pairs. One child in each pair blindfolded the other. Then the blindfolded child was led to a tree, at least ten paces away, and was instructed to feel the tree with her hands, from the ground up; and also to smell it. (Some children even licked it.) Next the child was spun around and led away from the tree, at least ten paces in a different direction. Then the blindfold was removed and the child was asked: Which tree were you just feeling? "*Ohne Augen zu sehen,*" the teacher told me: to see without your eyes.

Such an experience would be rare for American schoolchildren today. American students may occasionally go on field trips, but the trips are almost invariably didactic in tone. Pupils learn the difference, say, between an oak leaf and a maple leaf. It's all *Wissenschaft*. American education, today more than ever before, is characterized by a serious lack of understanding of, and respect for, *Kenntnis*. It's hard to overemphasize how much most Europeans value *Kenntnis*. When I smiled (perhaps somewhat patronizingly) at the children feeling and sniffing their trees, the teacher frowned at me. She insisted on blindfolding me herself and leading me to a tree, and having me touch it and smell it without being able to see it. Then she led me ten paces away from the tree, turned me around, removed the blindfold, and asked me: "Where is your tree?" I looked, and immediately recognized "my" tree from the dozens of others. It was an unfamiliar, exhilarating experience.

There is more than fifty years of research on the importance, for child development, of multisensory interaction with the real world. This work began with the investigations of the psychiatrist René Spitz into "hospitalism," the syndrome of stunted emotional and cognitive development that was seen in abandoned children raised in sterile and impersonal hospitals after World War II. This research demonstrated that children must have a rich, interactive sensory environment—touching, smelling, seeing, hearing the real world—in order for the child's brain and mind to develop properly.[32] Without such real-world experiences, the child's development will be impaired.

Kids need to experience the real world. Only in the past decade have developmental psychologists come to recognize that a curriculum that emphasizes *Wissenschaft* at the expense of *Kenntnis* may produce a syndrome analogous to the neglected child. Richard Louv, author of *Last Child in the Woods,* has coined the term "nature-deficit disorder" to refer to the constellation of symptoms seen in a child whose life has been spent indoors.[33] You can easily find high school students in America today who can tell you about the importance of the environment, the carbon cycle and the nitrogen cycle, and so on, but they've never spent a night outdoors. They have plenty of *Wissenschaft* but not a trace of *Kenntnis*.

For boys in particular, emphasizing *Wissenschaft* while ignoring *Kenntnis* may seriously impair development—not cognitive development but the development of a lively and passionate curiosity. "Nature is about smelling, hearing, tasting," Louv reminds us.[34] The end result of a childhood with more time spent in front of computer screens than outdoors is what Louv calls "cultural autism. The symptoms? Tunneled senses, and feelings of isolation and containment . . . [and] a wired, know-it-all state of mind. That which cannot be Googled does not count."[35]

Boys who have been deprived of time outdoors, interacting with the real world rather than with computers, sometimes have trouble grasping concepts that seem simple to us. Louv quotes Frank Wilson, professor of neurology at Stanford, who says that parents have been deceived about the value of computer-based experience for their children. Dr. Wilson says that medical school instructors are having more difficulty teaching medical students how the heart works as a pump,

> because these students have so little real-world experience. They've never siphoned anything, never fixed a car, never worked on a fuel pump, may not even have hooked up a garden hose. For a whole generation of kids, direct experiences in the backyard, in the tool shed, in the fields and woods, has been replaced by indirect learning, through [computers]. These young people are smart, they grew up with computers, they were supposed to be superior—but now we know that something's missing.[36]

Kenntnis and *Wissenschaft* are fundamentally different kinds of knowledge. Each is important. Imagine that my baby daughter, Sarah, is crying. Let's suppose further that a world-renowned expert on infant and child development, perhaps Dr. T. Berry Brazelton himself, has just walked into the room. If I hand Sarah to Dr. Brazelton, how effective will he be in calming her down? Probably not very effective. He doesn't know how Sarah likes to be rocked or bounced. All his knowledge about child development counts for nothing if he doesn't have some *Kenntnis* to go with his *Wissenschaft*. That principle generally holds true in the real world, I have found, at least as far as the practice of medicine and of psychology is concerned. Book learning is essential. But without *Kenntnis* you'll go far astray.

Louv provides a compendium of research demonstrating that when there is a profound imbalance in a child's early experiences—when nature has been replaced by computer screens and fancy indoor toys—the result is an increased risk for attention deficit disorder. For example, Louv cites a Swedish study in which researchers compared children in two different day-care facilities. One facility was surrounded by tall buildings, with a brick pathway. The other was set in an orchard surrounded by woods and was adjacent to an overgrown garden; at this facility, children were encouraged to play outdoors in all kinds of weather. The researchers found that "children in the 'green' day care had better motor coordination and more ability to concentrate."[37] Similarly, researchers at the University of Illinois have found that putting children in an outdoor environment, where they can actually put their hands in the dirt and feel and smell real stuff, as opposed to interacting with sophisticated computer simulations, is helpful in treating ADHD.[38] Ironically, the outdoor alternative is cheaper than the program with the fancy computers. Boys are at least three times as likely to be treated for ADHD compared with girls, and the rates of diagnosis of ADHD for both girls and boys have soared over the past two decades.[39] One wonders to what extent the shift from *Wissenschaft* to *Kenntnis* may have contributed to the explosion in the numbers of children being treated for ADHD.

The mental-health benefit of getting your hands dirty is not a particularly new insight. As Louv observes, Dr. Benjamin Rush, one of the men who signed the Declaration of Independence, declared more than two hundred years ago that "digging in the soil has a curative effect on the mentally ill."[40]

We have forgotten what our grandparents knew: All children need a balance of *Wissenschaft* and *Kenntnis,* a balance between sitting and standing, a balance between classroom work and field trips. That's true for girls as well as for boys. But if girls are deprived of that balance, if girls are saddled with a curriculum like ours today, all *Wissenschaft* and no *Kenntnis,* they will still do the homework—because for girls, as we discussed a moment ago, pleasing the teacher is a significant reward for its own sake. Not so for most boys. If boys are deprived of that balance between *Wissenschaft* and *Kenntnis,* they may simply disengage from school. If you ask a boy to read about the life cycle of a tadpole metamorphosing into a frog, but that boy has never touched a frog, never had the experience of jumping around in a stream in his bare feet chasing after a tadpole, he may not see the point. The shift in the curriculum away from *Kenntnis* toward *Wissenschaft* has had the unintended consequence of diminishing the motivation of boys to study what they're asked to learn.

How could such a change happen? How could the intelligent, well-educated people who write school curricula push the school format into such an unhealthy imbalance?

The answer is simple: computers

How Is a Child Different from a Programmable Computer?

Imagine a really good robot, the best robot money could buy, with the best possible "brain" and "eyes" and "ears." How would a human being differ from that robot?

Or to put the question another way: Will we someday—someday soon, perhaps—have robots that are able to simulate humans—simulate human behavior, maybe even feel emotions?

The entertainment industry offers us a continual diet of movies like *I, Robot* and *Bicentennial Man,* and TV shows like *Star Trek: The Next Generation* that portray robots (always played by human actors) that are indistinguishable from humans.

It's just a matter of time before reality catches up with science fiction, right?

Maybe not. Like the search for peace in the Middle East, or for a self-sustaining fusion reactor, the goal that we were once assured was nearly within grasp keeps receding further into the distance. Today, the idea of a fully mechanical device that can actually experience human emotions—and not merely simulate such an experience—seems more distant than it did thirty years ago.

I enrolled in the PhD program in psychology at the University of Pennsylvania in 1980. The period from the late 1970s through the late 1990s was the era when cognitive psychology ruled supreme. Cognitive psychology is that branch of psychology that focuses on how we process information.[41] And the University of Pennsylvania was a haven for true believers in cognitive psychology. For those two decades, roughly 1977 through 1997, cognitive psychologists were optimistic that their approach was the best way to understand human learning, development, and behavior.

Throughout that period, cognitive psychologists insisted that everything we do, everything we are, can be represented formally as a computational process and therefore could theoretically be transposed to any computational device, i.e., to a computer. Humans are just complex computers—or so the story went. The mind itself is a sort of computer program running on a very sophisticated computer made of neurons instead of microchips.

This way of thinking about the human mind, and human learning, continues to be influential among educators. If humans are sophisticated computers, and learning is in some way equivalent to programming that computer, then teachers are in some sense merely computer programmers. If we give teachers the correct set of instructions, or programs, then all we should need to do is flip the "on" switch and children should learn, infallibly and efficiently. The 1980s and 1990s saw the widespread adoption of programs such as Direct Instruction, in which teachers were expected essentially to read from a script for an entire class, with students answering questions in unison and by rote. If the script is written correctly, and the teachers do as they are told, then good results are inevitable.

Foolproof.

Failsafe.

. . . provided only that children are pretty much the same as programmable computers.

Which they aren't.

It turns out that a great deal was missing from the cognitivist perspective. This is not the place for a thorough critique of the arid cognitivism of the 1980s and 1990s. But for our purposes the most obvious and key deficiency of the cognitivist point of view was its failure to grasp the primacy of motivation and emotion.

Type an address in your Web browser and hit "Enter." If your computer is functioning properly, it won't talk back. It will do what you tell it to do. Your computer won't say, "I don't feel like it," or "Why go there?" or "How about if we go outside and play instead?"

Computers don't have to be motivated to do what you tell them to do.

But children do.

The colossal error of 1980's cognitivism, and of the educational strategies it inspired—many of which are still with us today—is that both cognitivism and cognitive-based educational strategies ignore the crucial question: What motivates kids to learn?

The first thing that happens when you ask kids to do stuff they have no interest in doing is they stop paying attention. Twenty-five years ago, attention deficit disorder was a relatively rare condition, with an incidence estimated at less than one child in one hundred. Today it's common. A study published in 2006, conducted jointly under the auspices of the University of Michigan and the University of Texas at Austin, found that the likelihood of a child being diagnosed with ADHD is a function of three main factors:[42]

- **Sex:** Boys are several times more likely to be diagnosed with ADHD than girls;
- **Race:** White children are more likely to be diagnosed with ADHD than black or Hispanic children;[43]

- **Socioeconomic status:** Affluent children are more likely to be diagnosed with ADHD than children from low-income families.

For white boys in affluent suburbs, the odds of being diagnosed with ADHD at some point in childhood may be as high as one in three. In one suburb, more than half of the boys were being treated with medications for ADHD.[44]

As we'll see in chapter 4, many cases of ADD/ADHD being diagnosed today may be overdiagnosed. Many of those boys who are being prescribed drugs may not need drugs. What they need first, is a curriculum that is developmentally appropriate; and second, teachers who know how to teach boys. Again, we'll return to these points in chapter 4.

The second thing that happens when you ask kids to do stuff they have no interest in doing is they get annoyed. They get irritable. They withdraw. "I hate school. It's stupid." Anything associated with school becomes uncool. Reading is uncool. Caring about school becomes uncool. Being interested in learning becomes uncool.

Computers don't have to care about frogs or be interested in frogs to learn about frogs. But children do. If children are not motivated to learn, they may stop paying attention. That's especially true for boys, for reasons we discussed earlier in this chapter. Computers are all about *Wissenschaft*. They don't need *Kenntnis*. But real children do—especially boys. The lack of respect for *Kenntnis* over the past three decades is an important part of the answer to the question, "What's behind the massive disengagement of so many boys from school?"

Good News: The Boys' Crisis Is a Myth!

On Sunday, June 25, 2006, I received a call on my cell phone from Jay Mathews, the lead education reporter for the *Washington Post*. Mr. Mathews wanted my opinion of a study that had just been released by an obscure nonprofit group calling itself Education Sector. He explained that his story on the study would appear the next morning on the front page of the *Washington Post*.[45] He wanted my opinion for a follow-up column that he planned to post online.

Mr. Mathews' front-page article announced "that widespread reports of U.S. boys being in crisis are greatly overstated and that young males in school are in many ways doing better than ever. . . . the pessimism about young males seems to derive from inadequate research, sloppy analysis and discomfort with the fact that although the average boy is doing better, the average girl has gotten ahead of him."

The article was picked up by many of the nation's largest-circulation newspapers. The *Miami News, Baltimore Sun, Buffalo News, Detroit News, Seattle Times, San Diego Union Tribune,* and dozens of other papers ran the story verbatim. *New York Times* columnist Judith Warner, in a column entitled "What Boy Crisis?" wrote that the study confirmed that the "boys' crisis" is a myth, after all. The facts, wrote Warner—echoing the *Washington Post*—are that boys are "doing better than ever on most measures of academic performance," with the possible exception of black and Hispanic boys from low-income households. Within twenty-four hours of Mathews' article in the *Post,* the story was featured on the *CBS Evening News,* with the headline "It's a Myth That Boys Are Falling Behind in School."

But is it true? Is the boys' crisis really a myth?

The answer is not so simple. Something strange has been happening with American boys over the past two decades: The reading and writing scores of fourth-grade American boys have improved somewhat, which has actually narrowed the gender gap separating them from girls. Jay Mathews' article focused on that fact. But during the same period of time, the reading and writing scores of twelfth-grade American boys have dropped. The gender gap separating twelfth-grade girls from twelfth-grade boys has widened, not because girls are doing better— they're not—but because boys are doing worse.[46]

You'll sometimes hear people claim that the gender gap is confined primarily to black and Hispanic students, or to low-income girls and boys, or to students whose parents didn't go to college. We'll talk about those issues more in a moment. But even among twelfth-grade white students with college-educated parents, the gender gap has become dramatic: One in four white boys with college-educated parents today cannot read at a basic level of proficiency, compared with only one in sixteen white girls.[47]

To repeat:

- Fourth-grade boys are doing slightly better in reading and writing than they were twenty years ago.
- Twelfth-grade boys are doing worse in reading and writing than they were twenty years ago.

How could it be the case that fourth-grade boys are doing better, while twelfth-grade boys are doing worse? How does better become worse?

This riddle is not hard to solve when you think about what we expect from fourth-graders compared with what we expect from twelfth-graders. When we test fourth-graders on their basic reading skills, we're trying to determine whether they have mastered the fundamentals of reading. Can they read what's on the page? Do they have some basic vocabulary? In the past twenty years, there has been increased emphasis on mastering the basics of reading. Elementary school students have also been drilled in specific test-taking skills in ways that would not have been imaginable twenty or thirty years ago. The drilling begins at an earlier age and lasts longer. As a result, elementary school students—both girls and boys—are doing somewhat better than they were twenty or thirty years ago, and the gender gap has narrowed somewhat.

Twelfth grade is a different story. Twelfth-graders are expected to be able to read for content. It's not enough just to be able to sound out all the words. If you're reading a passage about global warming, you need to be familiar with that topic; it also helps to know what the Kyoto Treaty is; and you'll write an even better essay if you can make some allusions to Al Gore's *An Inconvenient Truth*. If you read widely and extensively in your spare time, that's likely to be a tremendous help. In other words, you'll do best if you can read that passage in the context of a whole world of knowledge about science and politics.

You can drill third-graders on phonics and see improvements in their reading test scores, but rote drills and repetition don't work as a means of teaching high school students about how the world works. There's growing evidence that the intensive reading drills that now characterize early elementary education may actually disengage many students, particularly boys. What's important, as neurologist Judy Willis recently observed, is "for students not only to learn the mechanics of reading, but also to develop a love of reading." She cautions against any "approach that puts phonics first at the expense of intrinsic appeal and significance to the young reader."[48]

In order for high school kids to understand many of the topics we expect them to grasp, they have to be reading a wide range of material. Kids need to be reading in their spare time. Kids need to read for fun.

Boys used to read for fun. Mark Bauerlein, former director of research for the National Endowment for the Arts, and his colleague Sandra Stotsky recently published an important article on what teenagers do with their spare time. The National Endowment for the Arts surveyed a demographically representative sample of teenagers around the United States for twenty-five years, from 1980 through 2004: rich and poor kids; urban, suburban, and rural kids; white, black, Asian, and Hispanic kids. Bauerlein and Stotsky found that girls have always been more likely to read for fun than boys are. But that gender gap widened dramatically between 1980 and 2004. It has grown so wide that it has now become "a marker of gender identity," these authors found. "Girls read; boys don't."[49]

The gender gap did not widen because girls are reading more; they're not. In fact, girls are slightly less likely to read in their spare time today than they were in 1980. But roughly nine out of ten boys have stopped reading altogether. Why?

When I present this research to parents and ask them that question, a few raise their hands, confident that they know the answer. "Video games," they usually say. "Boys who might have read books twenty or thirty years ago are playing video games today." But the evidence suggests otherwise. Boys who play lots of video games are no less likely to read for fun than boys who don't play lots of video games.[50]

Video games have displaced a major activity in the lives of teenage boys, but that activity isn't reading; it's playing outdoors. In 1980, many boys spent lots of time playing outdoors. Today, those boys are more likely to spend that time indoors with the GameCube or the PlayStation or the Xbox. That may be one reason why boys today are four times more likely to be obese compared with boys a generation ago.[51]

So video games aren't the explanation. But there's a more plausible explanation: namely, that changes in education over the past thirty years have created a negative attitude toward education among many boys. Boys are less likely to read today simply because they don't want to. And that change in motivation is, at least in part, a consequence of the gender-blind changes in education over the past thirty years.

Let's return now to that cell phone call from Jay Mathews, the *Washington Post* reporter who wanted to talk about the study that purported to disprove the idea that boys are having problems in school. That study, like the reporter's article, rested very heavily on test scores of nine-year-olds nationwide, in fact, on scores on just one particular test, the National Assessment of Educational Progress (NAEP). The authors of the study showed that on this test, nine-year-old boys are doing better today than they were doing thirty years ago; on this test, the gender gap in the scores (girls doing better than boys) has been narrowing. White boys—particularly white boys with college-educated parents—are doing fine, according to the report. The real problems in American education are problems of race and social class, not gender, according to the report—a position echoed by the *Washington Post*.

Mr. Mathews had called to ask for my opinion of the study. "You don't need my opinion, Mr. Mathews," I told him. "You know how biased that study is. They focused on improvements in the scores of nine-year-olds, but they neglected what's happening to seventeen-year-olds! You know very well that the gender gap in reading is getting larger among seventeen-year-olds," I pointed out. "This study emphasizes the improvements among fourth-graders but completely ignores the decline in reading scores among twelfth-grade boys over the past twenty years. You know that one in four white boys with college-educated parents can't read proficiently. That means one in four white boys in high school won't be able to read your article saying how well white boys are doing."

Mr. Mathews thanked me and promised to include my remarks in his online column on Tuesday, June 27, the day after his front-page article would appear. And he was true to his word: that Tuesday, he did indeed post an online column that continued his coverage of the Education Sector report.[52] He apologized for the one-sided coverage in the previous day's paper. To give a more "balanced and comprehensive" coverage, he included not only my comments but also those of other researchers who pointed to the glaring shortcomings in the Education Sector report.

Unfortunately, though, the readership for Mr. Mathews' personal online column is trivial compared to the coverage afforded to a front-page above-the-fold news article in the *Washington Post*. Mathews' front-page article was widely picked up by the media. His online column wasn't picked up by anybody, wasn't featured anywhere, and hasn't been read by anybody, as far as I can tell.

So far, I've identified two ways in which education has changed in the past thirty years to make it likely that boys will disengage from school more so than girls:

1. the acceleration of the early elementary curriculum, and
2. the shift from *Kenntnis* to *Wissenschaft*.

We turn now to one other important change.

"How Would You Feel If You Were Piggy?"—And Other Questions Unfriendly to Boys

Your son is now twelve years old. His latest report card was a mess: an A in math, C's in social studies and Spanish, and D's in reading and English. "You can do better than this," you say to your son. "Your English teacher told me you didn't turn in even half the homework. Am I going to have to supervise you to make sure you do your homework every night?"

"I'm not gonna do that homework. It's stupid," your son Brett says.

"What's stupid about it?" you ask.

"It's TOTALLY stupid," Brett says.

"What do you mean by that? Can you give an example?"

He shrugs. "Do you want to see it?" he asks.

"Sure," you say.

Brett rummages in his knapsack, then produces a crumpled piece of paper. After smoothing it out, this is what you read:

> In *Lord of the Flies*, a group of boys finds themselves stranded on a tropical island. One of the boys, nicknamed Piggy because he is overweight, is the victim of vicious bullying by the other boys. Write a short essay in the first person, in Piggy's voice, describing how you feel about the other boys picking on you. Remember to
> - include lots of detail,
> - describe scenes from the book, and
> - mention specific boys.

"See what I mean?" Brett says, a note of triumph in his voice. "It's totally stupid!"

"What's stupid about it?" you ask.

"'Write an essay in Piggy's voice,'" Brett paraphrases. "That is total stupidness!"

"Why is it stupid?" you ask again.

"I'm not Piggy. I'm not some fat loser who probably couldn't even pick his own nose right. If I'd been on that island, I'd have smashed his face myself!"

This homework assignment boils down to: How would you feel if you were Piggy? When I spoke with the teacher who assigned this homework, she explained that she wanted to teach the children about empathy. With all due respect to the teacher, I submit that this assignment didn't teach this particular boy anything about empathy. Instead, the message the assignment reinforced for him is that doing homework is for girls, not for real boys. No self-respecting boy, in this boy's frame of reference, would do such a homework assignment.

In *Why Gender Matters* I reviewed research by Deborah Yurgelun-Todd and her associates at Harvard Medical School demonstrating that the regions of the brain associated with negative emotion in teenage girls are closely associated with the language areas of the brain. In boys of the same age, by contrast, brain activity associated with negative emotion is localized primarily in the amygdala, a nucleus with comparatively scant connections to the language areas of the brain.[53] It's easy for most middle school and high school girls to answer a question like "How would you feel if you were X?" because the area of the brain where the feeling is happening is closely linked to the area of the brain where talking happens. For boys, that's not the case. For boys like Brett in the example above, it's not easy to answer, in a genuine and articulate way, the question "How would you feel if . . . ?" He may attempt to produce the answer he thinks the teacher wants to hear, but it's a chore. A better question for most boys would be "What would you *do* if . . ." That question may sound similar, but it's actually a different question, and much more boy-friendly—for most boys.

The Right Kind of Competition

I've already pointed out that using the computer metaphor to describe how brains work fails to capture the importance of motivation. It also falls short in another important respect: it doesn't accommodate the enormous individual differences between one student and another. The differences between a PC and a Mac are trivial in comparison with the differences between Brett, who plays every kind of competitive sport, and his younger sister, Emily, who occasionally watches football games with her older brother but feels bad for the losing team, no matter who they are, because "it must hurt to lose."

Some kids—both boys and girls—thrive in a competitive atmosphere, even if they often lose. Others wilt and collapse, or withdraw, under the stress of competition. Is competition good or bad? It depends on your child. That's why there may be no such thing as "a good school."

The best choice for Emily may be a disaster for Brett. The school that is best for Brett may be the worst possible choice for Emily.

Think for a moment about boys who thrive on competition (not all boys do). Consider how changes in our schools and in our society over the past thirty years may have disengaged these boys.

- **Traditional physical education:** Gym class used to offer many opportunities for boys to experience "the thrill of victory and the agony of defeat"—even if the game was just kickball or dodgeball. But over the past thirty years, many school districts have eliminated sports such as dodgeball, in the belief that dodgeball and similar sports reward violence. Likewise, competition has been systematically eliminated from many districts' physical education programs, in the belief that competition alienates some kids from sports. And perhaps it does. But your son may need the zest of competition as a motivator. Without competition, he's likely to say "Why bother?"

- **"Zero tolerance for violence"** has changed the way that creative writing and language arts are taught. I remember when I was a seventh-grader, thirty-some years ago, and we were assigned to write a short story. I wrote about an American prisoner of war breaking out of a German prison camp during World War II (I was a huge fan of Steve McQueen in *The Great Escape*). I've seen boys who write similar stories today referred for psychiatric evaluation, just as if they had been caught passing notes about killing the teacher. "I'm sorry," the teacher says to the parents, "but your son Richie wrote a story about a man garroting the prison guard. We can't allow that here. We have a zero-tolerance policy for violence."

When a teacher or principal tells you that the school has a zero-tolerance policy for students writing violent stories, ask them whether the same policy applies to what students read. If students are not allowed to read violent fiction, then the librarian will have to remove novels by Hemingway, Steinbeck, Dostoyevsky, Tolstoy, and many others from the library shelves. If the school is really going to ban Hemingway and Dostoyevsky, then that school has some pretty serious problems. But if they're not going to ban Hemingway and Dostoyevsky, then on what grounds can they reasonably prohibit boys from trying to write in the same genre that they're allowed to read?

- **Competitive sports:** Schools have ballooned in size over the past thirty years. I commonly visit middle schools with two thousand–plus students and high schools with four thousand–plus students. One problem with a high school of four thousand–plus students is that only the most elite athletes get to play on the school team. In most metropolitan areas, at least one boy in five would like to play football. In a coed school with four thousand students, i.e., about two thousand boys, there might easily be four hundred boys who would like to play on the football team. But even big schools often have only one bus for the varsity and one bus for the JV team. That means only thirty-six boys can make the varsity team, and another thirty-six on the JV. The other three hundred–plus boys are out of luck. Most of those boys probably won't even try out: they know that only the best athletes can make the team, and they don't want to be embarrassed. So they stay home.

If your son is one of those boys who thrives on competition, and he can't make the team, what should you do? I used to suggest either transferring to a smaller school (where your son would have a better chance of making the team), or helping your son find another competitive athletic outlet. However, a recent article by Brooke de Lench—author, parent, and founder of MomsTeam.com, a Web site devoted to providing guidance to parents of athletes—changed my thinking on this subject. "The current public high school model—one first-year team, one varsity, maybe one subvarsity—might have made sense when it was adopted some 80 years ago," de Lench writes. "Back then, in many schools the number of roster spots on a team was roughly equal to the number who wanted to play. But it makes no sense today, when the number of those who want to continue playing sports in middle school and high school far exceeds the finite number of spots available." She argues that we need to reinvent high school sports, beginning with a new idea: nobody gets cut. "Adopting a policy of full inclusion would be especially beneficial for teenage boys," she observes, "for whom sports provide an outlet for aggression and a means of connecting socially with other boys."[54]

I know a boy, let's call him Tony, who is competitive in absolutely every aspect of his life. He's only eleven years old, but he finds a way to make everything a race or some sort of competition. At summer camp, he organized a contest among all the boys to see who could pee the farthest. Boys like Tony usually will respond well to any challenge so long as:

- there are winners and losers, and
- the outcome is in doubt. Anybody might conceivably win and anybody might conceivably lose. Everything depends on how hard you play.

Satisfy both criteria, and Tony will be on board. If either one of the criteria is missing, Tony won't see the point. He'll disengage. He'll lose interest. He'll stare out the window.

Mater Dei School is an all-boys elementary school not far from my home in Montgomery County, Maryland, where this principle is understood very well. On enrollment, every boy is assigned either to the Blue Team or the White Team. The assignment is arbitrary—in other words, it's random—and it is permanent.* Once you're a member of

---

*The only exception to random assignment is that if a boy has an older brother who attended the school, then the boy is assigned to the same team that his brother was on.

the Blue Team, you are forever a member of the Blue Team. The two teams compete in every aspect of school life. When the boys play soccer, it's Blue against White. On school examinations, it's Blue against White. The team that scores higher on the exams gets points. The team whose members donate more food to give away at Thanksgiving gets points. At the end of the year, the winning team is officially recognized and gets its name—"Blue" or "White"—the year of its victory, and the names of the team captains, emblazoned on a plaque in the hallway. This may seem silly to some people. But for many of these boys, it's highly motivating.

Team competition has another benefit for boys who are motivated by the will to win. Team competition socializes boys. It teaches boys to value something above themselves. It subordinates some of the ego and the egocentricity that these boys often manifest.

I've seen the principle of *team* competition engage many boys who otherwise don't care much about school. *Individual* competition is seldom as successful and is almost guaranteed to disengage many boys. Why is that? Remember the second principle we discussed a moment ago: the outcome must be in doubt. If you have individual competition in academics, for example, Daniel may decide that he's unlikely to win. Once he's decided that he's not likely to win, he's not interested in playing. "You think I care about this subject? Ha. I couldn't care less. Go ahead and flunk me. You think I care about your stupid contest?"

But if Daniel is a member of a large team, anything can happen. Either team might win. If the class examination is public, Daniel's performance might determine whether his team wins or loses. For example, if the class assignment were to read *The Lord of the Rings: The Fellowship of the Ring* and now there's an oral quiz, Blue Team vs. White Team, Daniel needs to be able to answer the questions. All the students in the class will have been warned, incidentally, that answers must be taken only from J. R. R. Tolkien's books, not from a movie version of the books.

The teacher, Mrs. Hofstadter, says: "It's the Blue Team's turn. Carlos, you're answering for the Blue Team this round. Here's your question: After Frodo is wounded by the Nazgûl and needs to be taken to Rivendell, what is the name of the Elf who takes him there?"

"Arwen?" Carlos guesses.

"Wrong!" Mrs. Hofstadter says. "Arwen plays that role in the movie, but not in the book. Daniel, you're answering for the White Team. After Frodo is wounded, what is the name of the Elf who takes Frodo to Rivendell?"

Daniel shouts "Glorfindel!"

"Right!" Mrs. Hofstadter says. Daniel's teammates on the White Team give him high fives all around, because this is a high-stakes test for sixth-grade boys. Each member of the winning team in this classroom will get a coupon for free pizza and ice cream at the popular corner store.

Daniel may not care that much about his grade in the class or about *The Lord of the Rings.* He may not even care that much about pizza and ice cream. But he doesn't want to let his teammates down. He doesn't want to risk being the one who got the wrong answer, whose one wrong answer cost the whole team the prize.

Why doesn't this approach work as well for many girls? Here's why: most girls value friendship above team affiliation. If Emily and Melissa are best friends, and you put Emily and Melissa on opposing teams, both girls may be uncomfortable. Emily doesn't want to make Melissa sad, so she may be reluctant to beat Melissa. She'd rather play alongside Melissa rather than try to make her lose. But if Justin and Jared are best friends, and you put them on opposing teams, Justin will happily run down the field and knock Jared down. In that situation I've seen Jared get up, dust himself off, and say to Justin, "You think that was a good hit? That wasn't anything. I'll get you better next time." That kind of good-natured competition actually builds their friendship. Boys are more likely to understand that friends don't have to be teammates, and teammates don't have to be friends. And boys are more likely to be invested in the success of their team regardless of whether any of their friends are on the team.

It's easy to see how the competitive team format might engage and motivate boys who otherwise wouldn't be inspired to do their homework or read the assigned text. But I've also seen team competition work in other, unexpected ways: for example, to motivate scholarly boys to become better athletes. When I visited Calgary, Alberta, in 2004,

I heard a story involving team competition that took place at a boys' school near Edmonton. At this school, all the boys were assigned to one of three teams. It happened that this particular year, the best athletes were on one team while most of the best students were on another team.

A twenty-kilometer snowshoe relay race was announced. Each team would nominate four boys to race. Everybody expected the team with the best athletes to win easily. But the scholars—the "geeks"—really studied up on snowshoeing. They learned that the key to success in snowshoeing is to run lightly over the surface of the snow. So they nominated their four lightest, fastest boys to represent their team. And those boys trained. The athletes didn't train for this event; they figured they didn't have to, they were already in excellent shape.

When the day of the race arrived, the scholarly boys were ready. They blew the other two teams away: the fourth boy on the scholarly team crossed the finish line about ten minutes ahead of either of the other teams. The strong football players representing the athletic team bogged down in the snow—their muscular build was a liability rather than an advantage. That event, I was told, raised the status of the scholarly team enormously in the eyes of the whole school. They had beaten the jocks at an athletic event. And the jocks saluted them.

The competitive format of this school in Alberta, or of the Mater Dei school in Maryland, might make those schools a poor choice for many girls (even if the schools enrolled girls, which they don't). And those schools might not be the best choice for some boys. But if your son loves competition—if you can imagine him competing to see who can pee the farthest—then you need to find your son a school like this one. If there is no such school nearby, then I hope you will lend your copy of this book to your school's principal and to some of your son's teachers. Ask whether they might make some effort to accommodate different types of boys. In the twenty-first century, most school formats allow little place for team competition. Indeed, any school competition with clearly defined winners and losers is disparaged in many schools nowadays, on the grounds that the loser's self-esteem might be in jeopardy in a competitive environment. We need to change that, and we can.

What About Self-Esteem?

"What if my son loses?" you may be wondering. "What if my son gives the wrong answer and the team loses as a result? Wouldn't that damage his self-esteem?"

To understand the answer to this question, you have to understand something about gender differences with regard to self-esteem. Let me tell you first about a study that was done recently at Harvard University. The researchers recruited Asian and Asian-American women from among Harvard undergraduates. The women were then randomly assigned to three groups. One group was simply asked to take a short written math examination and that was it. The second group was given a questionnaire that emphasized their Asian heritage. The questionnaire asked what language they spoke at home, whether they preferred traditional Asian foods over Western foods, and so on. The women in this second group scored significantly higher on the math exam than the women in the first group.

The third group was given a questionnaire that emphasized the fact that they were women. The questionnaire asked whether they preferred to live in a single-sex dorm or a coed dorm, whether they felt that there were adequate protections for women on campus. The women in this third group scored significantly lower on the math exam than the women in the first group.[55]

Just reminding women of their membership in a category that is negatively stereotyped—i.e., women supposedly aren't as good in math as men are—resulted in a significant impairment of the ability of these women to test well. Reminding women of a different stereotype—the supposed superior ability of Asians in math—significantly enhanced the women's ability to do well. These women weren't stupid. They were Harvard undergraduates. Similar studies of young girls and teenagers, with even larger effects, have been published.[56] For girls and for many women, if you believe you're smart, you'll actually be smarter—you'll learn better and do better on tests—than if you think you're dumb. A girl who thinks she's good in math will test better than a girl of the same ability who thinks she's bad in math.

But that effect simply doesn't hold true for boys. A boy who thinks he's smart in math won't necessarily test better than his equally bright peer who thinks he's not so smart. The boy who thinks he's smart may actually test worse than his peer, because boys who think they're smart in a subject tend not to work as hard studying the subject—just as the athletes at the school in Edmonton didn't bother to train for the snow-shoe relay. The correlation between a boy's self-esteem in a subject and his performance in that subject is zero at best—and may possibly be negative, after controlling for ability.[57]

I know many parents who are uneasy with the idea that their son needs a school with a more competitive format to get motivated. That idea clashes with the politically correct notions of the past twenty years, according to which competition is bad because it is harmful to self-es-teem. But those notions were not empirically based. We now know that self-esteem has a value for girls that it simply doesn't have for many boys, while competition—particularly team competition—has a value for many boys that it doesn't have for most girls. Some boys need the challenge and the risk of competition to care about the results. Parents and teachers and school administrators who don't understand that fact may actually disengage these boys from school.

Angie Romano is an acquaintance of mine who has coached both girls' and boys' sports for many years. She has found that most girls, even athletically talented girls, need encouragement. Otherwise, girls are likely to decide they're not good enough, they're not fast enough, they're not strong enough. They give up. "You have to build the girls up," Angie told me. But boys are different. Many boys—especially athletically tal-ented boys—have a tendency to overestimate their skills and their abil-ity. "You have to tell that hotshot that he may have some talent, but he's not nearly as good as he thinks he is. He still has a lot to learn. He's going to need to put in a lot of work if he wants to make it to the next level," Angie told me. "You have to break the boys down."

I'm a little uneasy with Angie's motto—"build the girls up, break the boys down"—but I have to admit that it captures the essence of the re-search on self-esteem. For many boys, failure is a spur to work harder. The competitive format gives these boys a structured environment in which they can easily determine whether or not they're making real progress. A noncompetitive format in which "everybody's a winner" is a sure way to disengage this boy from the whole process.

What About Columbine—and Virginia Tech?

The zero-tolerance policies many school districts have regarding anything that looks or sounds violent didn't spring out of nowhere. They were motivated by concerns about school violence. Some parents ask: "If you let boys write violent stories, and you encourage competition with winners and losers, aren't you creating conditions in which violent activity is more likely to occur?"

Those parents—and the district administrators who wrote the zero-tolerance policies—usually believe that prohibiting violent play or imaginary violence (e.g., boys' writing violent stories) will decrease actual violence. There is no shred of evidence to support this belief.[58] We actually know a good deal about the kind of boy who is the most likely to bring a gun to school. That boy is more likely than other boys to be an honor student; he's more likely to be shy, a loner; he is less likely than other boys to participate in aggressive sports such as football.[59] We now understand that aggressive play, such as dodgeball, does not increase the risk of truly violent activities such as a school shooting. Writing a story about a World War II prison break is not a violent act. Prohibitions on dodgeball and on writing violent stories do not in any way decrease the likelihood of school violence. They only accomplish one thing: they send a clear message that certain types of boys are simply not welcome at school. To do well at school, that boy must deny his true self and pretend to be someone else. More compliant. More willing to do what the teacher asks. More concerned about pleasing the teacher.

Consider these recent examples:

- In Arkansas, an eight-year-old boy was punished for pointing a cooked strip of chicken at another student and saying "pow, pow, pow."[60]

- In New Jersey, eight-year-old Hamadi Alston found an L-shaped piece of paper in a schoolbook. When he used it in a game of "cops and robbers" at the next recess, he was taken to the school office and then turned over to police for "threatening to kill other students"—because he had said "pow pow" while playing during recess. He spent five hours in police custody and had to make two court appearances before charges were dropped.
- In Alabama, nine-year-old Austin Crittenden was suspended for "possession of a weapon—replica" when he brought a tiny plastic G.I. Joe handgun to his elementary school. The third-grader's principal "had to tape the gun to a piece of paper to keep from losing it," Austin's grandmother reported.[61]

These stories are so outrageous that they made the newspapers. But I can tell you many stories from my own experience that don't make the newspapers: a boy whose story about a white family escaping from Zimbabwe was given a C because it included the suggestion of a violent act, while a girl's story of comparable quality in response to the same assignment—but with no hint of violence—received an A+. The end result of these episodes is the widespread belief among the children themselves that school isn't welcoming to real boys.

In *Why Gender Matters*, I quoted a famous saying attributed to the Roman poet Horace: "You can try to drive out Nature with a pitchfork; yet she will always return."[62] If your son is motivated by competition, then eliminating it from his school, throwing out his toy guns, and forbidding him to write stories with violent themes won't change him. Those policies may disengage him from school, however. The end result may be a boy who feels that the only place he is truly understood as he really is, is the world of video games.

And, as we'll see in the next chapter, that world has its own problems.

3

THE SECOND FACTOR
Video Games

Your son is now thirteen years old. He's a serious video-game player. He still plays with a few friends, occasionally, but more and more he prefers to play against other gamers online. Last month he was a runner-up in an on-line Halo competition that drew competitors from around the world.[1] That's OK, you suppose, but you're becoming concerned about how much time he spends playing, as well as the strangers he plays with online. Who are these people? How come they have so much spare time on their hands?

His grades are fine, more or less, so far. But he'll be starting ninth grade next fall. You and your spouse have decided it's time to lay down some rules. First of all, homework comes before video games. Your son's going to be in high school soon. No playing video games until all the homework is done.

Before you get to rule number two, you notice that your son isn't paying attention. He's not even pretending to pay attention. He's looking out the window. He's tapping his fingers on the table. Now he's actually humming something. And he's not looking at you. He just keeps looking out the window, nodding his head—not at you, but in rhythm to the song he's humming.

"You're not paying attention," you say.

"Sure I am," he says, still not making eye contact. "No video games until the homework's done. Got it."

"OK, then let's talk about rule number two," you say, "Rule number two is: no more than thirty minutes a day on video games, regardless, Sunday through Thursday when school's in session."

Now you've got his attention. He stops drumming his fingers on the table. For the first time he makes eye contact with you. Then he snorts contemptuously. "Not gonna happen," he says. "Sorry. Thirty minutes? That's barely enough time to get powered up and log on."

"But all the time you're spending on video games right now—it must be a dozen hours a week, at least," you protest. "You're spending all your free time on video games."

"But those games are basically the best thing I have," your son says. His tone is simultaneously angry and pleading. "Those games are who I am. I'm not some pathetic nerd geek who's going to spend six zillion hours a night studying."

"But those games aren't the real world," you say. "They're just games."

"What's real?" your son says. Before you can answer this unexpectedly existential question, he continues, "When I'm playing Halo, that world is more real to me than this one. I'm really good, too," he says, dreamily. "Although I do NOT expect you to have even the slightest clue what that means." He pauses, then adds softly, almost shyly, "I could win the championship. Next year maybe. Definitely a possibility. But not on thirty minutes a day."

Where's this coming from? How did this boy come to have such a monomaniacal drive to play some silly game? The answer will take you deeper than you might expect.

Boy World is a weird place. Many boys and young men are wrestling with drives and motivations that a lot of parents, especially mothers, don't understand. Fathers may understand these motivations, but fathers are sometimes contemptuous of the egocentricity and unreality that characterize the inner life of many teen and preteen boys. Dads may not want to be reminded that they were something like that themselves, once upon a time, decades ago.

I am not making a grand statement about all boys. I'm focusing only on those boys who seem unmotivated to do their best, boys who don't seem to care much about getting the best grades or getting into a good college, boys who are capable of doing the schoolwork but who just aren't motivated to do it.* Many of them could be good students, but they don't seem to care about that. What do they want?

Let's agree that physiologically, boys haven't changed much in the past thirty years: genetic makeup can't be significantly altered in only one generation, or even ten. Society has changed. Your son, who seems so unmotivated to succeed at school, may actually be highly motivated to succeed—just not at school, at least not at the particular school he is attending. I hear many parents say things like "My son doesn't care about school at all, but he can work incredibly hard at something that he does care about. He'll stay up till two in the morning to get to the next level in *SpyHunter*. He just doesn't care about school."

Why do some tasks engage your boy's motivational engine, while others don't? It's not sufficient to say that video games are fun and school isn't. That answer begs the question. Why do these boys find video games to be so much more fun than school? Most girls and indeed many boys wouldn't get much of a kick out of playing *SpyHunter*. For many girls, and for some boys, the main activity in *SpyHunter*—shooting the (virtual) bad guys while driving a car very fast down a (virtual) highway or while driving a (virtual) speedboat on a (virtual) waterway—would be as tedious as conjugating Spanish verbs in the imperfect subjunctive tense, or writing an essay on the Federalist Papers.

The answer, I think, lies in a concept that most of these boys have never heard of, something that contemporary psychologists refer to with

---

*I don't mean to suggest that studious, highly-motivated boys don't have any problems. They do. In fact these boys are, in my experience, somewhat more likely to be clinically depressed than the less-motivated boys we're discussing in this book. More information about the emotional problems of studious, highly-motivated boys is provided in chapter 9 of my book *Why Gender Matters*.

terms like "the reinforcing effects of contingent paradigms" or "learned mastery." The German philosopher Friedrich Nietzsche[2] was the first to write at length about the reinforcing effect I have in mind here: he called this drive simply "the will to power." To get a better handle on what has changed in the past thirty years, what hasn't changed, and to begin understanding how you might get your son's motivation back in gear, I think you'll find it helpful to understand Nietzsche's idea of the will to power.

First a disclaimer: Some unmotivated boys don't fit into the will-to-power category. We'll investigate what might be going on with those boys in chapters 4 and 5.

Let's start with Nietzsche's insight, follow that insight to help us understand the modern research, and figure out where and how twenty-first-century boys—including your son, perhaps—may have gone astray.

The Will to Power

The simplest version of what Nietzsche meant by the "will to power" is that individuals want to be in charge of their environment. This characteristic is clearly evident as early as two months of age. In one classic study, psychologists rigged up babies' cribs with motion detectors so that a colorful mobile over the baby's head would rotate for a few seconds every time the baby moved its head. These were two-month-old babies. Very soon these babies were moving their heads back and forth and cooing at the mobiles. Other babies were given the same crib and the same colorful mobiles, programmed to rotate every minute or two regardless of the baby's activity—but no motion detectors. These other babies had no control over the movement of the mobile. They lay still, not moving, not cooing. They appeared bored.[3] Another psychologist, commenting on this study, remarked that "infants, no less than we, prefer to exercise some control over their environments. . . . It appears that even a two-month-old infant wants to be master of its own fate."[4]

If you tell a boy who has a generous dose of this kind of motivation to sit down, he'll stand up. If you tell him to stand up, he'll sit down. He doesn't care so much whether he's standing or sitting. But he needs to know, and he needs you to know, that he's in charge of whether he stands or sits. He doesn't want you to tell him what to do.

Now of course many people will object and say, "I know girls just like that. I know women like that too. They don't like to be told what to do. They like to be in charge." And that's certainly true. But what distinguishes these boys from other boys and from most girls is that the will to power takes precedence over other drives and other perspectives. For most girls and women, being well-liked or being well-thought-of counts for more than being in charge. But some boys and some men would rather be in charge than be well-liked. That's true for a few women, but not many.

Again, I emphasize that I'm not making any sweeping statement about gender here. We all know women who want to be the boss, and we all know boys and men who are content to follow rather than to lead. What I have found in my twenty-one years of medical practice, however, is that many of the boys who seem unmotivated, from our perspective, are actually motivated by the will to power. The will to power is best understood perhaps not so much as a drive, per se, but as a worldview, a way of valuing traits and characteristics. Secretly, these boys often believe that they are special, that they are unique, that they have a destiny that will be revealed in time. As a result, they believe that rules that apply to ordinary people don't apply to them. Their "destiny" matters more to them than friendship or academic achievement—more than happiness, for that matter. They often do not expect other people, including their parents, to understand them. They may not even want other people to understand them, because they sense (correctly) that their worldview, with all its megalomania, will appear puerile and egocentric to most adult eyes.

Watch a teenage boy playing certain video games, particularly games in which the boy has to shoot and kill his way to victory such as *Halo* and *Grand Theft Auto*. Such video games offer a quick and easy fix for these boys. These games give the boys the feelings of power and control they crave: the power of life and death. "It's just a game"—but watch the seriousness with which these boys play. What happens when you tell your son that he needs to stop playing those video games? You tell him that he won't be happy if he doesn't get into a good college and get a good job. He says he doesn't care about being happy. You tell him that he needs to grow up, put the games aside, and get a real life. He may reply, quoting Nietzsche (but not aware that he is quoting Nietzsche): "This is what I am; this is what I want; you can go to hell!"[5]

Not all gamers are motivated by the will to power, of course, and not all video games are violent first-person-shooter games like *Halo*. Consider *SimCity* and its numerous progeny, all of which are games in which one constructs a city, landscape, worldscape, and more, according to realistic rules and constraints. *SimCity* and *The Sims* are not violent games, although they are games in which the player exercises great control over the lives and destinies of virtual people in a virtual world. But I don't know many teenage boys who are addicted to playing *SimCity* or even *The Sims*. What distinguishes the boy who's really addicted to video games, the boy for whom video games pose a real hazard, from the boy who plays occasionally but doesn't get hooked?

Remember that the average teenage boy today spends more than thirteen hours a week playing video games, compared with five hours per week for the average teenage girl.[6] I know some boys who don't play video games at all. I know other boys who play more than twenty hours a week, more than three hours a day, every day, including school days—which often means that their homework ends up being an after-midnight afterthought. Throughout this chapter we will continually ask "How much involvement in video games is OK for your son, and with what kind of video games?" We'll get to some specifics in a moment, but I can tell you right now that one key is balance. Moderation in all things is the key to good health. If time spent on video games is crowding out time spent with friends or time spent on homework, then clearly too much time is being spent on video games.

Video games aren't all bad. I know families where video games bring parents and kids together, instead of separating them. Shawn Hirsch of Gaithersburg, Maryland, always considered himself an "anti-video-game guy." Then he bought the Nintendo Wii system for his daughters. Now he enjoys playing video game tennis and bowling with his daughters, especially his seven-year-old, with whom he plays almost every night after dinner. Thomas Morgan of Potomac, Maryland, agrees that a good video game "absolutely reaches across the generation gap."[7]

I've had this experience myself. I own a GameBike. It looks like an ordinary exercise bike, but it plugs into a PlayStation and functions just like a game controller—except that if you want your virtual motorcycle to go faster, you don't press a button, you pedal faster. Kids around the neighborhood love to come over and play against Dr. Sax on video games like *MTX Motocross* and *NASCAR: Dirt to Daytona*. They always win: they can push the buttons faster than I can pedal. But they have fun beating a grown-up, and I get a great workout. For a while we had two GameBikes, which created a much more level playing field, because I can outpedal most of the eight- or nine-year-olds on the block. Then one of the GameBikes died, so we're back to me on the bike and the kid pressing the button.

So video games per se aren't necessarily evil. Neither is the will to power. It's not hard to see how boys motivated by the will to power might have been successful in earlier generations. They might have grown up to be successful entrepreneurs, daring innovators, explorers, politicians, or soldiers. They could readily create a productive niche for themselves. Most young men I have known eventually outgrow this stage when maturity arrives around age thirty and they gain a broader, less egocentric perspective on life. But some men remain motivated by the will to power for their entire life. General George S. Patton Jr. was certainly such a man, as was Henry Ford, Howard Hughes, and perhaps Richard Nixon. You may not like any of these men: they were all selfish, relentlessly self-centered and almost completely incapable of irony or of self-deprecating humor. But they each played a substantive role, for better or worse, in American culture and history.

If these men were reborn today, it is less likely that they would undertake a meaningful career. I suspect that a boy born today with the DNA of General Patton or Howard Hughes would more likely become a video game addict. He might have a job, but there's a real risk that his drive and his energy would be directed into the video games rather than into his career.

If you haven't played video games in the past five years, you may not understand how addictive some of them can be, owing to advances in technology—particularly for boys motivated by the will to power. Imagine that you are such a boy, the reincarnation of General George S. Patton. That boy can now play a video game in which he gets in a tank, hears the clang as he closes the hatch, feels the rumble (from three-hundred-watt subwoofers) as his tank rolls over the rubble of a demolished house, and fires depleted uranium rounds at enemy outposts as he enjoys the thrill of victory—or the agony of defeat when three enemy tanks blast him almost simultaneously. But the agony of defeat is lessened by the comforting knowledge that he can just hit "Restart" and play it all over again . . . and again.

Today, any boy with a high-speed Internet connection can play in real time against another gamer across town or on the other side of the planet. Sophisticated headsets allow boys to engage in simulated online combat in teams, arranging coordinated ambushes of enemy fighters using high-tech virtual weaponry. After your son has spent two hours leading a squad of fighters in a raid on terrorist headquarters, issuing commands through his headset-mounted microphone to his online comrades, and raced through a hail of virtual bullets to destroy the enemy power generator, well, studying Spanish grammar from a textbook can seem hopelessly dull. The virtual world is fast-moving, interactive, collaborative, and fun. The real world of homework and textbooks can't compete—not, at least, for the boy who is motivated by the will to power.

When military combat gets boring, he can carjack some geek's Corvette and drive around an astonishingly detailed simulation of 1980s Miami, right down to the music he can play on the (virtual) car's in-dash radio. Your son drives around the city for a minute, then slams on the brakes, bringing his (virtual) car to a screeching stop. A pretty young woman is walking toward the car. She smiles and asks, "You want a good time?" She's a prostitute. Your son lets her in the car and has (simulated) sex with her—then shoots her in the head with a pistol he stole earlier from a police officer he murdered. As she dies, blood pouring from her head, he retrieves the money he gave her. After all, in *Grand Theft Auto: Vice City* (from which this scene is taken), the player gets extra points for shooting the prostitute and recovering the money. Megapoints are awarded for shooting police officers.

In 2005, journalist Steven Johnson published *Everything Bad Is Good for You,* in which he argued that today's popular culture—including video games—is actually making us smarter.[8] Johnson's book enjoyed a short stint on the best-seller lists because his idea was just so audacious. Video games don't fry your brain, Johnson claimed. In fact, they make you smarter, he said—including video games such as *Grand Theft Auto: Vice City.* Reading books, on the other hand, is overrated; it dulls the senses, Johnson wrote. Johnson was fully aware of the paradox of writing a book that disparages reading. On several occasions he teases the reader on this point. He very nearly says: Why don't you put down this book and go play a video game?

Johnson's book has a light touch and a tongue-in-cheek style. It's a fun read, in part because the reader is never sure whether Johnson is being serious or just joking. Since his book appeared, however, other writers and researchers have followed up with books and articles supporting his position: video games are good for you. Video games help kids learn.

This position is rapidly gaining adherents—and money. In 2006, the Federation of American Scientists—which usually makes recommendations about terrorism and nuclear weapons—suggested major investment from government and the private sector to explore the educational potential of video games. Also in 2006, the John D. and Catherine T. MacArthur Foundation announced that it would spend fifty million dollars between 2007 and 2011 to support "the emerging field of digital media and learning,"[9] specifically with regard to the potential of using video games in the classroom.

Leading this vanguard are two professors from the University of Wisconsin–Madison: James Paul Gee, author of *What Video Games Have to Teach Us about Learning and Literacy,* and David Williamson Shaffer, author of *How Computer Games Help Children Learn.*[10] Professor Gee's book has an unreal quality to it: he defends violent video games such as *Grand Theft Auto* on the grounds that seeing the world from the perspective of a violent criminal helps the player to "transcend" one's "narrow" societal values, recognizing that "general conceptions of good really just hide the narrow interests of particular groups in a society. . . . "[11] The MacArthur Foundation has awarded Professor Gee and his associates three million dollars to bring video games into the classroom.[12]

Professor Shaffer's book is far more persuasive. Like me, he points out that American education has shifted away from "knowing how"—experiential knowledge, *Kenntnis*—and has placed too much focus on "knowing that"—didactic knowledge, *Wissenschaft*. He eloquently describes an unusual high school integrated into a large farm in Vermont. "The students planted and harvested all of the school's produce. They fed and mucked the cows, sheep, and chickens. . . . The rhythms of nature and the realities of life on a farm determined the things that needed doing and the times they had to be done." Paraphrasing John Dewey, Shaffer writes that at this farm/school, "these tasks were not about life, they were life itself."[13]

Then Shaffer makes a subtle shift. Most of us don't live on rural farms anymore, he observes. So what would education "based on life itself . . . look like in our high-tech, digital world?" His answer is that video games can serve the same function for twenty-first-century kids that working on a farm would have done in previous generations.[14] Video games are, he asserts, the best training to make kids smarter and better-prepared for the challenges they will face in the twenty-first century.*

Dumb and Dumber

Do video games actually make kids smarter?

---

*In defense of Professor Shaffer, we should note that he is promoting a specific type of video game that few teenagers play—a kind of game he calls *epistemic*. He provides five examples of such games, none of which are commercial successes or even widely available at this time. However, the broad title of his book—*How Computer Games Help Children Learn*—and the PlayStation-style game controller on the jacket cover, conceal such subtleties. Shaffer mentions but never condemns or criticizes games with a much wider audience such as *Grand Theft Auto*.

It depends on what you mean by "smarter." If you ask, "Do video games improve kids' reaction times, for example, if they're asked to push a button every time they see a flashing light?"—then the answer is yes. Kids who play video games will be faster at such a task—by about two-hundredths of a second (0.02 seconds)—compared with kids who don't play video games.[15]

But if you ask the questions "Do video games help kids to do better in school? Do the games help improve their grades or their test scores?"—then the answer is no. A series of studies over the past seven years has demonstrated clearly and unambiguously that *the more time your child spends playing video games, the less likely he is to do well in school*—whether he is in elementary school, middle school, high school, or college. This negative association between academic performance and playing video games remains strong even when investigators control for all possible confounding variables, such as personality traits. I regard this finding as "clear and unambiguous" because all studies of this question have yielded similar results. There are no studies pointing in the opposite direction. Every investigator who has correlated the amount of time that a child or adolescent or young adult spends playing video games with that student's academic performance has found a negative correlation.[16]

Is there a cause-and-effect relationship between playing video games and disengaging from school, or is the relationship merely an association? Maybe kids who are less motivated to do well in school are more likely to play video games. If this were the case, then playing video games might be a marker for lack of motivation, but the video games themselves would not be to blame for the lack of motivation. In a moment, we will consider other scholarly work suggesting that the link is in fact causal.

Many parents and teachers with whom I've spoken get frustrated with the scholarly papers, however. "You don't need to tell us about all those academic papers to know that video games are having a negative effect on boys' motivation," one parent told me. "Just listen to the teachers." Patrick Welsh has been teaching English at T. C. Williams High School in Alexandria, Virginia, for more than thirty years. He's "worrying about the young guys who spend so much time divorced from reality and the life of the mind as they zap away the hours before their video screens." At first he was amused by the stories of how the boys camp out all night at the local Best Buy or Circuit City to purchase the latest version of *Grand Theft Auto* or *Halo* on the day of its release. Mr. Welsh continues:

> But I didn't think it was so funny when some guys skipped school that day to stay home and try to beat the game. Senior Steve Penn (who wasn't one of the skippers) told me that the following weekend, he played for six hours straight (minus bathroom breaks) at a friend's house. When he got home at one a.m. on Sunday, he went at it for two more hours, fell asleep, got up at seven and fired up the game again. "My mother had to remind me to change my clothes and take a shower," he said.

Football coach Greg Sullivan, Mr. Welsh's colleague, says that he sees fewer and fewer boys playing outside when he drives around northern Virginia. "They are inside playing video games," he says. "More kids are finding real sports too demanding."[17]

I've talked with other football coaches who describe, with amazement, teenage boys who think that because they can win at *Madden NFL*, they therefore know something about playing the real-life game of football. "These guys are five-minute wonders," one coach told me. "They get out on the field, run around for a few minutes, and then they're done. They have no endurance. They're in pathetic shape. And they don't want to do the work that they would have to do, to train the way they would have to train, to get in shape."

I don't think the blame can rest solely on the scrawny shoulders of these boys. They are the logical product of an educational system that conveys so little understanding of the distinction between *Kenntnis* and *Wissenschaft* that these boys truly believe that because they know something about football, that's the same as knowing how to play football.

So let's return to the question: Do video games make kids smarter? There's actually some disturbing evidence that boys today, on average, are less intelligent—less able to understand and solve real-world problems—compared with boys just fifteen years ago. Professor Michael Shayer and colleagues tested more than ten thousand girls and boys who were eleven and twelve years of age. They used a special test that measures how well a child understands intuitive density, internal volume, conservation of liquids, and other concepts related to real-world science and math. This test, validated by more than thirty years of research with children, has been shown to be impervious to the so-called Flynn Effect—the tendency of children's scores on IQ tests to improve over time.

When these tests were first conducted thirty years ago, there was a substantial gender gap in the results, with boys outperforming girls. When the researchers repeated the tests in 2005, they found that the gender gap had vanished. The gap didn't disappear because the girls were doing better. These researchers found that girls are not doing better; in fact, the performance of eleven- and twelve-year-old girls in 2005 had deteriorated slightly in comparison with the performance of eleven- and twelve-year-old girls thirty years ago. Instead, they found that the boys' performance in 2005 was dramatically worse than it had been thirty years ago. "This is a huge and significant statistical change," concluded Professor Shayer.[18] Boys who are nearly twelve years old "are doing [only] as well as the eight- to nine-year-olds in 1976," he observed.[19] Why the drop? Professor Shayer suggested that "the most likely reasons are the lack of experiential play [Kenntnis] in primary schools, and the growth of a video-game, TV culture. Both take away the kind of hands-on play that allows kids to experience how the world works in practice."[20]

Professor Shayer's study isn't the only one to document a recent decline in the intelligence of boys and young men. Norwegian researchers published an analysis of test scores of Norwegian draftees between the 1950s and 2002. From the 1950s until the mid-1980s, test scores steadily improved, then leveled off, then began to decline in the early 1990s.[21] (Norway requires military service of all young men, so a selection bias can't explain this drop.)

Denmark, like Norway, requires a brief stint of military service for all young men. Professor David Owen of Brooklyn College recently collaborated with Danish researchers to look for a similar phenomenon

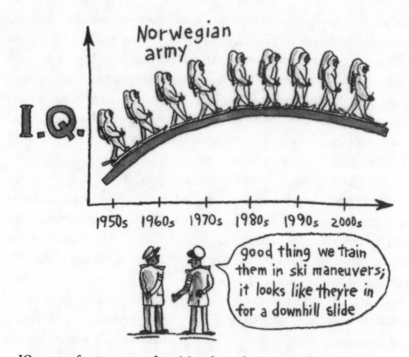

IQ scores of young men, after rising throughout most of the twentieth century, have now begun to decline, according to some studies.
Tom Dunne

among Danish recruits. Analyzing test scores for more than five hundred thousand recruits between 1959 and 2004, Owen and his Danish counterparts found a gradual rise in performance from 1959 through the 1980s, a plateau into the early 1990s, and a definite decline between about 1994 and 2004.[22]

And what about preparing for the real world? In the real world—unless you're a fighter pilot or a Marine sniper—being able to push a button 0.02 seconds faster than the other guy isn't such a valuable skill. Preparing teenagers for the demands of real life requires skills quite different from the cognitive and visuomotor skills required to master video games. Imagine a young father, in his twenties let's say, trying to comfort his crying baby daughter. There are no buttons to push, no photon torpedoes to fire. The right thing to do may be simply to rock the baby and

THE SECOND FACTOR: VIDEO GAMES 67

hum a lullaby. The chief virtue required may not be lightning virtuosity with a game controller, but merely—patience. If you need to get along with a belligerent coworker, the chief virtue you need may not be lightning speed. In most video games, the best way to deal with difficult people is to vaporize them with photon torpedoes. In the real world, what you need is not high-tech virtual weaponry, but patience.

The stereotypical pastimes of boys and men in previous generations were pretty good at teaching skills like patience. Thirty years ago, and even more so fifty years ago, it was more common for boys and men to go hunting and fishing together. Boys who go fishing with an experienced fisherman soon learn that a good fisherman has to be able to wait patiently. That sort of patience might serve a young father well. But video games do not teach that kind of patience.

So are boys getting dumber? Maybe. Are video games to blame? Perhaps in part. But I think we need to focus more on the *non*cognitive effects of video games. Instead of asking whether video games improve reaction times (they do, slightly, at least in some studies), we should ask: Do video games disengage boys from the real world? Does playing video games make boys more violent? Researchers at Yale University recently reported that playing violent video games such as *Doom* clearly and unambiguously causes young men to have a more violent self-image and to behave more violently; this report has not received any coverage in the media, to the best of my knowledge.[23] A comprehensive review of the research on video games recently demonstrated that playing violent video games leads directly "to aggressive behavior, aggressive cognition, aggressive affect, and cardiovascular arousal, and to decreases in helping behavior." The linkage between the violent game and the boy's antisocial behavior is unequivocally cause-and-effect, these researchers found; the end result is that boys who play these games are more likely to engage in "serious, real-world types of aggression." The more carefully researchers control for all the variables, the larger the effect size, suggesting that previous studies "underestimate the true magnitude of observed deleterious effects on behavior, cognition, and affect."[24]

Moreover, researchers have found that playing violent video games has a substantially more toxic effect than watching equally violent television programs, probably because when a boy is watching a violent TV pro-gram he's watching someone else commit the violent act, but when he's playing *Doom* or *Grand Theft Auto* or *Halo*, he's inflicting the death and destruction himself.[25]

Video games also tend to teach the wrong lessons about masculinity. A study entitled "The Emotional Appeal of Violent Video Games for Adolescent Males" found that boys prefer games that allow them to ex-perience "emotions that sustain dominant masculine identity," which sounds like something akin to the will to power. These games are grati-fying to boys, this study found, not only because the boys have the satis-faction of being the tough guy, but also because they are in charge of the game itself: they can turn it off any time they want to and move on to another game in another universe.[26] In real life, you can't just walk away from the havoc you create. In the world of video games, you can.

The destructive effects of video games are not on boys' cognitive abil-ities or their reaction times, but on their motivation and their connect-edness with the real world. These boys may be highly motivated, but their motivation has been derailed: I've seen boys who care much more about their success at *Halo* than about their grade in Spanish. They're motivated, but they've become disconnected from the real world. The video game world is more real to them than the world of homework and grades and college applications. Violent video games in particular tend to promote this disconnection, precisely because of the unreality of the violence. Your son knows that he doesn't get to fire photon torpedoes at the kids he doesn't like at school.

It's easy to see how some parents can be confused about video games. The experts don't agree, as we've seen. In my judgment, though, the re-search clearly indicates that boys who spend many hours each week playing violent video games are at greatly increased risk of disengaging from the real world. One of the highly regarded researchers in this field, Professor Craig Anderson, chairman of the department of psychology at the University of Iowa, has pointed out that the strength of the evidence linking video games to antisocial behaviors is every bit as strong as the evidence linking second-hand smoke to lung cancer or lead poisoning in infancy to lower IQ scores. Professor Anderson also notes that the controversy now surrounding video games is reminiscent of the controversy surrounding cigarette smoking in the 1960s or lead poisoning in the 1970s. After all, most people who are exposed to cigarette smoke will never get lung cancer. And some people who get lung cancer are not smokers and have never been exposed to cigarette smoke. Likewise (Professor Anderson would argue) not all boys who play video games twenty hours a week will disengage from real life, and not all boys who disengage from real life are video game players.[27]

So what rules should you lay down for your son? Professor Anderson has provided some practical guidelines based on the published research.[28] He recommends first of all that you either play the game yourself or watch it being played. Then ask yourself these questions:

- Does the game involve some characters trying to harm others?
- Does this happen frequently, more than once or twice in thirty minutes?
- Is the harm rewarded in any way?
- Is the harm portrayed as humorous?
- Are nonviolent solutions absent or less "fun" than the violent ones?
- Are realistic consequences of violence absent from the game?

If you answer yes to two or more of these questions, then Professor Anderson suggests that you reconsider whether your son should be allowed to play the game. The first consideration should not be how many hours per day or per week your son is allowed to play these games. The first question should be what kind of video games he is allowed to play at all. Violent video games that reward antisocial aggression—games such as *Grand Theft Auto* and *Doom*—should not be permitted in the house. Period. "Antisocial aggression" means aggression—such as killing police officers or prostitutes—that runs counter to all acceptable social behavior. A game like *SpyHunter*, on the other hand, in which the player is rewarded for killing terrorists and (just as important) penalized for any careless injury to innocent bystanders, is arguably less harmful—although it's still not as good a choice for your son, in my judgment, as racing his bicycle around a track.

Another consideration is what activities are displaced by playing video games. If your son is neglecting his friendships with non-gamer friends to spend more time playing video games, then he's spending too much time playing video games. If he refuses to sit down to dinner with the family because he's in the middle of a video game, then he needs some help from you getting his priorities straight.

Or maybe there's a more complex dynamic at work. I've seen more than one family where Dad is fighting with Mom, daughter Emily is perpetually angry at both Mom and Dad—and son Jared just doesn't want to deal with it. So he uses video games as an escape and an excuse. He just stays in his room with the door closed. So if your son seems to be using video games at least partly as an excuse to get out of family activities, you may have to ask yourself some hard questions about why that might be so.

I'm not the only person who's noticed how video games are displacing family activities such as having dinner together. Elinor Ochs is a cultural anthropologist and director of UCLA's Center on Everyday Lives of Families. She has studied how the electronic culture is changing family life. She's videotaped what actually happens in middle-class suburban homes. She found that when a parent arrives home, the kids are so absorbed by what they're doing that they often barely even raise their heads from their electronic gadgets. The returning parent is greeted only about a third of the time, usually with a perfunctory 'Hi.' "About half the time the kids ignored [the parent] or didn't stop what they were doing, multitasking and monitoring their various electronic gadgets," Ochs says. "We also saw how difficult it was for parents to penetrate the child's universe. We have so many videotapes of parents actually backing away, retreating from kids who are absorbed by whatever they're doing."[29]

And what about teenage boys having relationships with girls? Surprisingly, especially to those of us over thirty, many boys today seem to prefer playing video games to being with girls. Mr. Welsh, the teacher at T. C. Williams High School that I mentioned earlier, has heard any number of stories along these lines. Girls at his school have told him that at parties they "are often totally ignored as the guys gather around TV screens, entranced by one video game or another. 'Girls sit around watching the guys play until they get fed up and drive off looking for something else to do,' says junior Sarah Kell, for whom the games range from 'stupid and boring' to 'disgusting.' 'We try to tell them they're wasting their time, but they just keep going. Some guys stay up playing until three in the morning on school nights, and then they try to do their homework.'"[30]

Boys prefer video games over girls? In the summer and fall of 2006, the *New York Times* published a series of front-page articles entitled "The New Gender Divide." One of these described how many young men seem more interested in playing their video games than in being with their girlfriends. The reporter interviewed one young woman at college who had broken off her relationship with a young man, "in part out of frustration over his playing video games four hours a day. 'He said he was thinking of trying to cut back to fifteen hours a week,' she said. 'I said, "Fifteen hours is what I spend on my internship, and I get paid $1,300 a month. That's my litmus test now: I won't date anyone who plays video games. It means they're choosing to do something that wastes their time and sucks the life out of them.'"[31]

A young man at college today has unprecedented sexual opportunities. Unlike his father or grandfather, he is likely attending a school where men are outnumbered by women. Even boys who are not the best-looking or particularly popular now have an excellent chance of finding a young woman to date. Nevertheless, as the *New York Times* reported in a recent front-page story, college administrators are reporting that more and more young men show no interest in meeting young women (or meeting other men for that matter). They don't want to meet anybody. They just want "to stay in their rooms, talk to no one, [and] play video games into the wee hours. . . . [They] miss classes until they withdraw or flunk out."[32]

To summarize, here are some basic guidelines for the appropriate use of video games:

- **Content:** I strongly recommend you not allow your son to play video games in which the player is rewarded for killing police officers or noncombatant civilians. The video game industry itself provides a rating system for games, assigning an "M" for mature to this kind of antisocial violence. "M" games should not be sold to or used by anyone under eighteen years of age. But just because a game is rated "T" for teen doesn't guarantee that it's appropriate for your son. Familiarize yourself with the T-rated games. Even games rated "E" for "Everyone" cannot be assumed to be safe. In fact, Professor Anderson's team has found that some of the E-rated games were more violent—and engendered more violent behaviors—than some explicitly violent "T" games. Anderson and colleagues ". . . were somewhat surprised to find that even cartoonish children's violent games seemed to have the same short-term effect as the most graphic T-rated violent games. . . . what seems to matter is whether the game includes aggressive content, not how realistic or graphic the violence is."[33]

- **Time:** No more than forty minutes a day on school days, one hour a day on other days—and that's only after homework and household chores have been completed.

- **Activities displaced:** Make sure your son knows where his priorities should be. Family comes first; schoolwork comes second; friends come third; video games are last. If your family is one of the fortunate few in which most family members still sit down to share a common evening meal, then sitting down to dinner with the family is more important than playing a video game, more important than talking on the phone with a friend, more important even than finishing a homework assignment. Homework is more important than talking with friends or playing a video game. Taking a phone call from a friend should be a higher priority than playing out a video game, though.

The Polar Bear Club

If you've followed my argument about the will to power, you'll understand that just restricting your son's access to video games is at best only half the challenge. You want to help find a constructive outlet for your son's need to conquer. In some cases, competitive sports and a more competitive academic format—such as the team competitions discussed in chapter 2—might provide such an outlet. What kind of free-time activities and hobbies would be the best choice for this kind of boy? How can he best satisfy his need to be tested and to triumph?

Let me give you one example, from the boys' school near Edmonton that I mentioned earlier. At that school, every boy is required to participate in the Outdoor Challenge Exercise, which varies from year to year. One year, the Outdoor Challenge consisted of each boy having to take a swim in the frigid waters of the North Saskatchewan River in early spring. As one observer wrote:

> The water was frigid, with the ice breaking up only a week earlier. I could see the new boys' anxiety rise as time neared for them to tip their canoes over and take a swim in the 1° C water. Some chatted incessantly about being too young to die and how they were sure they would never have children, while others were sullen. . . . Canoes were dumped one after the other and, in due process, its former occupants were hauled into a "rescue canoe" and taken ashore to dry off. Every one of those boys arrived on shore with their chests puffed out, feeling like a man. Each boy claimed victory over the chilly waters of the North Saskatchewan. They also stated that no one at their old school has tried or would dare to try such an experience.[34]

In my firsthand experience, this sort of trial by fire is immensely satisfying, particularly for boys who are addicted to video games. It suddenly dawns on them: this is the real thing. The video games are just a simulation. This is reality. Once a boy achieves that insight, video games often lose much of their power over him.

The story of the canoe-dumping exercise in Saskatchewan reminds me of the experience of one of my own patients. At age twelve, Aaron Grossman was an avid video game player. His behavior bordered on addiction. The defining characteristic of addiction, incidentally, is loss of control: the boy knows that he shouldn't be spending so much time playing video games, he may not even want to play that much, but he just feels that he can't help it (the photo on the cover of this book captures the body language of the addicted player). So Aaron was spending three or four hours a day playing video games, mostly sports games like *Madden NFL*. When his parents asked him whether he'd like to try playing real football, though, he said no. He wasn't interested.

His mom and dad, Jennifer and David, decided to sign Aaron up for football anyway, Pop Warner football (a nationwide football organization for youth founded in 1929). They didn't ask Aaron. They just told him that he was going to play. I've found that parents can do this kind of compulsory sign-up for a boy only up to about age twelve or maybe age thirteen but generally no later. If you drive a fifteen-year-old boy to an activity he doesn't want to attend, he may simply get out of the car and walk away. But Aaron's parents judged correctly that their son was still young enough to go to the practice on their say-so.

Once Aaron was surrounded by the other boys who were doing their best to run, kick, throw, and catch, he joined in. After all, the format of the first day of Pop Warner football isn't much different from gym class at school. It's not unfamiliar.

On the drive back home that first day, Jennifer wisely did not ask whether Aaron had a good time. Asking whether Aaron had a good time would have been very nearly equivalent to asking him to admit he was wrong and his parents were right. Instead, she just said, "Practice tomorrow starts at eleven a.m., right?"

He nodded.

The practices were every day, Monday through Friday, sometimes lasting several hours. It was hot. The second week, the boys put on their equipment: helmets, shoulder pads, the whole deal. Mom gasped the first time she saw another boy knock Aaron to the ground. But Aaron got up immediately and trotted back to where the coach was explaining the next drill.

The next day was the first scrimmage. Aaron was knocked down several times, one time pretty hard. It was a hot, muggy August day. On the ride home, Aaron was visibly flushed and tired. After driving in silence for several minutes, his mom finally said, "Aaron, if you want to quit, it's OK. Daddy and I appreciate your making an effort."

Aaron shook his head "no." "Coach can kick me off the team if he wants to," he said, "but I'm not quitting."

The words were so corny, so reminiscent of Richard Gere's line to Louis Gossett, Jr., in *An Officer and a Gentleman*, that Mom almost laughed. But then she realized that her son had almost certainly never seen *An Officer and a Gentleman*. He was serious.

Aaron stopped playing video games altogether during football season. When the season ended in November and his team didn't make the play-offs, he said "Maybe next year."

He started playing *Madden NFL* again, on and off, after the season ended, but seldom more than thirty minutes a day. "It's nothing like the real thing," he told his mom spontaneously one day. That's the closest he ever came to thanking his parents for signing him up for real-world football.

In March 2006, I wrote an op-ed for the *Washington Post* about the growing problem of unmotivated boys. We'll return to that op-ed, and the response it elicited from readers, in chapter 6. For now I just want to share with you an e-mail I received from a parent in North Carolina:

Dear Dr. Sax,

I read your article in the *Washington Post*. I'm not an expert, just a Mom. I have my own theory. I think video games are the main culprits in this phenomenon [of unmotivated boys]. I wish I had somehow shielded my son from such games or at least put a strict limit on them. When I see guys in their twenties who are totally unmotivated, mooching on someone else and lack any social skills that will benefit them in the workplace or in life, I've noticed a common thread: an obsession with video games.

Video games teach these boys that if you manipulate things a certain way, you will get an easy win. These boys have little interaction with people during the years when such interaction is crucial in developing the skills they need to handle themselves as an adult. They shut themselves off to the real world and get caught up in their fantasy worlds. After a while, they prefer their fantasies to the real world. In the real world, things are not so easy to control. They can't rule with a joystick. In the real world they have to talk to people. They have to work.

That brings up another point. Laziness. A guy addicted to video games can waste hour after hour after hour without doing anything productive. Playing games is easy. Studying is hard. Taking care of daily chores is hard. Working on a real job is hard.

We parents are to blame for some of this because it started out as a way to entertain our kids. We justified it by saying they were developing their hand/eye coordination. They were home, we knew what they were doing, they were out of our hair and not causing trouble. Now they are in their twenties and we are scratching our heads wondering, "What's their problem?"

I think if you were to research the growing popularity of video games and compare it to the growing number of young men living at home, you would find a parallel. I know that sounds simplistic, but sometimes the answers to complex questions are as plain as the nose on our face.

Cheryl M.
North Carolina

In this chapter, I've argued that video games are one factor derailing many boys. In the previous chapter, I suggested that changes in the education system—including the shift away from competitive formats in school—constitute another factor. But those changes aren't the whole story. I can think of plenty of boys who aren't motivated to succeed but who don't play video games and who don't thrive on competition. They're not motivated by the will to power. They're just not motivated, period.

What's their story?

4

THE THIRD FACTOR

Medications for ADHD

From the age of two, Timmy was fascinated by trucks. He would bang his toy trucks together, then pick them up and race around the house going *vroom-vroom*. When he was three, Timmy and the family's yellow Labrador, Miss Demeanor, got into the bad habit of chasing the UPS truck down the street, after the UPS driver had been friendly to them one day. Aside from the fact that three-year-olds shouldn't be running down the middle of a street, even in our suburban cul-de-sac nestled safely off the main roads, the real problem with that habit was that once Timmy was outdoors he was *gone*. He would start running after the truck and just keep going. He'd forget to come home, and wander, fearlessly and aimlessly, through other people's backyards and driveways, with Miss Demeanor trotting faithfully behind. After one frightening evening driving around the development looking for Timmy and the dog, Carol (Timmy's mother) considered having an invisible fence installed and putting the collar around Miss Demeanor's neck—and maybe a collar around Timmy's neck, too.

Aside from chasing after delivery trucks, Timmy was the darling of our neighborhood. His energy and enthusiasm for life were contagious.

Then came kindergarten. Timmy's teacher, Mrs. Engelhardt, spoke with Carol after the third week. "Timmy seems hyperactive," Mrs. Engelhardt said.

"Isn't that pretty normal for a five-year-old boy?" Carol said.

"Not really. I know you may think so," Mrs. Engelhardt said, before Carol could interrupt. "But as a teacher, I see a whole range of children. I've seen hundreds of children in the eleven years since I started teaching, and I just thought you should know that Timmy may be having some difficulties staying focused."

"You mean ADD?" Carol said.

"Well, I'm not a doctor," Mrs. Engelhardt said. "I don't make diagnoses. I just want you to be aware that Timmy is having trouble staying in his seat. He just can't sit still very long before he starts wiggling. I tell him to sit still, and he does, and then five minutes later he's wriggling in his chair again and giggling. It's very distracting to the other children."

"I'll talk to him," Carol promised.

Carol talked to Timmy, told him that he needed to sit still and be quiet, but Timmy seemed not to hear. By late October, both Mrs. Engelhardt and the school counselor were encouraging Carol to have Timmy seen by the doctor. So Carol made an appointment with the pediatrician.

On the day of the visit, the doctor's office was crowded with crying children who looked sick. There wasn't any space left in the "well-baby" corner of the office. Carol tried to shield her son from the germs she could almost see wafting through the air. After a half-hour wait, Timmy's name was called.

Dr. Feldman looked over the note from the school. "I see that the school is concerned about Timmy, they think he may have ADHD,*" she said. "What do you think, Carol?"

"I don't see anything really wrong with Timmy," Carol said. "I mean, Mrs. Engelhardt is concerned because Timmy won't sit still. But since

---

*ADHD = Attention Deficit Hyperactivity Disorder. The older term, no longer "correct," is ADD, Attention Deficit Disorder. However, many parents still use the term ADD, and I use the two terms interchangeably here.

when does kindergarten mean sitting still in a chair all day long? I thought kindergarten was supposed to be about singing songs, playing games, that sort of thing."

"You're about thirty years out of date," Dr. Feldman said, but not in a mean way. "That's what kindergarten used to be about. Today's kindergarten is pretty much what first grade was thirty years ago. Kindergarten nowadays is mostly about sitting in a chair with paper and pencil and learning to read and write."

"But if my son isn't ready to do that, does that mean my son has a problem? Maybe the school has a problem," Carol protested. "Maybe the problem is with the school expecting a five-year-old boy to sit still in a chair all day long. You know his school has all-day kindergarten."

"That's a fair point," Dr. Feldman said. "There's some evidence that many five-year-old boys are less ready and less able to sit for long periods of time than most five-year-old girls are." Dr. Feldman's beeper went off. She glanced at it. "That's the NICU," she said. "I'm going to have to interrupt our visit, I'm afraid. But here are the options, briefly. Option number one: No medication, no change in the basic plan at school. Instead, you just work harder with Timmy. Try to get him to behave the way the teachers want him to behave."

"What's option two?" Carol asked.

"Option two would be to pull Timmy out of kindergarten now, put him back in pre-K, and try again next year," Dr. Feldman said.

"You're saying I should hold him back."

"It's not such a bad idea, really," Dr. Feldman said. "As you yourself said a minute ago, there's something crazy about schools expecting five-year-old boys to sit still at a desk for six hours a day. Some boys can do it. Many girls can do it. But for many boys—for the boys who aren't ready to sit still in a chair all day long—their first experience of school is one long frustrating bore. And once they get off to a bad start, things can snowball in the wrong direction. One year can make a big difference. Often a boy will be more willing and able to sit still in class when he's six than when he was five. That one year can make all the difference in the world."

Carol paused. Then she said, "But how would I explain to my friends, and my parents, that my son flunked out of kindergarten? They'd think he's retarded. And I know Timmy is bright." Carol saw Dr. Feldman look again at the message on her beeper. "No, I can't do that. I won't hold my son back. What's option number three?"

"The third option is medication. Adderall, Ritalin, Metadate, Concerta. I usually start with a low dose of Concerta with these boys. If that works, great. If not, we adjust the dose."

"But stimulants like Concerta and Adderall and the others—aren't they harmful?"

"All medications have the potential for harm," Dr. Feldman said, standing up, suddenly impatient. "A child can die from swallowing twenty tablets of Tylenol. I've seen it happen." She looked again at her pager. "I'm sorry, Carol, but I have to answer this page. Think about what we discussed. Call my office if you decide you want to start the medication for your son."

Carol agonized over her decision for a week. She talked to friends. She searched the Internet. Finally she called and asked for the prescription Dr. Feldman had suggested.

Timmy's initial response to the medication reassured Carol that she had made the right decision. Timmy's behavior in school improved instantly, the very first day he took the medication. "You did the right thing," Timmy's teacher told her. "Now we can see how smart Timmy really is. He really is a very bright boy."

Carol beamed.

Dr. Feldman recommended that Timmy take the medication every day including weekends and holidays. But Carol decided not to make him take it over Christmas vacation. The first two days he was off the medication, she was alarmed by his behavior. The old impulsivity and energy were back, but with an unfamiliar edge. He didn't come inside when she called for him. When she went to bring him indoors, he suddenly threw his plastic hockey stick at her—directly at her, as if he wanted to hurt her. He had never done anything like that before.

The next day, and every day thereafter for the next two years, she made sure he took his medication. Dr. Feldman increased the dose the following fall, in October of first grade, when the teachers again said that Timmy wasn't paying attention.

The following spring, Carol heard about a study showing that boys who took medications like Concerta were likely to be shorter as adults than boys who didn't take those medications—three to four inches shorter, if they began the medication at age five as Timmy had and stayed on it for ten years.[1] Carol is short, just 5'1" tall, and Timmy's father is on the short side, at 5'8". Timmy was already showing a love for basketball, and Carol didn't want to be responsible for Timmy ending up 5'7" tall when he might have been 5'11".

So, when school let out that June, she stopped giving Timmy the medication. As she expected, Timmy showed "rebound." He was more impulsive than ever. But she also noticed something she had never seen before: Timmy had become lazy. It wasn't just that he didn't want to do his chores. He didn't want to do much of anything. He used to be enthusiastic about any project she or Timmy's grandparents would propose. He'd go fishing with his grandfather, or pick weeds in the garden with his grandmother, and he would enjoy it. Nothing was boring to him. Now everything was boring, except for video games.

Carol came to me for a second opinion that August. "I just don't know what to do," she said. "If I don't start him back on the medication, I'm dreading what school will be like, the phone calls from the teachers, all that. But I'm really bothered by what I'm seeing in Timmy this summer. He's been off the medication for two months and he's not getting any better. The laziness—that's something totally new for him. The lack of motivation. Do you think Timmy would have been like that now if he hadn't ever taken the medication?"

"It's hard to say for sure what might have happened," I said.

"I stopped his medication because I was worried it might stunt his growth," Carol said. "Now I'm finding out all these other problems. But what other options do I have?"

The syndrome we call ADHD has probably always been with us. Despite some claims to the contrary, ADHD was not invented thirty or forty years ago by drug companies eager to sell more medications.[2] In fact, it's easy to find accounts of boys written one hundred or more years ago who would meet all the modern criteria for ADHD. Some of those accounts are in medical journals. Some are in short stories and novels.

Take Tom Sawyer, for example. If you've never actually read Mark Twain's novel *The Adventures of Tom Sawyer*, you may want to read it now—if only to get some perspective on how the normative view of American boys has changed in the past 150 years. The official guidebook containing all criteria for all psychiatric diagnoses is the American Psychiatric Association's *Diagnostic and Statistical Manual of Mental Disorders*, 4th Edition—usually abbreviated *DSM-IV*. Some of the official *DSM-IV* criteria for ADHD include:

- "Often fails to give close attention to details or makes careless mistakes in schoolwork . . . "
- "Often has difficulty sustaining attention in tasks . . . "
- "Often avoids, dislikes, or is reluctant to engage in tasks that require sustained mental effort, such as schoolwork or homework . . . "[3]

Tom Sawyer fulfills these criteria with exuberance. He has no interest in school or schoolwork. Any indoor task that requires sustained attention is a task that Tom will not do well, if he does it at all. And despite attending Sunday school regularly, he appears not to have absorbed any of the information imparted to him there. He does at one point decide that he wants to win a prize Bible so as to impress Becky Thatcher. Children in his town are awarded special tickets when they memorize verses from the Bible. Tom trades knickknacks with his buddies to garner the necessary number of tickets needed to win a prize Bible—corresponding to memorizing two thousand verses. He turns in the tickets and is awarded the Bible. At the award ceremony, Becky Thatcher's father is about to bestow the award Bible on Tom, when he asks Tom to mention the names of just two of the twelve disciples of Jesus. Tom is at a complete loss. He finally blurts out, "David and Goliath!"

Many thoughtful people have pointed out that Tom Sawyer and boys like him would be diagnosed as having ADHD if they were to show up in a twenty-first-century American school. These people have suggested, with good reason, that perhaps the pathology lies not in the boy but in the school. In *Why Gender Matters*, I told the story of a boy who needed to be on multiple medications for ADHD when he was in school; but when he was assisting a professional hunter in Zimbabwe, he didn't need the medications at all, even when he had to sit motionless in the bush for long periods of time. (Update: in the years since I wrote *Why Gender Matters*, that boy has gone on to college and has published his poems and short stories in his college's journals—without taking any medication for ADHD.)

The fact remains that if Tom Sawyer is going to graduate from a twenty-first-century high school and go on to college, he is going to have to be able to sit still and pay attention in class. To help him do that, his parents may ask their doctor for help. And the doctor is likely to prescribe a medication such as Adderall, Ritalin, Concerta, Metadate, Dexedrine, Focalin, or Daytrana.

Stimulant medications such as Ritalin and Dexedrine have been on the market for over fifty years. Newer versions such as Adderall, Concerta, Focalin, and Metadate have been available only since the 1990s. In the past two decades, there has been an explosion in the use of these "academic steroids" for the treatment of ADD, depression, and even overweight. Boys in 2007 are thirty times more likely to be taking these medications compared with boys in 1987.[4]

"Why Not Give It a Try?"

How come boys today are so much more likely to be taking these medications compared with twenty years ago?

Several factors account for the greater willingness of doctors to medicate young minds today, and the greater willingness of parents to accept and even to seek out such medication.[5] One factor is our cultural shift away from individual responsibility toward third-party explanations. Thirty years ago, if a boy cursed his parents and spit at his teacher, the neighbors might say that the boy was a disobedient brat who needed a good spanking. Today, the same behavior from a similar boy might well prompt a trip to the pediatrician or the child psychiatrist. And the doctor is likely to "diagnose" the boy with Conduct Disorder (*DSM–IV* 312.82) or Oppositional-Defiant Disorder (*DSM–IV* 313.81). The main criterion for both these "disorders" is disobedient and disrespectful behavior that persists despite parental efforts.[6]

Is there really much of a difference between a neighbor saying "That boy is a disobedient brat," and a doctor saying "That boy has oppositional-defiant disorder"? I think there is. If another parent whom you trust and respect suggests that your son is a disobedient brat who needs stricter discipline, you just might consider adopting a tougher parenting style. If a doctor says that your son has a psychiatric diagnosis, the next step might reasonably be to ask whether a medication would be appropriate.

You can see how the assignment of responsibility differs in these two cases. If your son is a disobedient brat, then your son and you (his parents) have to take responsibility. You have to own up to the problem. You will probably have to make some changes. But if your son has a psychiatric diagnosis, that means he has a chemical imbalance in his brain. He—and you—are no more to blame for that imbalance than if your son were diagnosed with childhood leukemia, right? Psychiatrist Jennifer Harris recently pointed out that today, "many clinicians find it easier to tell parents their child has a brain-based disorder than to suggest parenting changes."[7]

Another factor has to do with the inappropriate acceleration of the early elementary curriculum. We've already discussed in chapter 2 how the first-grade curriculum of thirty years ago has become the kindergarten curriculum of today. If five-year-old Justin fidgets and taps his pencil and sometimes stands up in class for no reason, he may be referred to my office. Mom brings along a piece of paper from the teacher explaining the school's concerns. "They think that Justin may have ADHD."

Result: there's been an explosion in the prescribing of medication for very young children, particularly preschoolers and kindergartners.[8] According to an international comparison published in 2006, children in the United States are now at least three times more likely to be taking psychiatric medications compared with children in any European country.[9] And it often doesn't stop with just one medication. One-third of American children who are taking psychotropic medications today are actually taking two or three or four medications, not just one.[10] It's increasingly common to find a young boy who is on Adderall for his ADHD, clonidine to control his outbursts, and Prozac to stabilize his moods.

Four years ago, I obtained funding from the American Academy of Family Physicians to survey doctors in the Washington, DC, area* about ADHD. We asked many questions, but the most important one was: "Who first suggests the diagnosis of ADHD?" Is it the doctor? Some other professional? Mom? Dad? A teacher? A neighbor? A relative? The doctors told us that in the majority of cases, the diagnosis is first suggested by a teacher.[11]

Don't get me wrong. There's nothing wrong with teachers referring students with a concern about the student's ability to pay attention. On several occasions, I've visited schools at the request of parents to observe their son in the classroom after a teacher has made such a referral. I've found that the teacher is always right. Justin isn't paying attention. He's looking up at the ceiling or staring out the window or tapping his pencil. In every case I investigated, the teacher's observation was correct. If the teacher says Justin isn't paying attention, he's not paying attention.

But why isn't Justin paying attention? Does he truly have ADHD? Or is there some other reason?

It's the doctor's job to determine whether Justin's problem is due to ADHD or to some other cause. Unfortunately, most pediatricians and family physicians simply do not have the training to perform a sophisticated neurodevelopmental assessment of a five- or six- or seven-year-old boy to determine whether that boy's difficulties are due to ADHD or to some other problem. To their credit, just about every pediatrician and family physician who responded to our survey recognized that fact.

So what do the doctors do when asked to evaluate such a boy? We found that in a few cases, the doctor refers the child to a developmental

---

*Our survey included doctors in the District of Columbia, suburban Maryland (Prince Georges County and Montgomery County), and northern Virginia.

psychologist who is qualified to perform such an assessment. That doesn't happen very often, for several reasons. One is that many health plans don't cover such assessments, or if they do they provide only reduced or partial coverage. The out-of-pocket costs for such an assessment usually begin around seven hundred dollars but can run much higher.

Another reason is that many doctors believe in an empirical trial of medication, a time-honored tradition in American medicine. It's a very simple idea. If you think Justin might have ADHD, try giving him a medication for ADHD. If that helps, great. If not, then maybe it would be appropriate to go ahead and spend the seven hundred dollars on the formal assessment. Or maybe just try a stronger dose.

These medications will, indeed, improve the attention span and academic performance of many of the boys for whom they are prescribed. And for many middle-class and affluent parents today, that's all they need to know. If their boy is struggling in school, and the teacher suggests that these medications might help, and the doctor agrees—and the parents know three or four other boys in the same class who are already taking these same medications, apparently with good results—why not give it a try?

In May 2006, I had the privilege of speaking at the "Learning and the Brain" conference cosponsored by Harvard University. I wish I could say that my presentation was the most interesting, but it wasn't. Not by a long shot. The most interesting presentation by far, I thought, was given by MIT professor John Gabrieli.

Dr. Gabrieli's team somehow obtained permission to give powerful ADHD medications to normal children. These researchers also obtained permission to withhold ADHD medication from boys (and a few girls) who undeniably did have ADHD. Then Dr. Gabrieli's team tested both groups, on and off medication, to see how well both groups could learn with and without the medication. There was an audible gasp in the audience when Dr. Gabrieli showed us the crucial slide: medication for ADHD improved the performance of normal kids by the same degree that it improved the performance of kids with ADHD.[12]

That's a tremendously important finding. Many times I've been asked to provide a second opinion of a boy who's already been diagnosed with

ADHD. The parents come to me for a variety of reasons. Sometimes the in-laws have told them that their son doesn't need, or shouldn't take, medication. Sometimes the parents have seen something scary on TV about these drugs. So I evaluate their son, let's call him Jake. Several hours later, after doing the evaluation, I have sometimes said, "Mrs. So-and-so, Mr. So-and-so, I'm just not convinced that Jake really has ADHD."

One of the parents answers, "But the other doctor prescribed Adderall, and it's made such a difference. Jake is doing so much better since he's been on the medication. He's much less fidgety in class. The teacher says he's much better behaved and more focused. And his grades are up."

In other words, these parents—and Jake's doctor as well, in this case—are using the response to medication to confirm the diagnosis. "If medication for ADHD helps Jake to learn better, doesn't that mean that Jake probably has ADHD?"

As many of us have long suspected, and as Dr. Gabrieli's study confirms, the answer to that question is no. These medications—Ritalin, Concerta, Metadate, Dexedrine, Adderall, and other stimulants—are likely to improve the performance of a normal child just as much as a child who truly has ADHD. Just because these medications improve a child's performance in class, does not mean that the child has ADHD.

"But where's the harm?" one parent asked me. "If the medication helps my son to do better in class, and it doesn't seem to be hurting him in any way, why not give it to him?"

And now we come to the crux of the problem. Where's the harm, indeed? Many boys do look and feel more or less OK while they're taking these medications. What these parents don't know—and what the doctor also may not know—is that even relatively short-term use of these drugs, for just a year or perhaps less, can lead to changes in personality. The boy who used to be agreeable, outgoing, and adventurous becomes lazy and irritable.

The Nucleus Accumbens

Professor William Carlezon and his colleagues at Harvard Medical School recently reported that giving stimulant medications—such as those used to treat boys with ADHD—to juvenile laboratory animals results in those animals displaying a loss of drive when they grow up.[13] These animals look normal, but they're lazy. They don't want to work hard for anything, not even to escape a bad situation.

The Harvard investigators suggested that the stimulant medications might cause a similar phenomenon in children. Children who take these medications may look fine while they're taking them. They may look fine after they stop taking them. But as adults—when they're no longer taking the medication—they won't have much drive. They won't have much get-up-and-go.

The stimulant medications appear to exert their harmful effects by damaging an area in the developing brain called the nucleus accumbens. Independent groups of researchers at the University of Michigan, the Medical University of South Carolina, the University of Pittsburgh, Brown University, as well as in Sweden, Italy, and the Netherlands, all have found that exposing young laboratory animals to these medications— even at low doses for short periods—can cause permanent damage to the nucleus accumbens,[14] the part of the brain that is responsible for translating motivation into action. If a boy's nucleus accumbens is damaged, he may still feel hungry, or sexually aroused. He just won't feel motivated to do anything about it.

What about girls? Would girls be affected the same way? It's hard to say. Professor Carlezon has studied only male animals. There's substantial evidence that the neurological substrate of ADHD in girls and women may differ significantly from the substrate of ADHD in boys and men.[15] So we can't assume that what's true for males holds true for females, or vice versa. More research on sex differences in the consequences of treatment for ADHD, and on the long-term consequences of these medications generally, is urgently needed.

One particularly disturbing recent study—conducted jointly by researchers at Tufts, UCLA, and Brown University—documented a nearly linear correlation between the nucleus accumbens and individual motivation. The smaller the nucleus accumbens, the more likely that person was to be apathetic, lacking in drive. These investigators emphasized that apathy was quite independent of depression.[16] A young man can be completely unmotivated—and still be perfectly happy and content.

Drug companies spend tens of millions of dollars every year promoting medications such as Adderall, Ritalin, Concerta, and Metadate. But nobody is buying ads to warn parents and doctors about the possible risks. To be sure, those risks are not proven. We don't know for sure yet whether the damage these medications cause in the brains of laboratory animals also occurs in children who take the same medications. Maybe it does. Maybe it doesn't.

Would you like to volunteer your son for the trial?

Video Games Actually Do Fry Your Brain

Prescription medications are not the only problem. New research suggests that video games may also affect the brain in ways that compromise motivation. The nucleus accumbens operates in balance with another area of the brain, the dorsolateral prefrontal cortex (DLPFC). The nucleus accumbens is responsible for channeling drive and motivation, and gives the drive a rewarding character. The DLPFC provides a target and a context for the drive. Both these areas of the brain need to be working properly in order for a person to be motivated, and working toward a real-world goal.

A recent brain imaging study of boys between the ages of seven and fourteen years found that playing video games puts this system seriously out of kilter. It seems to shut off blood flow to the DLPFC. In other words, playing these games engorges the nucleus accumbens with blood, while diverting blood away from the balancing area of the brain. The net result is that playing video games gives boys the reward associated with achieving a great objective, but without any connection to the real world, without any sense of a need to contextualize the story.[17]

In other words, video games may affect the brain in children in much the same way that medications like Ritalin and Adderall and Concerta do. Curiously, this point is not disputed even by the most ardent advocates of video games. In *Everything Bad Is Good for You*, Steven Johnson noted that research on video games suggests that these games stimulate "a part of the brain called the nucleus accumbens" in much the same way that crack cocaine affects the same area.[18]

As we saw in the last chapter, video games probably don't make anyone smarter. More important, video games have the power to displace and distort the motivation of boys and young men, so that they no longer have the same interest in real-world success and real-world achievement.

"An Antiquated Relic of the Victorian Era"

We have considered an array of evidence that the stimulant medications that are most often prescribed for ADHD may adversely affect children. And as we have seen, some studies suggest that these adverse effects may be lasting: studies in laboratory animals in particular have shown that taking these medications during youth or adolescence may negatively affect learning and motivation in adulthood.

But I've had first-hand experience with boys who have proven that these adverse effects can be overcome.

I first met Jared when I did his prekindergarten physical. He was five years old: bright, outgoing, and friendly. Kindergarten, first grade, and second grade all went fairly well. Problems began in third grade, when Jared was eight years old. He started complaining about school. "It's stupid." The teachers were beginning to tell the parents that Jared wasn't paying attention in class. He had tested in the gifted range, especially in creative writing and art, but the problems actually seemed to have started after he was put into these gifted and talented classes, despite the very small class sizes. And his grades were starting to suffer.

Jared's mother, Deborah Stolzfus, had researched the situation thoroughly. When she brought Jared to see me, she had already diagnosed the problem: Jared had ADHD, "predominantly inattentive type" (she was using the professional jargon quite appropriately). "The reason he doesn't like school is because he can't pay attention, because of his ADHD, so he doesn't do well," she explained to me. "Jared is a perfectionist. He hates to do something if he can't do it perfectly." Jared's mother didn't really even want me to do my own evaluation; she just wanted me to prescribe medication. "I'm concerned that if we don't take action now, while he's still young, the situation could snowball," she told me. "He'll decide he hates school, and he'll start to fall behind. We definitely need to do something."

This encounter took place in the fall of 1996, when I had less confidence in my own judgment and diagnostic skills than I have now. And Deborah was quite determined. I suspect that any doctor might have had difficulty persuading her to change course. I insisted on a brief (thirty-minute) evaluation. At the end of that evaluation, I still wasn't persuaded that Jared really had ADHD, of any variety. But Deborah said, "Why don't we just try a low dose of medication and see whether it helps?" (This was ten years before Dr. Gabrieli did his study, remember.)

So I agreed to prescribe Ritalin, 5 mg twice daily. It had no effect—no beneficial effect, at least. Jared and Deborah returned three weeks later.

"He needs a stronger dose," Deborah said authoritatively.

"I'm sorry," I said. "I'm just not persuaded that increasing Jared's medication is the right course of action. I tell you what. How about if you take Jared to see Dr. So-and-so"—and I named a renowned expert on ADHD. "He's a consultant to the NIH. He's written a book on the subject. Let's see what he has to say."

Mrs. Stolzfus took her son to be evaluated by the famous expert. He agreed with her; Jared needed a stronger dose of medication. When that didn't help, the doctor switched Jared from Ritalin to Adderall. When Jared became even more moody and withdrawn, he diagnosed a comorbid condition—depression—and added Prozac. When Jared began having angry outbursts at school, the doctor added clonidine. Jared was now nine years old, he still hated school, but now he was on three medications. At that point the family switched health insurance to a plan we didn't accept, and I lost touch with them.

Four years passed. Dad got a promotion and the family switched back to a plan that was in our network. One day I noticed that the name *Jared Stolzfus* was on the schedule for a routine school physical. I looked in the nurse's note under the listing of medications and saw "None."

Interesting.

I walked into the room. I barely recognized Jared. He was a totally different kid: not merely older, but transformed. He was now muscular and tan. But the biggest difference was that he was smiling—a big smile like I hadn't seen on his face since he was in kindergarten. "Hello, Jared," I said, "nice to see you again. So tell me: what's your favorite thing to do in your spare time?" This is a good break-the-ice question for girls and boys in this age group, I have found.

"My favorite thing to do in my spare time," Jared repeated, thinking the question over. "Hmm. Well right now, I think my favorite thing to do is to read about ancient Minoa," he said.

"How's that?" I asked.

"Well maybe ancient Crete. Or Mycenae." He launched into a fascinating lecture about the ancient island of Thera, in the Aegean Sea. This island was destroyed by a massive volcanic explosion around 1500 BC, he explained. "But the people living there must have known the volcano was about to erupt," he told me, "because when you excavate the remnants of the island—which is now called Santorini, but it's really just the caldera of the volcano that used to be Thera—when you excavate the caldera, you find sheep bones and cattle bones but no human bones."

I was just glad I knew what a "caldera" was.

Jared continued with his lecture. He taught me how that cataclysmic event may have served as the source of the myth of Atlantis, recorded by Plato roughly a thousand years after the event, about an advanced civilization crumbling into the sea as the result of a natural disaster. I was fascinated. Jared gave me the title of a book on the subject to read so that I could learn more.[19]

I went out to talk with Deborah. "I'm amazed," I told her. "I'm so glad to see—what a tremendous change! Tell me what happened," I asked, but before she could answer, I tried to answer my own question. "I bet I know what happened. I bet you stopped the medications. I was so uneasy about such a young boy taking all those medications."

Mom shook her head. "We tried stopping the medication, but he got worse. More withdrawn, more grumpy. The doctor you sent us to was worried Jared might be suicidal and talked about hospitalizing him. So we went back on the medications, even though they really didn't seem to be helping much."

"So what's the secret?" I asked. "What turned everything around?"

Deborah said, "We transferred him from Byron* to the Heights."

Now it was my turn to shake my head. "But Byron is an outstanding school," I said. "And so is the Heights. They're both excellent schools. How could transferring Jared from one excellent school to another excellent school make such a huge difference?"

Mrs. Stolzfus matter-of-factly responded, "The Heights is all boys. Byron is coed."

"What possible difference could that make?" I asked—and before she could reply, I said, "Mrs. Stolzfus, I don't mean to be disrespectful, but we're in the twenty-first century now. As near as I can see, single-sex education is an antiquated relic of the Victorian era. We live in a coed world. School should prepare kids for the real world, which is a coed world, so school should be coed. That just seems pretty straightforward to me."

Deborah responded: "You need to visit the Heights, Dr. Sax. Jared was miserable at the old school. The people at Byron had determined, quite correctly, that Jared is gifted in art and in creative writing. So they put him in special advanced classes in art and creative writing—where he was the only boy, or sometimes just one of two boys. Most of the other kids in the class were always girls. So the other boys teased him. "You like art, you must be a fag," they said. Jared asked to drop out of the art class. He came to feel that school was a waste of time. His talents just led to him being made fun of. But he couldn't pretend to like the things that the other boys like, that boys are "supposed" to like at a coed school. So he was just miserable. At the Heights, he's just blossomed. Obviously all the kids in the art class at the Heights are boys. Same with the creative writing class. And it's just amazing how rapidly his interests have expanded and matured in the years he's been at the Heights. Not just academically. His favorite teacher, the history teacher, is also the lacrosse coach. So Jared decided to try lacrosse, and you know what? He's pretty good!"

---

*The name I have given the coed school, "Byron," is fictitious; "The Heights" in Potomac, Maryland, is the true name of the school to which this boy transferred, www.heights.edu.

This was an epiphany of sorts for me. I had attended only coed schools. I had always thought of single-sex education as an out-of-date relic of a bygone era. Maybe I would have to reconsider.

I wanted to share this true story with you for two reasons. Most important, in the context of this chapter, I think it's important to stress that despite all the scary news about Adderall and Ritalin and Concerta and Metadate, the fact that a boy has taken these medications does not mean that he is doomed. In the six years since Mrs. Stolzfus told me about the benefits of a boys' school for her son, I've seen many other similar cases: boys who were put on medications when they attended a coed school, who were able to stop those medications after switching to a boys' school, and who blossomed into well-rounded students and athletes after making the transition. Those cases have led me to believe that, in many cases, boys are being put on these medications to fit the boy to the school. I've come to believe that we should not medicate boys so they fit the school; we should change the school to fit the boy.

Which leads me to the second reason I think this story is important. In this true story, the school provided Jared's salvation. The school made all the difference. The parents were as dedicated and concerned and involved as any parents can be, all along, but until they transferred Jared to a school that was a better match for him, Jared was heading in the wrong direction.

I'm not saying that the Heights is a "better" school than Byron. I know other families who much prefer Byron to the Heights. They feel that the Heights is too regimented, or too strict, or that it has too strong a religious affiliation. Recall the point I made in chapter 2: there's no such thing as the "best" school without specifying the particular child who will be attending there. The best school for Jared may be a bad choice for his brother Jason. You have to know your child and then find the school that is the best match for your child.

One of the central questions we are trying to answer in this book is why we are seeing so many boys today who just don't seem motivated. What has changed in just the past twenty to thirty years that might account for this emerging phenomenon? So far, we've identified three factors:

1. Changes in educational format and curricula over the past twenty to thirty years, in particular:
   - The acceleration of the early elementary curriculum
   - The shift from *Kenntnis* to *Wissenschaft*
   - The abolition of competitive formats
2. The advent of ultra-high-tech video games
3. The overprescribing of stimulant medications

In the brain, both video games (factor #2) and medications (factor #3) may adversely affect the delicate balance between the nucleus accumbens and the DLPFC,[20] resulting in boys who look normal, who feel normal, but who just don't see the point of working hard to achieve some objective in the real world.

When I first wrote about this topic for publication, I hadn't identified the three factors listed above. My first article on this topic[21] followed a completely different line of inquiry and evidence, tracking down the fourth factor: endocrine disruptors.

5

THE FOURTH FACTOR
Endocrine Disruptors

Fish on the Wild Side

I live in one of the outer suburbs of Washington, DC. The medical office where I work is located only a few blocks from my home. Some mornings I indulge my taste for *schadenfreude* by listening to the traffic reports on the radio. The Woodrow Wilson Bridge is often featured on those reports. The Wilson Bridge is the longest bridge on the Capital Beltway, crossing the Potomac River just south of Washington, DC. It's often a bottleneck. "And of course, the approach to the Wilson Bridge is stacked up again this morning. It's stop and go. You can expect about a twenty-minute delay between Route 210 and the Wilson Bridge. . . . "

In the fall of 2006, scientists studying fish in the Potomac River reported an unsettling discovery. Collecting fish near the Wilson Bridge, the scientists found that the females were normal, but the males weren't. When the scientists examined the male sex organs, they didn't find sperm, they found eggs.

This weird finding wasn't confined to the congested and polluted areas around the Wilson Bridge. The scientists collected fish at all seven tributaries of the Potomac, extending two hundred miles up the

Shenandoah River into Virginia and more than one hundred miles up both the Monocacy River and Conococheague Creek in Maryland. At every one of these seven sites, the scientists found that at least 80 percent of the male smallmouth bass they examined were feminized: the sex organs in the male fish were making eggs instead of sperm.[1]

This news was reported on the front page of the *Washington Post* for the excellent reason that most of the readers of the *Washington Post* get their drinking water from the Potomac River. What's in the river water that's causing the male fish to become feminized? Could that something, whatever it is, affect boys and men in a similar way? What about girls and women?

Vicki Blazer, a veterinary pathologist who specializes in fish, acknowledged that the results were "striking." She concluded that the Potomac River and its tributaries clearly have significant levels of "endocrine disruptors": substances that mimic the actions of hormones, specifically female hormones. The hormones themselves are not present in the river. In fact, Dr. Blazer and other scientists haven't been able to figure out exactly which chemical or combination of chemicals is causing the problem among the fish in the Potomac. "There is this sort of widespread endocrine disruption in the Potomac, but we don't know still what are the causes," Dr. Blazer told the *Post*.

Local agency officials were quick to assure the public that the water is safe to drink. But some consumers were skeptical. "If they can't tell us what the problem is," said Ed Merrifield, executive director of the environmental group Potomac Riverkeeper, "then how can they tell us that they've taken it out of the water?"[2]

The *Washington Post* previously reported—in a seemingly unrelated story—that more and more young men attending colleges and universities in and around Washington, DC, are struggling with impotence, and even losing interest in sex.[3] The fact that the Potomac River now appears to contain a substance or substances that can emasculate males puts that story in a new light. But at least those impotent young men aren't making eggs.

If this problem had been observed only in the Potomac River estuary and Potomac River tributaries, we wouldn't be discussing it. But this problem is far more widespread. Similar stories of feminized or emasculated wildlife, including a diverse array of mammals as well as fish, have now been described in Idaho and Washington, in central Florida, in the Great Lakes, in Alaska, in England, and even in Greenland.[4]

What's going on?

And could it be relevant to your son?

This issue obviously affects girls as well as boys. One of the best-documented recent stories about endocrine disruptors concerns their effects on girls. Let's take a look at that story, and then see how or whether it's relevant to boys.

She's Only Eight Years Old, But She Could Pass for Twelve or Fourteen

Doctors in San Juan, Puerto Rico, began noticing something strange as early as 1980. Girls as young as seven and eight years of age were going through puberty. Those girls' breasts were developing in ways that would be more typical of twelve- and thirteen- and fourteen-year-old girls. As reports of these physically precocious girls spread around the city, and as the number of girls reported grew from the dozens to the hundreds and then the thousands, pediatric endocrinologists in San Juan joined together to try to discover the cause of the girls' early development. They tested many hypotheses.

Hormones in beef? One of the first ideas the specialists considered was the notion that hormones in the meat the girls were eating might be partly responsible. For more than thirty years now, Americans have been eating meat that comes from cattle that have been fed anabolic steroids—sex hormones—to make the cattle more meaty. These are, in many cases, the same steroid hormones that human athletes are prohibited from using because of the health risks. The doctors conjectured that perhaps these hormones were causing the girls' breasts to develop.[5] The U.S. Department of Agriculture joined with the Puerto Rico Department of Health to investigate this notion thoroughly, but they found no evidence to support this hypothesis. Compared to normal girls, the girls with premature breast development didn't have higher levels of any hormones linked to the hormones given to cattle. And, it wasn't clear how the synthetic hormones fed to the cattle—which are usually male hormones—would cause precocious puberty in girls but not in boys.

Genetics? The next hypothesis the specialists tested was genetic. Maybe ethnic Puerto Rican girls are just more prone to precocious puberty than girls from other ethnic and racial groups—or so they hypothesized. The doctors then carefully compared the frequency of precocious puberty among Puerto Rican girls living in Puerto Rico with Puerto Rican girls living in Philadelphia. They found that the Puerto Rican girls living in Philadelphia were not at risk. Only the girls in Puerto Rico were at risk. Furthermore, girls in Puerto Rico were showing early breast development regardless of their race or ethnicity. Genetics didn't seem to have anything to do with it.[6] The cause of the problem wasn't in the girls' chromosomes: it had to be something in the environment, something in San Juan.

Plastics. Then the doctors heard about feminized alligators in central Florida. Scientists with the U.S. Fish and Wildlife Service had found emasculated male alligators in the wildlife preserves around Lake Apopka in central Florida. The alligators had shriveled testicles and high female hormone levels. The scientists had linked the emasculation of those male alligators to phthalates.[7]

Clear plastic bottles—the type used for most bottled water in the United States, as well as for soda beverages such as Coke, Pepsi, and Dr. Pepper—are made with plasticizers called phthalates, in particular polyethylene terephthalate (PET). Have you ever left a plastic bottle in your car on a summer day? Did the bottle contain Coke or Pepsi or Sprite or was it just plain bottled water? Did you take a drink from the bottle? Did you notice that it tasted just a little funny? Just a little—plasticky?

What you were tasting was PET, polyethylene terephthalate. When you let one of these clear plastic bottles get warm, the phthalate starts to leach into the beverage. The higher the temperature, and the more acidic the beverage, the more phthalate will leak into the beverage.

Lake Apopka is in the same watershed that serves Orlando. We're talking Disney World. Just imagine how many plastic bottles end up in the water, one way or another. And it's hot in central Florida. The alligators are getting a hefty dose of phthalates. That appears to be the best explanation for their shriveled testicles, according to the U.S. Fish and Wildlife Service. Phthalates mimic the action of female hormones (more about that below).

The doctors in Puerto Rico wondered whether phthalates might be disrupting and accelerating the girls' endocrine development. So they tested the levels of phthalate in the girls' blood and compared their levels to the levels in Puerto Rican girls who didn't have early breast development.

Bingo. The girls whose breasts had developed early had high levels of phthalates, about six times higher than the levels in girls whose breasts had not yet developed: an average of 512 parts per billion in girls with premature breast development, compared with 86 parts per billion in normal girls.[8]

This story is an extreme case, but many studies now suggest that something like this may be taking place right now, more subtly, among girls throughout the United States and Canada. Girls are going through puberty earlier than ever before. In the United States, the number of girls beginning puberty at age eight has become so great that pediatric endocrinologists—doctors who specialize in problems of the endocrine system and hormones—called a special conference to decide what should be done about the problem. Just think of all the options the specialists might have considered. They could have called for an ongoing study to determine whether girls who develop adult breasts at age eight are at increased risk for developing breast cancer twenty or thirty years later, as some have suggested.[9] They could have called for a moratorium on clear plastic bottles for beverages served to prepubescent children. They could at least have called for an all-out effort to study the problem.

But the American endocrinologists did none of those things. Instead they decided simply to redefine what's normal. The experts decided that a girl who needs to wear a bra at age eight should no longer be considered an anomaly.[10]

But this is a book about boys. So why are we talking about girls?

Puberty Out of Synch

The overwhelming majority of modern chemicals that mimic the action of human sex hormones, curiously, mimic the action only of female hormones. Synthetic industrial chemicals that mimic the action of male hormones are rare. As a result, the average child today is practically awash in synthetic chemicals that have the effect of accelerating a girl's sexual development. The effects on boys are more subtle. The net effect appears to be a slowing and/or warping of boys' sexual development. There is now substantial evidence that the very same endocrine-disrupting chemicals that accelerate puberty in girls may delay or disrupt the process of puberty in boys.[11]

As a result, middle school has become a very strange place. There has always been a disparity between the sexual development of girls and boys, but thirty or forty or fifty years ago the gap was measured in months rather than years. In that bygone era, girls began puberty around age twelve or thirteen, boys around age thirteen or fourteen. If you attended a bar mitzvah party thirty years ago, you might recall seeing tall, almost adult-looking thirteen-year-old girls standing next to boys the same age who were six inches shorter than them. Three decades ago, the months right around the thirteenth birthday were the period when the disparity was most noticeable. Today, the duration of that disparity has lengthened. Today, girls commonly begin puberty around age nine, boys seldom earlier than age twelve and sometimes as late as fourteen or fifteen. Girls have completed the process of puberty by age eleven or twelve—an age when most of the boys are just getting started.

Enter any middle school. Ask to see a sixth-grade class. Most of the girls are sexually mature. They're only eleven or twelve years old, but many could pass for fourteen, fifteen, or sixteen. The boys are the same age as the girls, but they don't look it. You'll see a similar gap in physical appearance among seventh-graders. By eighth grade, some of the boys have started to catch up. Others haven't. Even when you enter a ninth-grade class, you'll still find a significant cohort of boys who could pass for fifth-graders. I've seen this myself at many of the schools I've visited over the past five years. Most of the ninth-grade girls could walk into a classroom with college freshmen and pass for college students themselves. Few ninth-grade boys could do that.

There's growing evidence that exposure to synthetic chemicals may disrupt or slow puberty in boys—and only in boys. Consider endosulfan, a pesticide used widely in the United States and throughout the world. In the United States alone, roughly one-and-a-half million pounds of endosulfan are applied to food crops every year. But it wasn't until December 2003 that scientists discovered that this common pesticide can slow and disrupt the process of puberty in boys—only in boys—apparently because it blocks the action of testosterone and other androgens.[12] Despite this discovery, there has been no change in the use of this pesticide in the United States. It's being applied right now to food that your family may soon be consuming.

Bottled Water, Pacifiers, and Baby Bottles

What could be healthier than a pregnant woman drinking bottled water? What's wrong with a baby sucking on a pacifier? What's wrong with Mom putting some of her pumped breast milk into a clear plastic bottle so that Dad can feed the baby?

In the past five years, scientists have found that each of these activities introduces chemicals—bisphenol A or phthalates—into the baby's system that may actually damage a boy's brain. Rigid plastic bottles—the sort commonly used worldwide to feed babies infant formula or pumped breast milk—leach bisphenol A into the milk or formula.* That's because those bottles are usually made of polycarbonate, which is in very wide use in all developed countries. It is made from bisphenol A. When you put anything to drink—such as breast milk or water—into a polycarbonate bottle or container, a small amount of bisphenol A will get into that drink.

In December 2005, a team of researchers at the University of Cincinnati published research showing that the low levels of bisphenol A that

---

*Some parents use a soft flexible plastic liner within the bottle. Those liners are usually made with phthalates.

leach into milk or formula from such bottles irreversibly disrupt brain development in laboratory animals. And, even though bisphenol A mimics the action of the female hormone estrogen, the effects on the brain are not confined only or even primarily to the areas involved in reproduction or sexuality. Instead, brain areas involved in memory and motivation are disrupted.[13] These toxins do not affect girls and boys in the same way. A collaborative investigation by researchers from Harvard University and Oxford University recently demonstrated that environmental factors "resulted in more dramatic neurodevelopmental and behavioral changes in male neonates."[14]

Researchers in Italy have made a similar discovery. They found that when laboratory animals are exposed to these chemicals when they are young, the animals seem less curious about their environment when they are grown up. Male animals that have been exposed to these chemicals when very young subsequently behave less like males; their activity profile is "feminized, strongly resembling that of control females."[15] The same team of Italian researchers discovered in 2005 that these chemicals may damage the nucleus accumbens—the same area of the brain we discussed in the previous chapter—the vital pivot for motivation, the place where emotion gets translated into sustained and purposeful action.[16] Female animals exposed to these substances at a very early age grow up to be more curious and more active than females who are not exposed to these substances; but males exposed at the same age grow up to be less curious than males who were not exposed.[17] A different team of investigators found that females who were exposed early in life to these chemicals actually learn some tasks better and faster than females who were not exposed; whereas males exposed at the same age learn those tasks significantly less well, and more slowly, than males who were not exposed.[18]

Endocrine Disruptors, ADHD, and Motivation

Scientists have just begun to recognize the pernicious effects these chemicals have on the brain—particularly on the brains of boys—in ways not previously imagined. ADHD may be one result. The soaring rates of ADHD among North American boys in the last twenty years have only recently been linked to these chemicals. It wasn't until recently that neuroscientists recognized the mechanism by which phthalates and bisphenol A might actually cause ADHD.

In 2004, neuroscientists identified a crucial link between endocrine disruptors and ADHD. When young laboratory animals were exposed to tiny doses of endocrine disruptors—including bisphenol A and various phthalates—the scientists found that the endocrine disruptors appear to damage a brain system built around a substance known as PACAP (pituitary adenylate cyclase–activating polypeptide). These laboratory animals were, quite literally, hyper. They just couldn't slow down.[19]

Many researchers have pointed out that ADHD, which is very common in North America, is rare in India and China. The usual explanation has to do with differences in the educational system, culture, and parenting styles in North America compared with India or China. Many of those arguments have considerable merit.[20] But they do not exclude another possibility that also deserves investigation. Bottled water—water sold in plastic bottles—is rare in India and China. Where it is available, it's sold mainly to North American tourists.[21] Soda beverages sold in plastic bottles were until recently also rare in these countries. Is it possible that the dramatically higher rates of ADHD in the United States and Canada compared with India and China may be due in some part to an effect of environmental estrogens such as bisphenol A and the phthalates on the developing brain?

The damaging effects of environmental estrogens on American boys may well cause harm beyond increases in the rates of ADHD. In recent years scientists have begun to understand that the fountainhead of drive and motivation is very different in girls and boys. In boys, testosterone fuels more than just sexual interest: it fuels the drive to achieve, to be the best, to compete. Successful, high-achieving boys have higher testosterone levels than boys who are content to come in last. Girls can be just as competitive as boys are, but competitive girls don't rely on hormones for their drive. Competitive, high-achieving girls do not have higher testosterone levels than less competitive girls have.[22] This sex difference may be one reason why the flood of estrogenic chemicals in which today's children are immersed has not impaired the drive or motivation of girls. But the boys, increasingly, are lazy.

Infants, toddlers, and young children don't make sex hormones. Their bodies and brains are not meant to be exposed to them until puberty begins. When young children are exposed to substances that act like sex hormones—exogenous mimics, as the chemicals are sometimes called—the delicate balance is upset, with unpredictable results. Rockefeller University Professor Bruce McEwen noted years ago that "exogenous mimics can play havoc with brain development and differentiation."[23] More recently, Professor Neil MacLusky at Yale has called attention to the long-term effects of these substances on the ability of children to learn. MacLusky and his colleagues found high levels of the endocrine disruptor bisphenol A in the blood of pregnant women. Similar levels in pregnant laboratory animals have now been shown to cause learning disabilities in their offspring, leading Professor MacLusky to express concern that exposure at levels that people are currently being exposed to in the United States may have "long-term effects on children's learning ability."[24] Recent research suggests that young children are far more sensitive to these substances than was previously thought, and that the "safe" levels of exposure established by the FDA in the 1990s may be dangerously high. Until recently, concerns about these chemicals centered on the risk of cancer. In fact, they rarely cause cancer in the amounts to which most of us are exposed. But we now know they may disrupt brain development even at very low doses.[25]

Why Have American Kids Gotten So *Fat?*

Environmental estrogens often have profoundly different effects on girls and boys, as we have seen. But the effects of these endocrine disruptors are not confined to the brain. They may also be contributing to one of our most serious health problems: childhood obesity. Environmental estrogens appear to make kids fat—both girls and boys. Teenagers today are four times more likely to be obese and overweight compared with teenagers in the 1960s.[26] Of course, many blame the increase in the number of chubby teens on teenagers' fondness for pizza, french fries, and potato chips. But teenagers have always been fond of pizza, french fries, and potato chips. Why are teenagers so much more likely to be fat today than they were forty years ago? You might answer that teenagers are less active today, and that's true—if you're talking about boys. But it's not true for girls. Girls are much more likely to play competitive sports today than they were forty years ago. Forty years ago, we didn't have soccer leagues for seven-year-old girls. Likewise at the high school level: forty years ago, before Title IX, girls' high school sports at most schools consisted of badminton, softball, and basketball—and not many girls participated. Girls' involvement in serious competitive sports has soared over the past forty years—while boys' participation over the same era has remained relatively flat.[27] Yet both girls and boys are more likely to be overweight today, compared with forty years ago. The increase in the risk of overweight affects girls and boys about equally.

Why are so many kids getting so fat? Increasingly, investigators are pointing the finger at environmental estrogens. Scientists have known for decades that estrogens regulate the size of fat cells. Young children—whether girls or boys—don't make estrogens. Exposure to environmental estrogens in childhood "may have long-lasting consequences" that increase the tendency to overweight and obesity, according to Retha Newbold, a biologist with the National Institute of Environmental Health Sciences (NIEHS). These chemicals may directly affect fat cells (adipose cells), or they may disrupt the signals between fat cells and the pituitary and hypothalamus (endocrine feedback loops). "We're still trying to determine if it's a direct effect on the adipose cells and how they differentiate or proliferate, or whether it's a disruption of the endocrine feedback loops," Dr. Newbold says.[28] Either way, exposure to these chemicals in childhood appears to increase substantially the risk that a child will be overweight.

Professor Frederick vom Saal at the University of Missouri has highlighted the risk of obesity associated with exposure to bisphenol A. Even very low-dose exposure can activate fat cells, causing them to get bigger, Professor vom Saal warns. He has found that low-dose exposure to bisphenol A early in life causes both male and female laboratory animals to be fatter as adults; it also causes the females, but not the males, to begin puberty at an earlier age.[29]

Environmental estrogens may lead to overweight. In girls, overweight may accelerate the onset and tempo of puberty. In March 2007, investigators at the University of Michigan reported that if a girl is overweight as early as three years of age, she will be significantly more likely to undergo puberty earlier than a girl who is normal weight at three years of age.[30] So what is the cause and what is the effect? If environmental estrogens do contribute to the earlier onset of puberty in girls, do they do so via a direct effect—as a result of their endocrine-disrupting action—or do they do so via an indirect effect, by causing overweight—or both?

We have seen how exposure to environmental estrogens can lead to overweight, in both girls and boys. And while exposure to synthetic endocrine disruptors may accelerate puberty in girls, we've seen that exposure to the same synthetic substances can disrupt or slow the process of puberty in boys. We now know that these substances may cause ADHD. How about a triple whammy: all three together? Scientists are now reporting that these three conditions—delayed puberty, overweight, and ADHD—occur together much more often than would be expected by chance—but, again, only in boys. Researchers at Harvard Medical School and Children's Hospital in Boston found that almost one in five boys who were late to begin puberty also were diagnosed with ADHD, compared with fewer than one in thirty girls in the same study.[31] We're seeing a substantial increase in the number of boys who are overweight, inattentive, and late to begin puberty.

Are Boys Now the More Fragile Sex?

My patient, a ten-year-old boy I'll call Steven, tripped and fell on the grass in his own backyard. No big deal, right? Kids fall all the time, right? But Steven was screaming in pain when he stood up, cradling his right arm in his left. And the right forearm was bent horribly, in a way no forearm should bend. Steven had broken both bones in his forearm— the mid-shaft of both the radius and the ulna—from a trivial injury. He had to have surgery to set the bones in place.

Doctors call such injuries *pathologic* fractures, because they suggest underlying pathology. A boy should be able to fall on the grass without sustaining a complex fracture that requires surgery. In the past, a fracture like Steven's might signify some rare underlying bone disease such as osteogenesis imperfecta or hyperparathyroidism. No longer. Steven doesn't have any underlying disease. He's a normal American boy— which has come to mean, he's a boy who can break his bones just by tripping and falling.[32] By their fifteenth birthday, almost two-thirds (63.7 percent) of boys have now had at least one broken bone, compared with 39.1 percent of girls.[33] The risk of fracture for boys roughly doubled between the 1960s and the 1990s.[34]

Why are the bones of American boys more brittle today than they were thirty or forty years ago? Some of this change has been attributed to changes in diet, which is reasonable. Boys today drink less milk and more cola beverages than they did thirty years ago.[35] But that change alone can't account for the dramatic increase in the rate of fractures among teenage boys.

There's a real possibility that environmental estrogens may be the missing factor. Whereas environmental estrogens may strengthen bones in girls, they have a more complex effect on boys. We now know that environmental estrogens (particularly phthalates) appear to cause lower testosterone levels in young men.[36] Those lower testosterone levels will likely impair bone mineralization. In other words, young men will have bones that are more brittle than the bones of young men a generation ago. The disruptive effect of these chemicals on bone density has now been demonstrated in species as diverse as monkeys and alligators.[37] We can't say for sure that these chemicals are to blame for declining bone density in boys. But it's a possibility that merits a closer look.

Neither Male nor Female

Sex differences are not unique to humans. Almost all higher mammals show sex differences in behavior. These differences are particularly pronounced among primates, the mammalian class to which we humans belong. These differences are present as early in life as behavior can be reliably tested.[38]

Here's what's scary: scientists are finding that exposure to environmental estrogens early in life, particularly in utero and in early infancy, blunts or eliminates sex differences in behavior. Females become less feminine. Males become less masculine. For example, when young laboratory animals were exposed to extremely low doses of these chemicals—comparable to the doses you might get by drinking bottled water or Sprite or Coke or Sierra Mist or Pepsi from a clear plastic bottle—the males stopped acting like males. They stopped engaging in the rough-and-tumble play characteristic of males, for example. Instead, they demonstrated "play characteristic of females rather than untreated males."[39] In the fall of 2006 researchers at Tufts University reported that when young laboratory animals were exposed to very low doses of bisphenol A—doses comparable to what a baby might get if her mother is in the habit of drinking bottled water—the distinctive sexual differentiation of female and male brains was eliminated. Brains of female and male animals that had been exposed to the chemical were no longer distinguishable from one another, unlike the brains of unexposed animals. Likewise, the characteristic sex differences in the behavior and play of the animals were eliminated as well.[40]

There's growing evidence that the end result of our increasingly toxic environment is girls who are both masculine and feminine, and boys who are neither masculine nor feminine. The deleterious effects on girls is a complex topic beyond the scope of this book. Right now, we need to consider the possibility that the very hardware that makes a boy a boy may be in jeopardy.

Private Parts

Your son may be less than half the man your father was.

American boys today are three times more likely to be born with genital abnormalities such as an undescended testicle compared with American boys thirty years ago. Young men today have lower testosterone levels than their grandfathers had,[41] and there is growing concern that male infertility is on the rise.[42] Over the past thirty years, according to one comprehensive study, there has been

a synchronized increase in the incidence of male reproductive problems, such as testicular cancer, genital abnormalities, reduced semen
quality and subfertility. Temporal and geographical associations, as
well as frequent combination of more than one problem in one individual, strongly suggests the existence of a pathogenetic link. The
association of male reproduction problems is probably not coinci-
dental but reflects the existence of a common underlying cause....

These authors conclude that the most likely underlying causes are
"adverse environmental factors such as hormone disruptors."[43]

The problem may start very early. I've suggested that if a woman
drinks water or soda from a clear plastic bottle while she's pregnant, the
baby boy growing in her womb may be adversely affected. That's a
testable hypothesis. Shanna Swan and her associates at the University of
Rochester, in association with colleagues at the University of Missouri,
the University of Iowa, and at UCLA, set out to test it. They analyzed
the urine of pregnant women to see which women had high levels of
phthalates in their system and which women didn't. They then studied
the sons born to those women a few weeks or months later. The researchers were careful to recruit women from diverse areas of the
country—Minneapolis, Missouri, and Los Angeles—to make sure their
results were not confounded by regional effects.

Dr. Swan and her colleagues found what they had feared. Mothers
who had high levels of phthalates in their system were roughly ten times
more likely to give birth to boys whose genitals showed subtle anomalies.
The most common malformations in American boys were smaller-than-
normal penises; undescended testicles; and hypospadias, a condition in
which the opening at the tip of the penis isn't at the tip, but is farther
down the shaft of the penis[44]—leading Dr. Swan to conclude that in these
boys, "the process of masculinization was incomplete."[45] Dr. Swan's findings did not come as a surprise, because previous research had already
clearly demonstrated a causal association between phthalate exposure
and genital malformations in laboratory animals—but only in males.[46]

Dr. Swan was already well known in this field because she had previously published some of the most important work demonstrating that

in many industrialized countries, including the United States, there has been a decline in sperm counts over the past fifty years.[47] Dr. Swan has also shown that men living in communities with low exposure to fertilizer and pesticides have the highest sperm counts, while men living in communities with high exposure to these chemicals have the lowest sperm counts. Curiously, the urban vs. rural distinction doesn't seem to play much of a role. Farmers living in the country—where they are often heavily exposed to pesticides and fertilizer—have lower sperm counts than men living in some big cities.[48] Other scholars have reported a direct association between exposure to phthalates and sperm quality.[49]

Moving to the country, then, is not the solution. You have to fix this problem where you are.

Dr. Jane Fisher at the University of London, in consultation with Dr. Niels Skakkebæk and his colleagues in Denmark, has assembled a disturbing array of evidence indicating that boys today just aren't growing up to be the men their fathers and grandfathers were. They are more likely to have problems with fertility than their fathers and grandfathers had; they are more likely to have congenital abnormalities, and they may be as much as ten times more likely to develop testicular cancer. Even today, the risk of testicular cancer in Denmark—a highly developed country with lots of plastics—is almost ten times higher than the risk in Lithuania, a less developed country.[50]

Here are some suggestions that Dr. Swan has prepared to help you safeguard your children, and yourself, from the damaging effects of environmental estrogens:

- Don't give your son soft vinyl toys or pacifiers made with phthalates—look for products labeled "PVC-free".
- Don't microwave food for your children in plastic containers. Use glass or ceramic instead.

- When heating or reheating a meal in the microwave, use a bowl rather than a plate. You can use Saran Wrap or a similar wrap over the top of the bowl, but make sure that the food does not come into contact with the plastic wrap.
- Avoid plastic bottles for your own beverages and for your children's beverages. Use glass instead.
- Don't use clear plastic baby bottles. Use glass instead.
- Don't allow your dentist to put sealants on your children's teeth unless the dentist can assure you that the sealants are phthalate-free.[51]

In the closing chapter, I will put Dr. Swan's recommendations in the context of an overall program for safeguarding your son.

6

END RESULT

Failure to Launch

Let's start with a lawyer joke.

So there's this lawyer. He lives in a big mansion in a really expensive suburb. His toilet clogs up. He tries using the plunger. Doesn't do any good. So he calls the plumber. The plumber arrives, fixes the toilet, and writes up the bill. The lawyer takes one look at the bill and protests. "You've put down a charge of $250 for labor," the lawyer says. "But you spent less than half an hour doing that repair. You're billing more than $500 an hour! That's a lot more than I bill my clients, and I'm a lawyer!"

The plumber nods sympathetically. "I used to be a lawyer too," he says.[1]

What Happened to Money?

Neal Brown started a plumbing business more than twenty years ago, not far from my home in northern Montgomery County, Maryland, near the border with Frederick County. In recent years, Mr. Brown has had trouble finding any young men who want to learn the plumbing trade or any trade.

"We approached Frederick County Public Schools," Mr. Brown told me. "We asked them whether they would help us set up an apprenticeship program in plumbing. They said fine, provided that we could recruit twelve students in the county for the program. Now Frederick County has over forty thousand students spread over sixty schools. How hard could it be to find twelve students, just twelve, not twelve hundred, just twelve?"

"How hard was it?" I asked.

"We found ten. In the whole county, only ten students wanted to learn plumbing. Ten boys, no girls. We couldn't persuade any girls to give it a try."

"I guess the idea of fixing backed-up toilets didn't appeal to the girls," I said.

"Actually, we hoped that at least some girls would be interested," Mr. Brown said. "We figured they might like the independence of being able to take care of plumbing problems without having to call someone. But we didn't get any girls. Not a one."

"I understand that girls have a better sense of smell than boys have,"[2] I said. "So what did the school district say when you told them you only had ten students?"

"They said fine. Ten was enough. And the need for trained plumbers is so great in the county, we told every one of those boys during the first week of training that we could guarantee them a job if they just stuck with the program. Even an apprentice plumber can earn fifty thousand dollars a year right now if you're willing to put in some hours. And a master plumber . . . "

"What does it take to be a master plumber?" I asked.

"Four years as an apprentice, two years as a journeyman, then you take the exam. If you pass, you're a master plumber," Mr. Brown explained.

"And a master plumber can earn how much?"

"Easily eighty thousand dollars a year, and that's just working forty hours a week. If you're willing to put in the overtime hours, you can crack one hundred thousand dollars, no sweat."

"Without a college degree?"

"Without a college degree," Mr. Brown said. "And we explained this to every boy in the class. We said, just stick with this, just learn this trade, and you are literally set for life. No college loans to pay back. You're set.

Your job is secure. No engineer in Bombay, no factory clerk in Beijing is going to be able to fix somebody's toilet in Buckeystown, Maryland. If you learn this trade and you do honest work, you are set for life."

"What happened?" I asked.

"After one month, more than half the boys had quit. They just had no interest in working. They just didn't care. Earning lots of money just seems to have no appeal to them. We were down to three boys by the middle of October. That's when the district shut the program down."

"I would have thought young men would have been motivated by the prospect of earning lots of money straight out of high school. Not many eighteen-year-olds can earn fifty thousand dollars a year," I said.

"I would have thought so too," Mr. Brown said.

John Craft's Dilemma

John Craft* never went to college. He started working in home construction right out of high school, thirty-five years ago. Twenty years ago, he started his own company specializing in custom remodeling of luxury homes. It's been a good business for him. "Most of the jobs I do now start at half-a-million. Quite a few run more than a million dollars," he told me. "And I've got a waiting list of work that's more than a year long. Now of course I don't take all that money home. Most of it goes for expenses, subcontractors, all that stuff." But John isn't complaining. His personal income is more than three hundred thousand dollars a year. Not bad for a guy who never went to college.

But John has a problem. He can't find good help. "It's been more than ten years since I've been able to hire any young man born in the U.S.A. and keep him for more than a month. Number one, these young guys nowadays have no idea of craftsmanship. Number two, they don't have any interest in learning. None whatsoever."

John has a crew of six men, all in their forties and fifties, most of whom have been with him for ten years or more. "I figure I'll keep

---

*This man's name has been changed to protect his confidential information.

everybody together another five, seven years, ten years tops, build up my retirement fund, then I'm done. When my guys are ready to retire, I won't have any way to replace them." He paused. "Boys today are lazy," he said at last. "They don't want to work. They'd rather play video games. They just don't have any motivation."

"But human nature can't change in one generation," I said. "If boys today are lazy, it's because our generation or our society made them that way. So what did we do wrong? What should we be doing differently?"

Miller & Long is the largest concrete contractor in the United States.[3] They built the huge new stadium for the Carolina Panthers. When the Internal Revenue Service decided to build new headquarters, Miller & Long poured the concrete for their 1,275,000-square-foot complex. In recent years, Brunei, Egypt, Ethiopia, Ivory Coast, Singapore, and Turkey have all built new embassies in Washington, DC, and guess who was hired to pour the concrete in each case: Miller & Long.

Miller & Long has also built a small clinic in El Salvador. That seems a bit strange, because Miller & Long does no business outside the United States. They are headquartered in Bethesda, Maryland. So why did this huge company build a clinic in a foreign country, at their own expense?

"More than three-quarters of our work force is from El Salvador," is the answer I received from Myles Gladstone, vice president for human resources at Miller & Long. "They live here, but they still have family back home, and they're naturally concerned about their family back home. Building this clinic was one way we can support their community. Miller & Long also built about one hundred homes in El Salvador after the big earthquakes in January and February 2001. The company spent a lot of money on that project. But Miller & Long wasn't the only company down there. All the big American construction companies were down there, helping out. All the companies get a big chunk of their work force from El Salvador."

"So you have trouble recruiting young people from the United States?"

"That's right," he says. "We're doing several ongoing projects to try to recruit young people, women and men, to get them to check us out. We work with the local high schools. We also recruit men and women who have just been released from prison."

"How successful have those programs been?" I asked.

"Terrible," he said. "We have maybe half a dozen success stories. They're the poster boys for these projects. Only half a dozen."

"Half a dozen out of how many recruits?" I asked. "Fifty? One hundred?"

"Hundreds," he said.

This was starting to sound familiar.

I first heard about Miller & Long's good works in El Salvador from Jeff Donohoe, a neighbor of mine. He and his relatives operate a large commercial contracting company, Donohoe Construction Company. For several years, Mr. Donohoe made valiant efforts to recruit young people to enter the trades: to become an electrician, a plumber, a welder, or other skilled craftsman. He would begin his talks by asking all the students: "How many of you plan on going to college?"

Almost all the students would raise their hands. Then he would ask, "How many of you can tell me why you're going to college? What do you want to do that requires a college education?"

Usually only about five or six students raise their hands to answer this question. So he would continue: "For those twenty of you who plan on going to college, but don't know why you're going to college, I'd like to make a few suggestions before you take on twenty or thirty or forty thousand dollars of college debt. I'd like you to consider a career in the trades. If you become a licensed electrician or carpenter, you can earn as much or more than your friends who go to college. You'll be earning good money right out of high school, and you won't have any college loans to pay back."

He seldom found any student who was interested. In fact he's given up doing the talks. "I just don't get it," Mr. Donohoe told me. "Most of these kids have no particular interest in going to college. They can't even tell you why they're going to college. But then when you explain that there are good jobs in the trades that don't require a college education, they just give you a blank look. I don't understand it."

"How come nobody wants to go into the trades?" I asked. Mr. Donohoe replied:

> I think it starts with the parents, and the teachers. They look down their noses at what they call "blue collar" work. They think we're just digging holes and throwing bricks around. They don't have a clue that modern construction techniques are more high-tech than most desk jobs. We upload the architect's plans directly into our earthmoving equipment, which uses laser guidance and GPS systems to grade the site to extremely close tolerances. It's more like brain surgery than it is like building sand castles at the beach. But the parents and the teachers think that if a kid doesn't go to college, that kid's a failure. We require smart people, highly motivated people who totally understand what they're doing. We're just not able to find those people in this country any more. So we have to hire people from El Salvador or from Mexico or Guatemala, and train them.

Mr. Donohoe isn't alone in his observation. The social critic Dr. Charles Murray observed early in 2007 that many high school students from middle-class families "go to college because their parents are paying for it and college is what children of their social class are supposed to do after they finish high school."[4] Those kids may have very little idea what they want to do at college. Few of them have given any thought at all to the trades.

Dr. Murray's analysis is harsher than Mr. Donohoe's. "A bachelor's degree in a field such as sociology, psychology, economics, history, or literature certifies nothing," he writes. "It is a screening device for employers. The college you got into says a lot about your ability, and that you stuck it out for four years says something about your perseverance. But the degree itself does not qualify the graduate for anything. There are better, faster and more efficient ways for young people to acquire credentials to provide to employers." Murray observes further that we have entered a peculiar age, an age in which physicians and lawyers are more plentiful than good plumbers.

> The spread of wealth at the top of American society has created an explosive increase in the demand for craftsmen. Finding a good lawyer or physician is easy. Finding a good carpenter, painter, electrician, plumber, glazier, mason—the list goes on and on—is difficult, and it is a seller's market. . . . [M]aster craftsmen can make six figures. They have work even in a soft economy. Their jobs cannot be outsourced to India. And the craftsman's job provides wonderful intrinsic rewards that come from mastery of a challenging skill that produces tangible results. How many white-collar jobs provide nearly as much satisfaction?[5]

Forty years ago, even thirty years ago, there was no shame in a young man choosing a career in the trades. Beginning in the early 1980s—and particularly after publication of the *Nation at Risk* report in 1983—a consensus grew in the United States that every young person should go to college, regardless. "Vocational education" lost whatever prestige it had, and came to be viewed in some quarters very nearly as a dumping ground for the mildly retarded. Principals and superintendents began to see classes in auto mechanics or welding as expensive diversions from the school's core mission of ensuring that every student would go on to college.

The consequences go beyond plumbers who charge exorbitant rates. The downside is a growing cohort of unproductive young men who see no meaning or purpose in their lives.

The Lesson of the Pribilof Islands

In May 2005, Professor Judith Kleinfeld of the University of Alaska Fairbanks invited me to Alaska, where I spent several days meeting with Native American leaders who are concerned about what's happening to Alaskan native boys. A growing proportion of those boys are disengaging from school, dropping out as early as sixth or seventh grade, drinking beer, and getting in trouble. Larry Merculieff, a Native Alaskan and deputy director of the Alaska Native Science Commission, made a comment during one of these meetings that I found disturbing. I stayed after the meeting to ask him to explain what he'd said.

"When I was growing up," he told me, "I learned to hunt the sea lion with the older men of my tribe. I learned about patience. I learned about using my senses. All my senses. I would go out on the ice with the older men and we would sit for hours, waiting for the sea lion. Hours."

"What'd you do while you were waiting?" I asked. "Play a game? Talk?"

Larry shook his head. "Think of a Buddhist monk meditating," he said. "That's the closest thing to what we were doing. We were silent. We were aware. I could sense the sea lion approaching when it was still five miles distant. I can't tell you how I did that, but there is no doubt that I knew, with absolute certainty, when the sea lion was approaching."

"So how did you actually do it? Kill the sea lion, I mean," I asked.

"Our traditional life depended on the sea lion," he answered. "You must kill the sea lion at precisely the right moment. Its lungs must be filled with air. Otherwise, the animal will sink to the bottom when you shoot it, and you will not be able to retrieve it. You must be patient. You can't shoot it as soon as you see it. You must wait for it to take that deep breath. You may have to wait several minutes after you spot it. Then the leader will give the signal."

"He tells you when to shoot?" I asked.

"He doesn't say anything. You watch him out of the corner of your eye. He fires first—then all of us fire within a tenth of a second of his shot. All the shots hit the animal in the head. That's how it is supposed to be. And that's how it was, every time. The animal dies instantly, floats on the water, and we retrieve it."

"So what's different about the young men you saw?" Larry had said something during the meeting about how the young men in his tribe now insist on going out on their own. They don't want any guidance from the older men, and the lack of guidance shows in the way they hunt the sea lion. I wanted to hear more about that.

"Those young men were talking. Laughing. Joking. Punching each other. Drinking beer," Larry said. "They weren't watching the sea. They weren't paying attention to the wind. They were never quiet. A sea lion appeared and they didn't even notice. Then one of them saw it and yelled. They all grabbed their guns and started shooting wildly. They didn't kill it. They wounded it. It swam away. You could see the blood trail in the water. That's the worst possible outcome. A wounded animal. The sea lion will die, but when it dies it will be of no use to the tribe."

Fifty years ago, Larry explained, young men and old men spent whole days and nights together in traditional underground structures they called "men's houses" (*gayjiq*). In these small, confined spaces—only somewhat larger than the sweat lodges used by Native American tribes in the southwestern United States—the art of hunting was passed from one generation to the next. "Then the missionaries came. They destroyed the men's houses," Larry said. Because Native religious ceremonies were occasionally conducted in the men's houses, the missionaries regarded the houses as pagan temples that had to be demolished. Larry believes that the destruction of the men's houses was a factor in the severing of the bond between the generations.

But, as Larry explained, many other factors contributed to the isolation of the younger generation. The introduction of grocery stores probably did more than the razing of the men's houses to wipe out the original Alaskan native way of life. Once a native woman could go to the store and buy food, she no longer needed the men of the village to hunt for her. When the men no longer needed to hunt, the central purpose of the men's houses was lost (or so Larry and other Native Alaskans have told me). The nature of hunting changed. The hunt was no longer an activity essential to sustain life. Hunting became a mere entertainment, a pastime.

More fundamentally: the young men of the island no longer see any mission or purpose in their lives. The young women are doing better in school and are usually better-qualified for the jobs that are available: jobs as a teacher, clerical worker, home health aide. The men don't want those jobs. Professor Kleinfeld told me that Inuit women in Barrow have the same labor force participation rates as women in New York, while men lag far behind national labor force participation rates.[6] Larry told me that on his island, 70 percent of the young men are either incarcerated, disabled by alcoholism or drug abuse, or dead from suicide. More than two out of three.

The Pribilof Islands are located in the Bering Sea, about one thousand miles west of Anchorage. The only way in or out is by plane, which is expensive, so most residents are essentially marooned on the islands. They have their own names for the four seasons: Tourist Season (June and July), Almost Winter (August and September), Winter (October through March), and Still Winter (April and May). The islands are among the most remote and inhospitable inhabited locations on the planet.

You and I don't live on the Pribilof Islands. So what does this story have to do with us?

In November 2006, Professor Kleinfeld sent me an e-mail about a recently published analysis of young men who don't want to work. The author of this analysis had suggested that the disengagement of so many young American men from the work force is due to changes in the North American economy about which we've all heard so much: fewer good jobs in factories, with the good jobs now primarily in the service sector.[7] Professor Kleinfeld wrote:

> Let me add a complexity based on my unique vantage point in Alaska, where traditional male jobs in construction and natural resources and mining have NOT declined. Many young men are not taking these jobs. . . . Many are floundering. Many don't want jobs requiring physical strength and hard labor. Even apprenticeships which offer high wages and benefits are going begging.

What's Going On?

A team of reporters for the *New York Times* recently documented a growing trend among young and middle-aged men throughout the United States: more and more able-bodied men are out of work and are not even looking for work. These men aren't included in the unemployment statistics because they've given up looking for a job. They may be from middle-class families, most of them are white, and many have some college education. Their ranks are growing rapidly. In Michigan, 18 percent of able-bodied men between the ages of thirty and fifty-four—almost one man in five—are not working and not looking for work. In West Virginia, that figure is now up to 24 percent, almost one man in four. Forty years ago, in the same age group, only about one able-bodied man in twenty was unemployed and not looking for work. Today, nationwide, it's about one man in seven. Most of these men could find work if they had to, according to the *New York Times* investigative team. But these men "have decided they prefer the alternative [i.e., not working]. It is a significant cultural shift from three decades ago. . . . [These men are] in the prime of their lives [but] have dropped out of regular work. They are turning down jobs they think beneath them . . . even as an expanding economy offers opportunities to work."[8] Instead, they live off the income of their wives or families, or off their own savings.

The traditional male provider roles—hunting among the Alaskans, factory work and the trades for American men—have been eliminated or made obsolete or, as in the case of the trades, have simply lost their appeal. The new jobs in the service industry don't interest many young men. Our situation is not as dire as that of the Native Alaskans of the Pribilof Islands. Not yet. But the more I listened to Larry and the other Native Alaskans, the more I saw parallels between their situation and ours.

I am not suggesting that we should try to turn back the clock to the days when the man was usually the sole or chief provider for the home. But I am suggesting that the emerging twenty-first-century economy, in which many women will earn more than their husbands—if they have husbands at all—requires a rethinking of the role of men. If a thirty-year-old man is not the principal wage earner in his home, then what is his role? Certainly the man could take over the principal responsibilities for child care. But men staying at home full-time to provide not only all the child care but also to clean the house and do the laundry and cook the meals are still a rarity in North America.[9]

More and more lazy men:
percentage of men age 30 to 54
not working and not looking for work

1950 · 1960

1970 · 1980

1990 · 2000

2004

Percentage of able-bodied men
who are not working

5% 10 15 20 25

The proportion of able-bodied men who choose not to work
has been rising steadily over the past fifty years. These men
are not included in unemployment statistics because they are
not looking for work.
Andrew Beveridge and Susan Weber-Stoger, Queens College.

So what is the man's role, if his wife is the principal wage earner? The answer, in too many cases that I have personally witnessed, is that this man becomes a parasite in his own home. The wife is still saddled with many or most of the child-care responsibilities and housekeeping chores in addition to the burden of being the chief breadwinner. Tension between husband and wife commonly ensues.

Let me stress that I fully endorse the idea of a full-time homemaker father. I applaud a man who makes the choice to stay home and raise the children, clean house, do the laundry, and so forth. But very few men make that choice. More often, the stay-at-home dad is not vacuuming the carpets, he's seldom making more than a token attempt to do the laundry, he's not preparing the meals and cleaning the kitchen, and he's not taking primary responsibility for child care. Mom's working full-time while Dad is working part-time or not at all, but nevertheless Mom is stuck with more than her share of the chores. That's a situation many Moms will put up with for only so long. Sooner or later it occurs to them that they might just be better off single.

The Changing American Household

Within the literary genre of "chick lit," there is an even faster-growing subgenre of books about productive young women saddled with under-achieving boyfriends or husbands. One of the most successful such books in this genre is Allison Pearson's *I Don't Know How She Does It.* The heroine is a woman named Kate Reddy. She's a hedge fund manager working seventy hours a week and earning a salary in the high six figures. She is also the mother of two small children. Her laid-back husband earns a small fraction of her income but does less than half of the child-care chores. There's lots of dark comedy in the story because her husband just doesn't understand what motivates her. If you're so tired and overworked, he asks her at one point, why not just call in sick and sleep late? At Christmas, her husband wonders why the nanny received a much nicer present than he did. Because the nanny is more important in my life, and helps me more than you do, is Kate's response.

For all the popularity of this genre, it's not what the future holds, for better or worse. Not many young women willingly sign up for Kate

Reddy's position—earning most of the money and still having to do most of the child care. What's actually happening is quite different. The marriage rate among young Americans continues a decades-long downward spiral. The household of the future—indeed, the household of the emerging present—does not look like Kate Reddy's home. The emerging norm is young and middle-aged men who have never married and are unlikely ever to marry, on one side; on the other side, young women with or without children, using professional help (nannies, day care) to raise their children. When one investigative team asked college students whether it was better to get married or to go through life single, two-thirds of the young men said it was better to get married. More than half the young women said it would be better to go through life single.[10]

The American household is changing. In 1930, 84 percent of American households were led by a married couple—and most of the remaining 16 percent were led by a widow or widower. Households led by single, never-married adults were rare. Not any more. In October 2006, the *New York Times* reported that for the first time in American history, households led by a married couple are now in a minority. The greatest demographic change over the past fifty years has been in the rapidly surging number of adults living alone. Adults living alone now comprise 27 percent of American households.[11]

It used to be unusual to find a man between the ages of thirty-five and forty who had never married. Just twenty-five years ago, only 8 percent of American men in that age group had never married. That proportion has nearly tripled in just the past thirty years: it's now up to 22 percent and still rising rapidly.[12]

The *Washington Post* reported in March 2007 that married couples with one or more children now constitute less than one-quarter of all households in the United States. This proportion is roughly half of what it was forty years ago. Isabel V. Sawhill, a senior fellow at the Brookings Institution, has concluded that "The culture is shifting . . . [Before 1970], if you looked at families across the income spectrum, they all looked the same: a mother, father, kids. . . . " Not any more. Marriage with children has become "the exception rather than the norm." And there's no sign of any taper in this trend. Examining the numbers, University of Michigan sociology professor Pamela Smock has no doubt that "the percentage of children born outside of marriage is also going to increase."[13]

The decline in marriage rates cuts across all demographic groups. "It is a mistake to think of this [drop in marriage rates] as just happening to the underclass at the bottom," says Christopher Jencks, professor of sociology at Harvard.[14] Likewise, the proportion of young men (age eighteen to thirty-five) living at home with parents or relatives has surged over the same thirty years. That proportion has roughly doubled, while the proportion of young women in the same age group living with parents or relatives has remained constant.[15]

Young women and young men are now following different life scripts. Young women are getting jobs, establishing themselves in the workplace, then (in many cases) thinking about having children. But a growing number of young men are just not on the same page. As a consequence, having children without being married—which would have been unusual for middle-class white women just thirty years ago—is now common. In 2004, 36 percent of babies born in the United States were born to unmarried women.[16] Right now, for the first time in American history, there are fewer adult women who are currently married than there are women who are unpartnered (either single and never married, or divorced and not remarried). Fifty years ago, married women outnumbered unpartnered women by roughly two to one.[17]

Whatever Happened to Money and Sex?

Traditionally, one of the factors driving Western society has been the fact that women prefer successful, affluent men over men who are less successful. Because men understood that women would be reluctant to marry men who couldn't comfortably support a wife and children, men were motivated to be successful. That simple mechanism has suffered a double whammy in the past forty years. First, sex has been divorced from marriage. Second—and here's what's really disturbing to those of us in the over-thirty crowd—sexual satisfaction has been divorced from women altogether. If you don't work with today's teenage boys on a regular basis, you may not understand the extent to which pornographic images of women have replaced the real thing. In the general population, the best estimates are that roughly 70 percent of college-age men now use pornography regularly.[18] Among those men, use of pornography can readily escalate from an occasional diversion to a daily pastime and finally, to becoming the preferred sexual outlet.[19] In one Harvard study, 69 percent of men who sought help for sexual problems were experiencing "compulsive masturbation"—meaning that they were masturbating more than they thought they should be, and/or they were sometimes masturbating in inappropriate places or at inappropriate times. Fifty percent of the men in the same study were described as being "pornography-dependent," meaning that they could not achieve an erection without pornography.[20] More and more boys are discovering that they prefer a sexy image on a computer screen to a real live woman with expectations, a woman who has her own agenda, a woman who may say things that the boy doesn't want to hear.

I've been seeing more and more young men in my office—men age eighteen to twenty-eight—who are dealing with the consequences of their overuse of pornography by asking for Viagra or Cialis or Levitra, because they find it difficult to get aroused by real women. One in three college men now reports erectile dysfunction.[21] And I'm seeing other young men who use a different strategy: they disengage from the dating scene altogether, using pornography as their only sexual outlet.

Here's an excerpt from an e-mail I received from a man in his late twenties after I wrote an article for the *Washington Post* related to this topic.[22]

> Dr. Sax, I think you're being very narrow-minded. Recently I've really gotten into Japanese anime, especially the videos. I love the girls in those videos. There [sic] sweet and submissive and nice. The real girls I know aren't anything like that. I would rather watch the anime girls than be with real girls. Why is that so bad? It's not my fault. It's the fault of the girls I know. They're too demanding. They expect the guy to do everything, pay for everything, make them laugh, do it all. Why is it so bad to prefer something different?

The problem is that the technology has gotten so good, and the images are so lifelike, so real, that when those girls bat their eyelashes at him it's easy for him to forget that they're just pixels on a computer screen, not real girls in his room.

Not everyone agrees on this point. A recent scholarly monograph concludes that the young man for whom masturbation is the preferred sexual outlet may merely be responding, appropriately, to "today's fast-paced social life characterized by individuality, impersonality, materialism, and social isolation."[23] Another critic dismissed concerns about pornography as the outdated prejudice of "moralists and religious conservatives."[24]

Recently, a number of critics have bemoaned the extent to which the culture of pornography has been mainstreamed in our society.[25] Lingerie has become evening wear. Young women can take classes at the local fitness club in aerobic striptease. "Girls Gone Wild" has very nearly become primetime fare.[26] These critics understandably see this development as a sign of cultural decadence. But I think they may have misdiagnosed the underlying dynamic. I asked a sixteen-year-old girl, as gently as I could, why she was wearing a Hooters outfit to a school Halloween party. Her shorts were very short, and her top displayed her natural endowment in a manner that invited comparison with Dolly Parton. "Why?" she mused. "If you don't dress like this, nobody will even notice you." To get the attention of the crowd, girls increasingly tell me that they have to dress like the models in *Maxim* photo shoots—or act like the ditsy girls on "Girls Gone Wild."

The Stick of Duty

Traditionally, boys who wanted money and/or sex were motivated to be successful in their job or career, because success was the surest route to money and sex. But there have always been boys who were not particularly motivated. The carrots of money and sex were not sufficient for them. A stick was needed. In some cultures, the stick went by the name of "duty." Korean culture still has this sense of duty, and English culture once did. In Victorian England, a young man might undertake a life of work that was not particularly appealing to him because his family would be dishonored if he did otherwise. In South Korea today, and among first-generation Korean immigrants to the United States, it is not unusual to find young men and young women who are doing a particular job, or even pursuing a particular career, not because they prefer it but because they believe that their duty to their family requires it.

The stick of duty was never as strong in North American culture as it was in British or some East Asian cultures. In any case, it is weak today. American boys today are unlikely to take a job they find demeaning or boring, or pursue a career that does not interest them, solely because of a sense of duty to parents or family. In this regard I think we can perhaps sense the primate tendency of young females to affiliate with their parents, and young males to abandon them (we discussed this aspect of primatology in chapter 2). Girls will follow societal norms unless they have a good reason not to. But the boy who disrespects society's norms may raise his status in the eyes of other boys. The culture of Victorian England, like the culture of present-day Korea, managed to overcome these primate tendencies. But in modern American culture, "duty" doesn't have much influence for most boys or young men.

Failure to Launch

Paramount Pictures released the movie *Failure to Launch* on March 10, 2006. Matthew McConaughey stars as a funny, friendly, good-looking thirty-five-year-old who is utterly devoid of ambition. He lives at home with his parents. His mother cooks his breakfast, washes his laundry, and vacuums his room. His character has no clue that his parents want him to leave. Their desperation leads them to hire a professional "interventionist," whose assignment is to motivate McConaughey's character to leave his parents' home and get a life.

Failure to Launch was the number-one movie in the United States for the first three weeks after its release, grossing more than ninety million dollars at the box office just in the three months between its March opening and the release of the DVD in June. I was struck by how accurately the movie captured a phenomenon I'd been tracking in my office for seven years. Two days after I saw the movie, I wrote an op-ed for the *Washington Post* entitled "What's Happening to Boys?" I began by pointing out how the movie captured key features of the phenomenon I've been seeing in my practice: in particular, the fact that the main character was intelligent. He is perfectly capable of success and achievement, but he simply has no motivation to accomplish anything real.

I wasn't prepared for what happened next. For three consecutive days, my article was the most e-mailed article on the *Post* Web site. The *Post* invited me to host an online chat on this topic. The chat line was open for just sixty minutes. Staffers at the paper shut the line down after 395 posts, which they told me was more than double the previous record for a sixty-minute chat of about 170 posts.

I was fascinated by the variety of comments I received, some of which were from men who were completely unapologetic about their situation. Here's one, from the online transcript of the *Washington Post* chat, from a twenty-six-year-old living at home:[27]

> Well, what IS the problem? If my parents are happy to have me, why shouldn't I stay with them? Why should I be in any hurry to have a career, wife, and children? Am I really obligated to have "direction"—direction towards where? You say there's something wrong with young people like me, but I would say it's worse to imagine that following the prescribed path to career and family will magically transform your life into a constant state of bliss.
>
> Today's hero is not the blazing, iconoclastic industrialist of Ayn Rand, but the slacking, chilled-out Dude of *The Big Lebowski*. Why is he wrong, while Taggart and Rearden* are right? Until you can answer that, the idea that I merit some kind of concerned examination is ridiculous.

Author's note: Taggart is Dagny Taggart and Rearden is Hank Rearden, both of whom can fairly be described as "blazing iconoclastic industrialist[s]" in Ayn Rand's novel *Atlas Shrugged*.

Another young man asked, "Why is the definition of adulthood wasting most of one's income on a rent or mortgage?"[28] He was a twenty-nine-year-old man living at home with his parents. He didn't see anything wrong with that.

I replied:

> The definition of adulthood is not how you spend your money, rent vs. ownership, and so forth. The definition of adulthood, I believe, is being independent of your parents.* You can live in a tent in a forest and not pay any rent at all. But if your room and board are subsidized by your parents, you are still a child, no matter what your age.
>
> You may not place a high priority on independence. You may prefer being comfortable, well-fed and warm over being independent, uncomfortable, and hungry. That's your choice.
>
> My concern is that we are seeing many more young men who seem to value being comfortable and well-fed over being independent and grown-up. Like you, these men don't see the problem. They attach very little value to economic or spiritual independence.

But the online chat was only the beginning. Over the next two weeks, my article was reprinted in about three dozen major newspapers around the United States. On April 4, I went to the studios of National Public Radio in Washington, DC, to be the featured guest in a forty-minute interview on the NPR program *On Point,* broadcast nationwide.[29] By the end of April I had received over one thousand e-mails from all around the country.

I threw out my original draft of this chapter. The e-mails I received turned out to be more interesting than anything I could say. In the remainder of this chapter, I'm going to share with you a few of the most provocative, most outrageous, and most profound of those e-mails.

---

*In suggesting this definition, I was thinking not sociologically but biologically. From a biological perspective, an individual has reached adulthood when one is A) independent of one's parents and B) sexually mature.

From: yogabody125@yahoo.com
Subject: Shortest Date in History

Dear Dr. Sax,

I read your op-ed in the *Washington Post* with great interest. I'd like to add a different perspective. I'm a 35-year-old single woman, with my own house, car, career etc. I've worked hard to get where I am, and I've had to move a lot to move up. Now I'm finally in one place for a bit and can actually date. But many of the single men I meet still live with their parents, or else they are STILL figuring out what they want to be when they grow up. Mostly, I just want to smack them. Would that be OK?

Case in point. Two weeks ago I had the shortest date in history. It was at a coffee shop with a guy named Michael. Michael is 32. He's always wanted to be a journalist but quit a couple jobs along the way (red flag #1) and now works writing proposals for an architecture firm. But he hates that job too (red flag #2) and is thinking of quitting and getting his MFA and teaching creative writing. Me: "How can you teach creative writing if you haven't done any?"

I asked Michael how he spends his free time. Mostly he hangs out at bars with his friends. He hasn't been to any of the local museums or theaters or anything remotely requiring intelligence (red flag #3).

He asked if I had an apartment nearby. I said I owned a home. He freaked. "Wow, you're quite the grown-up, aren't you?" he said. Well, uh, yeah, dude, I'm 35.

Total date time: 2 cups of coffee. 35 minutes.

I can't tell you how many times this has been repeated. I go out with a guy, turns out he's a total slacker. I don't want to date these guys. I want to tell them: Get a grip! Get a job! Have a dream! Do I need to go all JFK/MLK* on their sad sack selves?

Anyway. Last year, after more bad dates than I can count, I gave up. I got myself a nice 25-year-old boy toy, whom I call when I want and ignore when I want. He's not that bright, but who cares? There's no future. He lives at home with his parents.

Sigh.

Datelessly yours,
Rachel

Dear Dr. Sax,

As a 24-year-old college graduate, I knew that after graduating, I was supposed to get a job and move out of my parents' home, so I moved to the other end of the country. I love the independence, the freedom, and my personal space. My brother is a different story. I see so much of him in the comments people posted [on the *Washington Post* chat]: especially the young men who added their two cents. My brother went to college, dropped out, worked in a restaurant for a while, broke up with his live-in girlfriend, and ended up back in my parents' basement. He still works in a restaurant, but he doesn't do ANY chores, he never makes any attempt to help out, and he doesn't seem to care about moving on with his life, though he's made some half-hearted attempts. He's got a good thing going: no rent, few responsibilities other than entertaining the family dog,

*_Author's note:_ JFK/MLK is an abbreviation for John F. Kennedy / Martin Luther King Jr.

free food, sleeping till noon, and the knowledge that my parents will help pay for college again if he decides that's what he wants.

Why look to the future when he can have a wad of bills at the end of a shift in the restaurant? It's easy money, and it's a lot of money, but it won't get him anywhere. He doesn't care. I think a lot of young men have a very short-sighted view of the future: the next party, the next short-term job, the next free meal. He's not living at home for the family aspect; he's there because it's free and it's easy.

Another example: my boyfriend of over six years. He's never lifted a hand at home. His mother does everything for him: laundry, meals, picks up his dishes (which he leaves scattered in various rooms around the house), she makes his bed, etc. I told him that if he was going to spend time with me, he was going to do chores, especially washing the dishes. I made it very clear that I wasn't going to be his mother and pick up after him. Neither was I going to put up with laziness in getting things done. I've had to explain to him that sometimes you just have to do unpleasant things so you can enjoy yourself later. He wants instant gratification—and I know he gets that from video games. Your comment about Steven Johnson's book was right on. I've read Johnson's book. My boyfriend thinks that book is as close to the Truth as you can get. Play more video games and pretend it's mental development. Gladly! It's very frustrating. I'm worried, especially as we intend to move in together this summer, and I like to have a very neat and clean apartment.

Thank you for the chance to comment. I fully intend to show this to my boyfriend. Keep up the good work!

Anna M.

Dear Dr. Sax,

I read your article on the *Washington Post* website today and I was struck by your description of what I am going through right now. I am a 25-year-old woman, married eight months to one of these "boys." My boy will be 29 in August. I am experiencing what it's like to live with one of these boys after they finally leave their parents.

My husband and I met online. He and I graduated from college the same semester in 2002. I graduated with two majors in four years. He graduated with one major that took seven years. When we met in early 2004, we were both living with our parents. At that time, I was looking to leave the nest. He seemed content to be at home. I fully believe that if he hadn't met me, he would still be there.

He told me that he passed his time playing Nintendo, surfing the Net, watching TV, etc. He lived in luxury with a nice car, nice clothes and spending money—all on his parents' dime. He worked a retail job that didn't pay much, but it fit his laid-back, jovial, "not serious" personality. He claims that he didn't pursue a professional career because he didn't know what he wanted to do. He once wanted to do outdoors work with DNR* etc. but he claims that the chemistry and biology required were too steep of a price to achieve his dream job. I overlooked all of this as just being who he was. He is intelligent. I thought the way he lived was not because of him necessarily, but rather might be due to the foundation of money and security—and lack of responsibility—which his parents had set up for him.

I thought this would change when we got married, that he would grow up and do things on his own: balance a checkbook, get his own insurance, do at least some of the housework etc. I have learned that he doesn't know how to do any of these things. He is so

Author's note: DNR is the abbreviation for Department of Natural Resources.

financially inept that he has practically crippled our young marriage. I am the professional. I make twice what he does at his job at the mall. Couple that with the late hours he works, and I am pretty much by myself in running our household.

It frustrates me that what seemed to me to be a lack of motivation due to others enabling him has developed into a lack of understanding of adult responsibilities. I am perplexed. How can such an intelligent person be so utterly clueless? I feel like his mother. If I relied on him to pay the bills, file our taxes, get loans, clean up etc. it simply would not get done. We would be out on the street. As much as I tell him that I need help with the bills and that I need his understanding and support, the ignorance just gets that much worse. The thing is, his family always bailed him out and they still try to. I forbid it. He gets upset that I am upset but he never takes any interest in things even though he says he will. I think he just believes everything will magically work out every month like it has in the past. Luckily, I have made it work so far. But I know that eventually our reserve finances are going to run out. I can't imagine what will happen then. I don't see any motivation in him to improve. If I try to pull him from the Xbox or the TV, I'm the bad guy. He doesn't seem to realize that his $10/hour salary cannot cover everything that he wants: cable, Internet, car, cell phones. But I magically make it happen every month—because I'm working my butt off. Sometimes I even have to coerce him to shower and to shave.

I love my husband. But I am constantly haunted by something he once told me. He said that I might need to lower my expectations in life because he didn't know whether he could provide them for me. What I find funny now is that I'm the real provider. I don't feel like part of a team. It's wearing on me.

He has no idea.

Thank you,
Sarah C.

From: "Rachel Riggs" rachelriggs@hotmail.com
Subject: What's Happened to Boys?

Dear Dr. Sax,

I believe that what's happened to boys is directly related to what's happened to girls. Girls today feel that they don't need boys so much anymore. And boys have figured that out. Girls used to give motivation to boys to be successful so that the boys could "take care of them." Without that motivation, what is left for the boys? Video games, where they can still be the hero. Sleeping around—because, as you succinctly stated, girls still have sexual needs—but we've learned how to satisfy ourselves in that aspect, also. No, it's not the same, but it will do in a pinch.

If you'd like to take it one step further: what if women decide that they've had enough of men and their huge egos, and their testosterone-fueled wars, and start stock-piling frozen sperm until they really DON'T need men anymore? Do you think men, at least subconsciously, haven't thought about that scenario?

I love men. As a divorced woman, I really miss a male presence in my home. There's just something about men and testosterone and physical strength that really turn me on. The world would definitely be a worse place without men. But women are evolving, not necessarily in a good way, and men are reacting.

Rachel Riggs
Coeur d'Alene, Idaho

Dear Dr. Sax,

As a 29-year-old woman, I'm smack in the middle of the "failure to launch" generation. I grew up in Northern Virginia. I went to my 10-year high school reunion last year. All of the girls I went to school with have moved out, gone to college, gotten real jobs, etc. Almost all the boys live at home, have menial jobs, and don't know what they want out of life.

I think the boys' laziness started in high school. Honestly I think at least some of the blame lies with parents. All the girls had curfews in high school. We all had to tell our parents where we were at all times. We had to keep our grades up. Not a single boy I knew had a curfew. Most were allowed to slack off in school because they had "difficulty focusing" or they were diagnosed with "sensory integration disorder." The girls had jobs at the mall. The boys got allowances from Mom and Dad. Even within the same family, there were different rules for boys and girls.

Now we've reaped what we've sown. The girls have discipline. The boys have PlayStations.

I'm newly divorced. I'm not sure I want to remarry. There just aren't any worthwhile men out there. My generation of men aren't looking for partners—they're looking for a new Mommy. I'd much rather be on my own than be with a man who can't stand on his own two feet.

Sincerely,
Sharon S.

Dear Dr. Sax,

Thank you so much for bringing attention to this phenomenon. I'm a 28-year-old woman and I've noticed that my friends and I, instead of talking about our future weddings, families etc. are now talking about the fact that having a relationship with one of these boy/men works against our eventual goals: successful careers and having children. Instead we talk about how we're going to work on our careers, and if we haven't found someone by the time we're of a good age, we'll adopt or find some other way of having children on our own and we'll just support ourselves. The "Failure to Launch" phenomenon is precisely the reason for this shift. Why take on some boy/man who would then move into our homes and expect to be taken care of by us?

Thanks again, and keep us all posted if you come across a solid conclusion as to why this is happening.

Allie

Dear Dr. Sax,

I read your *Washington Post* article and it really hit home. My never-married fiancé who still lives with his mother called off our wedding a little over three months ago. He's a teacher with a master's degree. He pays his mother $250 a month for room and board (way below market rates). He doesn't even have a savings account. He has spent every cent he has ever made on electronics, car stereos etc.

I knew all this, but because we are both Christians, both teachers, and have many things in common, and because I fell in love with him, the thought never occurred to me that he would back out. He kept reassuring me that he would leave home. I thought he meant it when he spent $7,300 on a ring.

Oh well. Now I'm glad he backed out because it would not have worked out.

I have never married. I own my own home.

Thank you for listening.
Maxine C.
Georgia

Dr. Sax,

I sent this to NPR during their interview with you:

Perhaps the men-staying-at-home phenomenon is a reaction to the feminist era. Before that era, there was no other option than men going to work and women staying at home. Now perhaps there are men hoping to be "found" by a rich woman and marry her and not have to work. I know MANY men who want to marry me simply because I am a lawyer. It's gotten to the point that I don't want to tell a man what I do for a living until after we've decided to date steadily. My boyfriend was depressed for a week after I told him I want to practice PUBLIC INTEREST law. "What?!" he said. "There's no money in that!" He never recovered.

Thanks,
Penny
Reston, Virginia

Dr. Sax,

I read your article in the Washington Post and found it very inter-esting. While you raise some valid points, I find some of your points to be highly culturally biased. I come at this as a native-born American of Pakistani heritage.

In every other country in the world, it is completely normal and expected that children live with their parents in adulthood. This is seen as mutually beneficial. The older generation is revered in those countries, unlike this country. I believe this comes from a joint family system where parents and children are actively in-volved in each other's lives. Children can live with their parents to save money and they will take care of their parents when they are old.

Many in the United States seem to feel that family ties stop at age 18. Kids can't come home. Those kids will be unlikely to help their parents when they may need help in their old age. We have somehow established that a Mother's Day card and a Christmas card suffice for familial obligations. I believe this generates severe social consequences. Children benefit from growing up close to their extended families or in joint families.

I take your point that kids living with parents can create disincentives to work. I also concur that in some cases, maybe they do need to be evicted. But I believe it is a case by case matter. I find your advice to charge rent to be offensive. Families are not money-making endeavors.

Best regards,
Aliya Husain
Washington DC

I received several responses like Ms. Husain's, mostly from people who were born and raised outside of North America. These people observed that in countries such as India, Pakistan, Italy, Portugal, Spain, and many Latin American countries, it's common for adult children, both women and men, to live with their parents. That's true. But in those other countries, the adult children are more likely to be integrated into the household. In many cases, those adult children may help to operate a family business. The distinctive feature of the "Failure to Launch" phenomenon is that the American young man is coasting, slacking off, relying on his parents to provide everything for him while he has a good time.

This is something new. There is no country with a tradition of parents working while their adult children slack off at home. In Italy, there is a centuries-old tradition of the *mammoni,* men who choose to live at home with their mothers for their entire life. However, such men are still expected to be productive; it would be profoundly un-Italian for such a man to expect his mother to provide all the household income while he plays video games and surfs the Net.[30] Likewise, in Japan, demographers have expressed concern about the growing number of adult men who are living at home with their parents, refusing to work, while the young man's mother serves the son meals and cleans up his room. These boy/men are referred to as *hikkikomori*, literally "pulling away, being confined." One key difference between the Japanese *hikkikomori* and the American "failure to launch" is that the *hikkikomori* men themselves are, with very few exceptions, miserable. They wish that they had more motivation.[31] The American slacker dude, by contrast—epitomized by McConaughey's character in *Failure to Launch* or by Owen Wilson's character in *You, Me, and Dupree*—is perfectly content to be dependent on others.

From: "Ian Farache" ian.farache@gmail.com
Subject: NPR interview

I just finished listening to your interview on NPR. I'm 23 and living at home. I've been wondering why I lack either the motivation or the willpower to leave.

Maybe having ADHD as a child has something to do with it. I did hear you say that Ritalin and Adderall might cause a lack of motivation. That to me is not a huge leap of logic. I remember taking the medication at the age of 8 or 10 and becoming completely despondent.

The term "slacker" runs through my mind constantly.

If you would e-mail me some information about this subject I would appreciate it.

Ian
Glen Carbon, Illinois

What does society tell us should be our goal? A career spent in a cubicle on the phone trying to convince people that Bunco spark plugs are the best spark plugs in the world? And then, after 30 years, your company moves to Mexico and cuts your pension? No thanks.

From a bored 23-year-old.
Jeff

Good afternoon Dr. Sax,

I'm male, 27 years old, married, and in grad school, working toward a doctorate in medieval literature. I also teach Latin. My wife and I don't have a TV because of how much time it wastes and how much mindless junk there is on it. However, I have played computer games in some form since my parents got me a computer when I was in high school. Before that I sometimes used to go to friends' houses and play computer games there. Once I got to college, I had more time to play computer games if I wanted to.

I don't think you understand the computer game phenomenon when you talk about it sapping the motivation of male 20-somethings. That's only part of the picture. The other part is that computer games allow people to do things that feel as significant or important as the things they wish they could do in real life but don't see any way of doing. I don't mean that people are playing Battlefield 2 because they wish they could be shooting lots of people. But they do wish that they could be doing something that mattered. When they're playing that game, they can, for a few hours, feel like they're doing something significant.

When I started grad school, I had a rough first year or so. Many times I came home feeling like I was never going to be any good as a scholar, like I had no hope of ever actually doing anything significant, or making any serious contribution even just in the academic community. But I could turn on the computer and play X-Wing and feel like I was helping to defeat the Galactic Empire. If you want to feel significant, feeling like you just destroyed the Death Star helps for a little while. Or a few years later, I would play Morrowind. As I wandered around that world, I could help a wounded traveler, or rescue captives from bandits, or discover a secret upon which the survival of a city depended. And there, at least in that world, I could succeed. One thing that's key in most computer games is that there is positive feedback. In flight simulator games, you don't just defeat the other pilots: you also get a badge. There's an implicit pat on the back. And you get a sense of achievement. If you're not getting a sense of achievement anywhere else in life, computer games are pretty tempting as a way of getting that feeling. It's built into them.

Not only is there the sense of achievement, but there is also in many games beauty and adventure. In Morrowind, you can wander through a really beautiful, detailed, vivid world. Now I prefer reality. But I live in South Bend, Indiana. There aren't lots of places to hike or even to walk. I can't afford to travel much. I would love to wander on a misty shore and hear the waves, or hike through mountains and valleys. I can't do that here. I daydream about the one time I went to the Pacific Northwest, or the years when I lived in Switzerland. Or, instead of daydreaming, I can play a game that gives me something similar, though of course nowhere near as real or as good. The desire for beauty is very strong—so strong that one might accept all sorts of false substitutes if one couldn't find the reality.

Of course the sad thing is that spending lots of time on computer games can keep you from achieving the very things the desire for which sent you to computer games in the first place. Who has time to study and get involved in urban development if he spends all day playing *SimCity*?

Of course I agree that people should stop wasting time in front of the PC/Xbox and go do something real. But in order to treat a problem it may be helpful to know something about how it seems to those who suffer from it. I hope this is helpful.

Sincerely,
Richard R.
Notre Dame
South Bend, Indiana

Another post from the *Washington Post* chat:

WhatisanAdult: Doc,

I fall into that mold. I tend bar for a living. I live at home. I have fun. I pick up more pretty girls than I can count, so what is my motivation to have a family, career, etc? What if my happiness is defined differently from yours?

I've dated more than one attractive, highly-paid professional woman and stolen her away from her boring corporate boyfriend who makes multiples of my income. The women tell me they are sick of their non-exciting life. The burbs, playing the role of the little home maker.

We have FUN together. We talk about music, art, cool stuff. They don't seem to miss their "successful" exs much at all.

I am not hurting anyone. So why do I need the suit, the tie, kids, stroller, the BMW, just because I am 30? Seems sort of shallow to live that way.

My response to Casanova:

I'm glad that you are enjoying life.

You wrote that you are picking up "more pretty girls than I can count, so what is my motivation to have a family, career, etc.?"

What is, or should be, the motivation for having a family or a career? The motivation to have a family and a meaningful career is not (and should not be) grounded in the desire to pick up pretty girls. It should be grounded, rather, in the desire to be of use, to serve others, to give your life some meaning beyond the pleasure of the moment. If those objectives have no real meaning to you, then nothing I or anyone else says will have much impact. If FUN (capitalized, as you capitalized it) is the be-all and end-all, then by that standard you're doing extremely well.

I think at some point that you may find that having FUN is not satisfying, and that a meaningful life requires more than picking up pretty girls. At that point, you may see the point of having a career and a family.

Or you may not.

But I wonder what your parents would have to say about this?

From: "Max Geller" ms_geller@coloradocollege.edu
To: leonardsax@prodigy.net
Subject: I am that kid

Listening to your interview on NPR today, I needed about 15 seconds before I realized you were talking about ME. I'm a white, suburban, semi-affluent male who has been on academic steroids* since the third grade. I have no work ethic. I'm graduating in a month and a half.

Can I be of service to you?
Max Geller

---

*Author's note: "Academic steroids" is a slang term, growing in popularity, referring to medications such as Adderall, Ritalin, Concerta, Metadate, and so on.

My name is Mike. I'm 33 years old. I don't live at home, but rather in a home paid for by my parents. I'm in graduate school, but my efforts there have been lackluster.

Like many of the young men you mentioned, I play too many video games. I agree that they offer a fantasy world with a beginning, middle, end, and accomplishments. All with no risk, and nearly certain achievement.

I wonder about my lack of motivation. All the way back to grade school, I hated academics. It's not that I dislike learning. On the contrary, I love to learn. I just hate school. Always have. I used to be a teacher at a small private school working with autistic kids. Before that, I had a string of dead end jobs, which seldom lasted as long as a year. My days were punctuated with pot, video games, and beer. I lived hundreds of miles from home, but my parents have sent me money every two weeks for—many years. They make enough that it doesn't impede their own comfortable existence. Still I do have occasional guilty moments.

I was married for a time—for 6 years. Ironically, I always considered her lazy. At the end of a day's work, her favorite thing to do was watch TV and drink beer. It bored me to tears. My answer was to get into video games. That's when my fixation started. I was a late bloomer in the video game world, discovering them in my mid-twenties. Before that, I preferred to get high—or read—or see a documentary—or take in a museum.

My parents are enablers. They make it easy for me to do less than I might otherwise have to do.

I did live for one year once without any support from my parents. It started out exhilarating. I worked hard at a bookstore, earning raises and respect. But eventually I burnt out. Beer and pot sapped my energy. Depression took hold. Yes I was independent, but I was still a self-destructive mess.

Now I am back in the fold. I struggle with motivation. I struggle with depression and anxiety, but I do live a cleaner and healthier life. I have a year and a half of grad school done, but I'll be lucky to make any use of this degree by the time I get it, at the pace I'm going.

I don't think the answer is "your parents are enablers, they should cut you off." Of course you might predict that I would say that. But the issues are complex.

I hope that this is useful information for you. Thank you for the opportunity.

Mike

Dear Dr. Sax,

You've perfectly described my 31-year-old son, adopted in Taiwan at 5 weeks of age. It may interest you that it used to describe his twin sister as well. Both had high IQs and difficulties fitting into the small New England town we lived in. In college they both suffered from depression and dropped out. She found housing near her school, did some entry-level jobs, finally got married and now has some sense of direction. She talks of going back to school, getting a real job etc. He does not. He flunked out several times, came home, pretended to get jobs but never did— until we gave him an ultimatum: either get a job or get out. He got a job. Later he also moved into an apartment. The job moved away and he has not found another for several years. He seems content to exist on his leftover college fund. He plays video games and online role games with a few friends. He's a nice person—but with no ambition and no desires. He has never shown motivation.

I often wonder if the overwhelming importance for males of achievement in sports early in life offers some explanation for this total giving up if one is not oriented toward sports.

[no name given]

I often hear from parents who, somewhat like this mother, are convinced that their son's lack of motivation can be traced to the day when he wasn't asked to play in the pickup basketball game, or when he didn't make the junior high football team, or when he discovered that he just wasn't particularly good at sports. However, I also hear from parents of other boys, athletically talented boys, who are convinced that their son's lack of motivation is due to the fact that he grew accustomed to being the star, the best athlete, the golden boy. Once he finished high school and realized that he was never going to be good enough to play professional sports, he lost interest in life.

I agree that much of mainstream culture puts a tremendous emphasis on boys' being good at sports, just as it puts an overwhelming emphasis on the physical attractiveness of girls. Boys who are athletically talented are far more likely to be popular than boys who aren't any good at sports, just as girls who are slender and pretty are far more likely to be popular than girls who are obese. But the *Failure to Launch* phenomenon appears just as likely to occur in athletically talented boys as in klutzy boys. Parents often attribute their son's lack of motivation to his athletic prowess—or to his lack of athletic prowess. I think both attributions miss the point.

Another post from the *Washington Post* chat:

Missoula, Mont.: Hey, Mr. Sax, being out of the nest isn't so great for everybody. My advice to young men: take as much time as you need. The real world is very rough. The people advising you to move out are the ones who've made it. Others may not see it the same way.

My response: I agree that the real world is very rough. My question for you is: what's the best way to help young people to face that reality? If your child is ten or fifteen years old, then by all means, shelter him or her from that harsh reality. But what if your child is twenty-one, or twenty-six, or twenty-nine? How long is a parent expected to shelter a child who is not mentally or physically handicapped?

My own belief, based in part on my twenty years of medical practice, is that if parents continue to shelter their adult child after the age of twenty-one years, the parents may make it less likely that the adult child will ever be willing and able to meet the challenges of the real world.

Of course one has to make reasonable distinctions. If your son has just graduated from college and he's 22 or 23, looking for a job, I see no harm in his living at home while he's conducting his job search—provided that you and he have discussed, openly and up front, how long this situation can last before you will expect him to find some kind of part-time job to help pay his expenses. One month? Fine. One year? Too long.

Dear Dr. Sax,

I have 3 sons. My 25-year-old has an honors degree, a good job, he's married and a homeowner. Successful launch. My youngest is in college. He is very likely to launch: when he is home during summer we barely see him and he is very uncomfortable about accepting money from us for tuition or car insurance or anything else.

Our middle son, now 23, is a classic failure to launch. Despite 6 years of college, some of it part time, he only has a 2 year degree. Of my 3 boys, he's the only computer game player. He is addicted to video games.

I believe that in certain susceptible individuals, playing video games gives them control of a fantasy world without the discomfort and uncertainty of real world social interactions. This same son was diagnosed as ADD in first grade. We tried Ritalin, but after getting to a dose that caused palpitations without any noticeable behavior changes we decided that was not his problem. He tested in the gifted category, did well on the SAT, but his grades were all over the map due to lack of focus and a bout of depression in his senior year.

Thank you for focusing on this.
Carol in South Carolina

This e-mail highlights two recurring issues. First: variation within a family. It's not unusual to find a situation like this one where one son "fails to launch" while his brother does just fine. I agree with what Carol said about individual susceptibilities. Second: it's common to see these boys struggling with depression. It's often hard to say which comes first. Is the boy depressed because he's unmotivated and failing to launch, or is he unmotivated because he's depressed?

Dear Dr. Sax,

I listened with great interest to you on NPR yesterday. I'm the mother of a 33-year-old male—handsome, charming, personable, tall, college graduate (that took 6 years and 4 schools).

He has "failed to launch" no matter what my husband and I have done to help him, beginning right after he graduated from college. We bought him a car and clothes for job interviews. He wasn't interested. He liked the good life: hanging out with a bunch of kids he met in college who did drugs and stayed out all night and slept the better part of the day.

Finally, after consulting with a psychologist who encouraged us to let him fall to the very bottom, we let it happen. He became homeless. Out on the street. When he called us in desperation, we offered him yet another opportunity to launch. He joined the Army. He completed Basic and even did months of Advanced Individual Training.

Then just as the war with Iraq broke out, he figured out a way to get out of the Army. But we did not allow him to live with us again.

We are still helping him financially or he would not be able to live on his own. He's living in our beach place rent-free for 8 months a year. He has been working somewhat more steadily but he is still not capable of saving for a rainy day or even cover the basic costs of living. He has no aspiration to become anything. He says he dislikes "corporate" America. He is resentful of us, yet at the same time he needs us to help him.

My husband and I have been self-starters, self-made successes. Over the years, with hard work, we have managed to become financially comfortable. We are in our mid–60s, but we still work, because we enjoy what we do.

So how can we help our son to get on with his own life?? And stop leaning on us???? We have told him countless times that when we die then no one is going to be able to help him anymore.

I would love to hear from you.
D.G., near Boston

From: "Mike Cleveland" Mike.Cleveland@dhs.gov
Subject: Failure to Launch

Dr. Sax,

I read your article and the chat in Washington Post online. I was struck by the pervasiveness of this "Failure to Launch." Professor Kleinfeld's web site* indicated that this trend began in the early

*www.boysproject.net

70's. I find that timing interesting because that's when the military draft ended and we went to an all-volunteer force. The draft may have had a significant effect on young men in ways not readily apparent.

The military was a place for many boys to finish growing up.

- The additional supervised time after high school, age 18–24, may have provided the "catch up time" boys need to be on the same level with their female counterparts
- Mature role models. Older and wiser heads were in positions of authority and exercised that authority.
- Responsibility. Boys learned that they would be held accountable. Rewards and punishments were easily understood.

The draft—or more precisely, the threat of being drafted—may have encouraged young men who did not want to do military time to apply themselves in college. Dropping out of college could lead you to be drafted into service.

I do not advocate returning to a draft. But, programs which give boys a structured environment with more time to mature seem to have merit.

Regards,
Mike Cleveland
Elkview, West Virginia

Dear Dr. Sax,

I heard your interview this morning on NPR. I tried to call but could not get through. I too have a son, 26 years old, who is a "failure to launch." My son's situation is a little different from many of the young men you talk about because he doesn't live with me. He lives in a house that his Dad left to him, with conditions, before his death six years ago.

My son was a smart student who did not apply himself to his studies. He seemed to lack discipline to study and really did not put very much effort into his studies. He scored very well on his SATs though. He entered Northwestern University but dropped out after one year. Now, five years later, he seems to be sliding down the slippery slope of "failing to launch" his life.

My son is a wonderful conversationalist. He is interested in history, biology, space exploration, etc. There is a myriad of subjects that he is really knowledgeable about. He is charming, respectful, polite—and tall and handsome! He has so much enthusiasm for other areas of his life—but it doesn't seem to apply for planning for his own life. What will he become? What will he do? What will be his life's work? It troubles me. It doesn't seem to trouble him at all.

My son has had every opportunity. He has chosen not to return to college. Did he make this choice with full understanding of what it would mean for his future? I don't believe he ever really thinks about the future.

I want him to do something with his life. His Dad would have wanted that for him too. I know that my son misses him very much, but it's been 6 years and he must find a path for himself.

I would so appreciate a reply whenever you have the time.

Thank you.

Sincerely,
A Most Concerned Mother,

Mary W.

From: "Kent Robertson" kent@costreview.com
Subject: NPR interview

I thought I would share an epiphany I experienced during your interview.

With 4 sons, teen and pre-teen, this "Failure to Launch" trend is one I need to get in front of. You mentioned that these men are quite content despite their lack of motivation. Well, why the hell not. These man/boys have it all. Their material needs are handed to them. The over-indulgent Moms will see to that (didn't the mother who called in make that clear?). Their emasculated fathers usually have little say.

Here's the epiphany—or confession, if you like. I sense that I am only a marital separation away from sinking into such a funk. When I think how little I would need to be content, compared with how much I produce, it's amazing. But somehow it works. I work ridiculous hours and earn ridiculous money. Yet I personally expend only about $200 per month of it on food, haircut, sundries. Whatever new clothes I have are given to me as gifts, because I have little interest in how I look. I live in a comfortable home in a pleasant neighborhood, and a whole wonderful busy suburban lifestyle, but only because I want that for my wife and children. *Take my dear ones away and I need none of it.* [emphasis in original]

I have seen many grown men, when their marriage fails, drift toward the man/boy zero-ambition style of life, living in a shanty or maybe back home with parents, in pursuit of personal gratification over everything else, exploiting every sexual opportunity, not unlike the man/boys you described on NPR.

You mentioned "the engine that runs the world." As for me, I think that the engine is the love of a good woman and the ambitions we have together for the family we are raising and for the world we want them to inherit.

Has our intellectual elite and our popular culture tinkered with "the engine that runs the world"? Have we violated something that the ancients knew intuitively but which we have arrogantly ignored?

Kent Robertson

7

THE FIFTH FACTOR

The Revenge of the Forsaken Gods

How does a child become an adult? The transition from childhood to productive adulthood involves more than mere biological maturation and the passage of time. Children take their cues from the grown-ups they see around them. Girls look to women they know, as well as to the images they see on television, in magazines, in movies. Likewise, boys look to the men they see in their lives and in the media. In his memoir *The Tender Bar*, author J. R. Moehringer describes how he found his community of men at a local bar, beginning long before he was old enough to buy a drink.[2] The men at the bar were not all model citizens or great fathers or manly men. But collectively they provided Moehringer with what he needed. "Manhood is mimesis," Moehringer wrote. "To be a man, a boy must see a man."[3]

A boy does not naturally become a gentleman—by which I mean a man who is courteous and kind and unselfish. That behavior is not hardwired. It has to be taught.

In May 2006, I delivered the commencement address at Avon Old Farms, a boys' school in Connecticut. I noticed that there were a great many teenage girls in the audience—far outnumbering the boys. "You guys all seem to have about four sisters apiece," I said to some of the boys.

"Those aren't our sisters, Dr. Sax," one of the boys told me. "Those are friends."

"You mean girlfriends?"

"Some of them are girlfriends, most of them are just friends," he said.

This piqued my interest. I spoke with some of the girls. A few were from Miss Porter's School, a girls' school about five miles away, but most were from the Westminster Academy, a coed school right next door to this boys' school.

"A coed school?" I said. "So what are you girls doing here? Why would you want to hang out here at a boys' school, when you have boys at your own school?"

One girl rolled her eyes. "The boys at our school are all such total losers," she said. "Being around them is like being around my younger brother. They're loud and obnoxious and annoying. And they think they're so tough. It's totally—nauseating." The other girls laughed and nodded their agreement.

"And the boys here are really that different?" I asked.

They all nodded their heads again. "Totally," another girl said. "The boys here are, like—gentlemen. I know that sounds really strange and weird and old-fashioned, but that's just the way it is. Like, they stand up when you come in the room. They open doors for you."

"And they don't interrupt you," another girl said, interrupting. "I hate trying to talk to guys at our school 'cause they are always interrupting you."

"You should come here some weekend, Dr. Sax," another girl said. "You would totally not even know that this is a boys' school. There are probably more girls here than boys on the weekend. We just totally mob the place. Not even to hang with the guys necessarily. Last week a bunch of us girls went down to the hockey rink here at the school just to slide around on the ice, just us girls."

"But why bother to come to this school at all? You could have just gone to a public ice skating rink," I said.

She shook her head 'no.' "It wouldn't be the same. It's fun to hang out here, because. . . . "

"Because it's like we're family," another girl said.

"Because it feels safe," another girl said.

This boys' school is not unique. I have heard similar comments from other girls who like to congregate at boys' schools, for example at Georgetown Prep in Bethesda, Maryland. I hasten to add that I have heard very different comments at certain other boys' schools: I have heard girls say that they would never ever in a million years hang out at certain boys' schools. Just establishing a boys' school doesn't make that school a place where girls like to gather. On the contrary, when you put teenage boys together in groups, without the right kind of adult leadership, they can easily become a gang of bullies and thugs, "crashing through several moral guardrails," to borrow David Brooks's memorable phrase.[4] The *Animal House* frat-house party exemplifies the stereotype of young men without the right kind of leadership. *Lord of the Flies* exemplifies a different stereotype, but illustrates the same underlying idea: Teenage boys without strong leadership can easily become barbarians.

Leadership from responsible adults makes the difference between boys' schools where girls feel safe and welcome, and boys' schools where girls feel unsafe. Boys' schools like the one in Connecticut where I spoke don't leave this to chance. They make a point of teaching boys to be gentlemen. At this particular school, the boys are taught the school's eight "core values," which are:

- Scholarship
- Integrity
- Civility
- Tolerance
- Altruism
- Sportsmanship
- Responsibility
- Self-discipline

"It's not enough for a boy to become a man. We want him to become a gentleman," the headmaster, Kenneth LaRocque, explained to me. A gentleman doesn't pretend to make farting noises to amuse his buddies. A gentleman doesn't harass girls or women. A gentleman doesn't interrupt a girl when she is speaking. At this boys' school, all these points are explicitly taught to the boys. "You can't assume that boys today know these things. Many of them don't. But they can be taught," Mr. LaRocque said. "A boy does not naturally grow up to be a gentleman. You need a community of men showing boys how to behave. And that's what we have here."

Almost every culture of which we have detailed knowledge takes great care in managing this transition to adulthood. One example: The !Kung bushmen of southwest Africa, who call themselves "the harmless people." Their culture is nonviolent: war is unknown. They have no warriors and no tradition of combat. "Yet even here," according to anthropologist David Gilmore, "in a culture that treasures gentleness and cooperation above all things, the boys must earn the right to be called men by a test of skill and endurance. They must single-handedly track and kill a sizable adult antelope, an act that requires courage and hardiness. Only after their first kill of such a buck are they considered fully men and permitted to marry."[5]

Professor Gilmore devoted several years to researching the various manifestations of masculinity in cultures around the world, including the !Kung. "There are many societies where aggressive hunting never played an important role," Gilmore writes, "where men do not bond for economic purposes, where violence and war are devalued or unknown, and yet where men are [even] today concerned about demonstrating manhood."[6]

What happens when a culture—like ours—neglects this transition? For a decade or two, or three, perhaps, the culture can coast along. But after thirty-plus years of neglecting this transition, one might expect problems to begin developing.

We are now seeing a rise in violent crime committed by young men. I suggest that one of several factors driving the current rise in crime may be our collective neglect of this transition to adulthood. Teenage boys are looking for models of mature adulthood, but we no longer make any collective effort to provide such models.

> *USA Today*, November 1, 2006: Violent crime rates are increasing in dozens of cities across the nation, according to a recent analysis by the Police Executive Research Forum, a police advocacy group. The police group's report led the Justice Department to launch a review of possible demographic and economic triggers for violence in cities from Philadelphia to Sacramento. . . .
>
> Across Florida, police are reporting spikes in violence after a decade of historically low crime rates. Homicides are up 27% [in 2006 compared with 2005] . . . Ron Stucker, criminal investigations chief for the Orange County Sheriff's Department, reports seeing a new and increasingly deadly escalation of behavior in which offenders are quick to use lethal force. . . .
>
> "It goes from zero to 100 mph and sometimes murder, just like that," Lee says. "You see minimal confrontations blow up, and there is no hesitancy to kill." The random nature of the robbery-related murders makes it more difficult to identify and pursue suspects, he says, and has contributed to a decline in clearance rates—from near 70% in previous years to about 50% today.[7]
>
> *Boston Globe*, November 9, 2006: Six members of a Beverly gang were arrested after they allegedly attacked two men with a baseball bat as part of what police called a gang initiation. . . . Once isolated in [Boston's] congested urban core, gang activity has begun to spread to the suburbs, according to local law enforcement officials and crime reports. "We're a very mobile society, and at this particular point, gangs are not just staying stationary," said Lieutenant Mary Butler, with the Salem department.[8]
>
> The *Post and Courier* (South Carolina), September 30, 2006: Many of Colleton County's most dangerous gang members still live at home with Mom and commit crimes in their parents' cars. They dress like the guys from the big cities but mostly hail from secluded, tight-knit hamlets. . . . Gang violence has become so bold and prevalent in this county of 28,000 people that deputies with the

year-old gang task force say it's just luck that a bullet has yet to hit
its target or an innocent bystander.[9]

If we fail to provide boys with pro-social models of the transition to
adulthood, they may construct their own. In some cases, gang initiation
rituals, street racing, and random violence may be the result.

Of course, not all enduring cultures follow the same template in
guiding boys to manhood. Without doubt, significant attributes of masculinity are constructed differently by different societies. One example
has to do with attitudes toward homosexuality. In some cultures homosexuality is seen as a deviant, unmasculine orientation. In numerous
other cultures, however, homosexuality is seen as a normal masculine or
even hypermasculine orientation. Among some Native American tribes,
for example, the most masculine men have sex with other men; having
sex with women is perceived as less masculine.[10] Likewise, among samu-
rai warriors in Japan, particularly in the period from the establishment
of the Tokugawa shogunate in 1603 to the Meiji Restoration in 1867, the
homosexual orientation was held in high regard as a sign of the truest
masculinity. A similar cultural bias in favor of homosexuality was preva-
lent in ancient Sparta.[11]

Each culture differs somewhat, then, in terms of what is considered
masculine behavior. But these variations in cultural attitudes should not
confuse us. There are certain constants. There is no enduring culture in
which cowardly men are esteemed, or in which brave men are held in
contempt. There is no enduring culture in which lazy men are celebrated while hardworking men are despised.[12]

Enduring Cultures Have One Thing in Common

What do cultures that have lasted for hundreds or thousands of years
have in common? Orthodox Jews and Navajo Indians seem at first
glance to have almost nothing in common, except that both cultures
have endured more or less intact for more than a thousand years. The
religious beliefs of the Orthodox Jew conflict fundamentally and profoundly with those of the Navajo Indian; rules about what may or may

not be eaten differ enormously between the two; and they dress very differently.

But they have one thing in common, having to do with how these cultures pass the rules for what is expected of mature adults from one generation to the next. Both these cultures—like almost every other enduring culture of which we have detailed knowledge—pass this information from one generation to the next in gender-separate communities. Women teach girls what is expected of adult women in their community. Men teach boys.

I'm not talking about teaching reading, writing, social studies, math, or science. Women can teach these subjects to boys effectively and well (just as men can teach these subjects to girls). I've visited boys' schools where some of the best and most beloved teachers are women, just as I've visited girls' schools where some of the most effective teachers are men. But when it comes to showing boys how a gentleman behaves— how a gentleman interacts with women, how he responds to adversity, how he serves his community—then there is no substitute for having a male role model. That's where boys can benefit most, in my judgment, from seeing a man, perhaps a teacher or a coach, who loves to read in his spare time, who participates in projects for Habitat for Humanity or in community service with his local synagogue or church, who's a regular guy—not a saint, not Rambo, not John Wayne. Just somebody real.

In some cultures, this process—the transmission of adult gender roles from one generation to the next—is explicit and formal. Shortly after a Navajo girl experiences her first menstrual period, she is sequestered in the hut of her grandmother for four consecutive days. During those four days, all of her adult female relatives call on her. She engages in a series of rituals illustrating her new status as a woman in the community. She is welcomed into the community of adult women.[13] Likewise, in this chapter we have already glimpsed a few examples of the ways in which various traditional cultures guide boys to manhood.

Not all enduring cultures have such formal ceremonies. In many cultures, the transition to adulthood is more gradual and incremental. But in every enduring culture, girls are led into womanhood by a community of adult woman; boys are led into manhood by a community of adult men. The mother and father play an important role in some cultures, a less important role in others such as the Navajo where the process is more communal rather than familial. But there is no enduring culture in which parents attempt this task alone. As the saying goes, it takes a village to raise a boy to manhood or a girl to womanhood.

When I speak to parents' groups, I'm often interrupted at this point. "I don't have a community of men to raise my son," one mother told me. "I don't even have his father, and I wouldn't want his father back in any case. He's out of the picture. So what am I supposed to do, as a single mom, as far as this 'transition to manhood' business is concerned?"

I suggested to that mother that she must do the same thing that every other parent of a boy has to do: find a community of men that can give your son healthy and life-affirming examples of what it means to be a man. This question has been addressed thoroughly by psychologist Peggy Drexler, who has studied how unmarried heterosexual women and lesbians raise sons. Based on her research, she has this advice for women who don't have men in their personal lives: "Actively recruit male figures from [your] family and from the community—including babysitters, tutors, coaches, and Big Brother–type pals—to be in [your] sons' lives. As a result, [your] sons wind up with more, rather than fewer, men upon which to model themselves."[14] It's hard for parents, even happily married parents, to do this alone. The community you choose might be a Boy Scout troop, an all-male Bible study or Torah study, or a sports team coached by men you know and trust.

If a boy does not have a community of men, then he is likely to look elsewhere for his role models. He may look to the media, where he will encounter a blizzard of images of men like Eminem and Akon and 50 Cent—all of whom make their money by writing songs that are degrading to women. He may look to his peers, to boys his own age. The results of teenage boys looking to other teenage boys for guidance are often confused and self-destructive. Teenage boys are seldom competent to guide one another to manhood. That's what men are for.

Enduring cultures often imbue the transition to adulthood with sacred meaning, as we have seen already from some of the examples in this chapter. We twenty-first-century Americans smile condescendingly at such traditions. We think we have no need for such rituals. We are amused by the customs of other peoples and other places, customs that are designed to placate gods we don't believe in.

Think twice before you look condescendingly at the traditions of other cultures that have lasted far longer than our own. Our culture's neglect of the transition to manhood is not producing an overabundance of young men who are sensitive, caring, and hardworking. Instead, there is growing evidence that our society's neglect of this transition results most often either in the "slacker dude" portrayed in *Failure to Launch,* or in the bully and criminal personae exemplified by convicted felons such as Akon and 50 Cent.*

The forsaken gods will have their revenge.

When I say that "the forsaken gods will have their revenge," I am not suggesting that I believe in the literal reality of the gods and goddesses who oversee the sacred festivals of the native communities that Professor Gilmore describes. Allow me to ask you to go back to the final e-mail message at the close of chapter 6, from Kent Robertson. Mr. Robertson asked, "Have we violated something that the ancients knew intuitively but which we have arrogantly ignored?" I think Mr. Robertson is on to something. We ignore the importance of these traditions at our peril. Manhood isn't something that simply happens to boys as they get older. It's an achievement—something a boy accomplishes, something that can easily go awry. If we ignore the importance of this transition, and fail in our duty as parents to guide boys through it, then we will learn the hard way why traditional cultures invest this transition with so much importance.

---

*I make reference to the fact that these men are convicted felons in part because both of them are quick to mention their criminal record at every opportunity. Both regard their criminal past as an essential ingredient to their current success. Neither man publicly expresses remorse or regret for the criminal offenses that led to imprisonment.

In all the cultures he studied, Gilmore found

> . . . a constantly recurring notion that real manhood is different
> from simple anatomical maleness, that it is not a natural condition
> that comes about spontaneously through biological maturation
> but rather is a precarious or artificial state that boys must win
> against powerful odds. . . . [This belief] is found among the sim-
> plest hunters and fishermen, among peasants and sophisticated ur-
> banized peoples; it is found in all continents and environments. It
> is found among both warrior peoples and those who have never
> killed in anger.[15]

The recurring theme is that "culturally defined competence . . . leads
to reproductive success."[16] In some cases, such as among traditional Orthodox Jews, "culturally defined competence" is completely intellectual.
An Orthodox Jewish boy must prove his knowledge of Torah and Tal-
mud. In other cultures the travail is more physical. But the underlying
theme is the same.

According to Gilmore, all enduring cultures agree "that regression to
a state of primary narcissism is unacceptable in and of itself as a threat
to adult functioning."[17] Similar ideas permeated American culture a century ago, Gilmore observes. The explicit motivation behind the founding of the Boy Scouts was to "make men of little boys" and foster "an
independent manhood."[18] There was no assumption that an independent manhood would just happen naturally. As in other cultures, there
was an urgent awareness that boys must be led to manhood.

The idea that manhood is conditional was a major theme in twentieth-
century American literature, Gilmore continues, at least until the mid-
1970s. William Faulkner, Ernest Hemingway, John Dos Passos, Studs
Terkel, Norman Mailer, James Dickey, and Frederick Exley all communi-
cated the idea that manhood is something you must earn.

American literary critic Alfred Habegger, commenting on the American tradition, notes that masculinity in American literature "has an un-
certain and ambiguous status. It is something to be acquired through a
struggle, a painful initiation, or a long and sometimes humiliating ap-

prenticeship. To be male is to be fundamentally unsure about one's status . . . "[19] Gilmore found this idea—that manhood is conditional—in
almost every culture he studied. He adds that the idea that manhood
must be achieved is "true of almost all U.S. ethnic subvariants of manhood, not just some hypothetical Anglo-Saxon archetype."[20]

Gilmore adds that "this heroic image of an achieved manhood . . . has
been widely legitimized in U.S. cultural settings ranging from Italian
American gangster culture to Hollywood Westerns, private-eye tales, the
current Rambo imagoes, and children's He-Man dolls and games." But
these gendered images have changed in the past fifty years. Fifty years
ago, these stories of boys becoming men were mainstream cultural stories of real boys becoming real men—by which I mean men you might
plausibly encounter in your daily life. Think of *The Hustler*, or *Rebel
Without a Cause*, or *On the Waterfront*. The characters played by Paul
Newman, James Dean, and Marlon Brando in those movies were ordinary boys or young men, not superheroes. In each of these stories, an
immature, lazy, cocky boy experiences personal hardship and the death
of a friend, and matures into manhood as a result of overcoming various trials. Each of these movies was set in its own time. Each story took
place in the era in which the movie was filmed, depicting stories that
might actually have occurred (*On the Waterfront* was actually based on a
Pulitzer Prize–winning series of articles for the *New York Sun*).

Such movies are rare today. We still have masculine heroes in our
movies—think of *Braveheart* and *Gladiator*—but scriptwriters seem un-
able to write a believable story about a boy becoming a heroic man set in
our era. The scriptwriters go back five hundred years or more, or set
their heroic epics in a science fiction past (*Star Wars*) or in a fantasy
world (*Harry Potter, Lord of the Rings, Eragon*).

The Samburu, who live in the region just south of Lake Turkana in
Kenya, are dairy farmers. When a Samburu boy is on the threshold of
manhood, he must solemnly renounce drinking milk. This action "conveys a public confirmation that he has renounced the breast voluntarily

in favor of delayed gratifications of work culture. All women will hence-
forth be treated as receivers rather than givers of food; the boy will no
longer need mothering."[21]

Farther south, the Masai tribes, living in the hills along the border
between Kenya and Tanzania, likewise view "manhood [as] a status
that does not come naturally, but rather is an elaborate idea symboli-
cally constructed as a series of tests and confirmations. . . . "[22] A high
point of Masai male adolescence is "the sacrifice of his first ox. The
major portion of the meat is then given to the boy's mother, an act that
is described as a thank-you to her for having reared and fed him as a
boy. . . . For the Masai, as for the Samburu, the idea of manhood contains also the idea of the tribe, an idea grounded in a moral courage
based on commitment to collective goals. Their construction of manhood encompasses not only physical strength or bravery but also a
moral beauty construed as selfless devotion to national identity."[23]
Many cultures have stories such as these, in which the young man
must reject the "puerile cocoon of pleasure and safety"[24] to achieve real
manhood.

Our culture used to tell such stories as well.

We no longer do.

American Culture—Toxic to Boys—and to Girls?

In 2003, Dartmouth Medical School professor Kathleen Kovner Kline
gathered together a distinguished panel of experts in child and adolescent development. The charge to the panel was to study problems facing
American children and teenagers from an interdisciplinary perspective.
Among the experts were Dr. T. Berry Brazelton, the renowned pediatrician; Robert Coles, arguably the world's leading expert on how children
learn morality; Dr. Stephen Suomi, who has spent more than three decades studying parent-child bonding; and about two dozen others. The
group included leading scholars in developmental pediatrics, sociology,
primatology, and adolescent psychology—the first and only time such
an interdisciplinary array of talent has been gathered to take a careful
look at what's going on with American children and teenagers.[25]

The panel began by reviewing what's happened in the United States with regard to the health and welfare of children and teenagers over the past fifty years. First the good news. Death rates among children and teenagers in the United States due to cancer and unintentional injuries have dropped by more than 50 percent over the past fifty years. But over these same fifty years, homicide rates among U.S. youth have risen by more than 130 percent, while suicide rates have risen by almost 140 percent. Suicide is now the third leading cause of death among Americans under eighteen years of age.[26] Among Americans age fifteen to nineteen years, young men are five times more likely to kill themselves than young women are; among Americans age twenty to twenty-four years of age, young men are seven times more likely than young women to die by their own hand.[27]

Who's better off: the children of new immigrants to the United States, or children born into families that have been in this country for generations? Remarkably, the panel found that on many parameters, children of new immigrants to the United States fare better than children born to families that have been in the United States for generations. Adolescents from immigrant families are significantly more likely to attend school faithfully, and they appear to be more motivated. They try harder. They are also significantly less likely to engage in risky behaviors such as early sexual encounters, substance abuse, delinquency, and violence.[28]

But it doesn't last. Although children in the families of new immigrants are healthier in many respects and more motivated compared to their American-born peers, "this relative advantage tends to decline with length of time in the United States and from one generation to the next."[29] The Dartmouth panel concluded that the longer an immigrant child lives in the United States, the more likely that child is

> . . . to be less healthy and to report increases in risk behaviors. The implication of these findings is unmistakable. For the children of immigrants, and for U.S. children overall, some of the basic foundations of childhood appear currently to be at best anemic, in the sense of [being] weak and inadequate to foster full human flourishing, and at worst toxic, inadvertently depressing health and engendering emotional distress and mental illness.[30]

Alison Cooper lives in Bethesda, about half an hour's drive from my home. The *Washington Post* recently published an article by her that provides an interesting perspective on the differences between native-born Americans and recent immigrants. On a Saturday morning, she was sitting in her car in the parking lot of a local supermarket, talking on her cell phone, when

> . . . a dad and his two sons, roughly 8 and 10, piled into the car next to mine, and in so doing one of the boys carelessly flung his door open so far that it scraped the side of my car. . . . I was appalled to see the dad backing out of his parking spot, apparently with no intention of stopping. I aborted my call and leaped out of my car, screaming at the driver. At this point he stopped, got out of his car and began [yelling]: It's a ding! This is a parking lot, what do you expect?! What's the big deal?! Get some touch-up paint! . . . I let him go, feeling slightly . . . sick about the lessons he had just taught his boys:
>
> 1. When you damage someone else's car, try to get away without having to face the owner of the car, and
> 2. If this fails, come out swinging aggressively, minimize the damage, and assert that parking-lot dings are a fact of life . . .

The next day my 7-year-old daughter pointed out to me fresh and severe damage to the bumper. It was badly crunched. We were home in our driveway, but the damage could have occurred any-time during the previous 24 hours while we were out and about on errands. There was no note on the windshield. I sadly accepted that I'd never know who did this to my car. . . .

The next day, a husband and wife come to her home to explain what happened. The wife, in halting English, explained that their son had panicked after hitting the car and rushed to [them . . . They] notified their insurance company and then went looking for the damaged car. . . . They provided their insurance information and apologized profusely.

These parents have taught their teenage son:

1. Take responsibility for your actions, even if you can get away with not doing so, even if it's not convenient or easy, and even though your insurance rates are certain to increase with this acknowledgment, and
2. Don't make excuses, don't lie, be forthcoming and apologize.

I am struck by the contrasting lessons taught by the Bethesda dad and the Kensington housepainters.[31]

The Kensington family were immigrants. The wife could barely speak English. Some pundits, such as CNN's Lou Dobbs, have argued that we should tighten restrictions on immigration to the United States, because immigrants are less likely to understand our American culture.[32] Stories like these make one wonder whether we should instead encourage immigration so as to improve the moral fiber—and indeed the general health—of young Americans.

The Significance of Gender

Gender was not mentioned in the initial charge to the Dartmouth panel. But as the experts met and consulted with one another about what they were seeing in their research and what they were hearing from adolescents, they kept coming up against one truth: gender matters. "Assigning meaning to gender in childhood and adolescence is a human universal that deeply influences well-being," the panel wrote. They concluded:

In much of today's social science writing, and also more generally within elite culture, gender tends to be viewed primarily as a set of traits and as a tendency to engage in certain roles. Yet the current weight of evidence suggests that this understanding . . . is seriously

incomplete. Gender runs deeper, near to the core of human identity and social meaning—in part because it is biologically primed
and connected to differences in brain structure and function, and
in part because it is so deeply implicated in the transition to
adulthood.

In recent decades, many adults have tended to withdraw from
the task of assigning pro-social meaning to gender, especially in the
case of boys. For some people, actual and desired changes in sex
roles, including a desire for greater androgyny, make some of our
culture's traditional gender formulations appear anachronistic and
even potentially harmful. We recognize the important issues at
stake here.

But neglecting the gendered needs of adolescents can be dangerous. Boys and girls differ with respect to risk factors for social
pathology. . . . We recognize the perils of oversimplifying or exag-
gerating gender differences. But as the medical world has discovered, the risk of not attending to real differences that exist between
males and females can have dangerous consequences.

Ignoring or denying this challenge will not make it go away. Indeed, when adults choose largely to neglect the critical task of sexually enculturing the young, they are left essentially on their
own—perhaps with some help from Hollywood and Madison Avenue—to discover the social meaning of their sexuality. The resulting, largely adolescent-created rituals of transition are far less likely
to be pro-social in their meaning or consequences.

Young people have an inherent need to experience . . . sexual
maturing within an affirming system of meaning.[33]

The Changing American Father

The stature of the father figure in the American family has taken a considerable tumble in the past forty or fifty years. American popular culture illustrates this point dramatically. Forty years ago, television shows
such as *My Three Sons* with Fred MacMurray and *Father Knows Best*
with Robert Young were popular fare. The father figures played by Mac-

Murray and Young were wise, caring, and competent. Fast forward to the 1980s and watch an episode of *The Cosby Show*. Bill Cosby's character, Dr. Cliff Huxtable, was a wise, caring, and competent father to five children and a loving husband to an intelligent wife. Unlike the characters portrayed by MacMurray and Young, Cosby's character was often the butt of jokes, but it was all in good fun. At the end of each show, Dad's stature as the father was never in doubt. *The Cosby Show* debuted in 1984 near the top of the ratings and stayed there through most of its run, going off the air in 1992.

Three years before *The Cosby Show* signed off, *The Simpsons* went on the air. *The Simpsons* is now the longest-running sitcom in American history, having aired over four hundred episodes in eighteen seasons, and shows no signs of slowing down despite (or because of?) the static nature of the lead characters. In particular, the father—Homer Simpson—is always an idiot, always a klutz, always the least intelligent character in any episode, with the possible exception of his son, Bart, or the family dog. By contrast, Homer's wife, Marge, is generally practical although sometimes silly. The most intelligent character is consistently daughter Lisa, who routinely ignores her father's advice, advice that is often hysterically awful.

I don't want to overstate the importance of a TV show, not even a show as iconic as *The Simpsons*. My own assessment is that TV shows reflect our society more than they shape it. Either way, the success of *The Simpsons* clearly demonstrates that the image of the American father in the American mind today is quite different from where it was forty years ago.

Our purpose here is not to debate whether it is "good" or "bad" that the popular image of the American father has been transformed from wise patriarch to bumbling buffoon. What's important for purposes of our investigation here, is that this transformation has muddled the idea of mature manhood in the minds of American boys. Forty years ago, if a boy were told to "grow up!" he knew what that meant. It meant acting like the characters portrayed by MacMurray and Young in *My Three Sons* and *Father Knows Best*, or by Gary Cooper in *High Noon*, or by Jimmy Stewart in *It's a Wonderful Life* or by Sidney Poitier in *In the Heat of the Night*.

But if you ask a boy today to "grow up!" what does that mean? Who is he supposed to act like? Homer Simpson? Michael Jackson? Rambo? Akon? Mel Gibson?

What does it mean to be a man today, a mature adult man?

———————

In 2006, a tenured professor at Harvard University published a book entitled simply *Manliness.* The author, Harvey Mansfield, was distressed by the devaluation of masculinity he saw in contemporary American culture. As any good scholar ought to do, Mansfield began his book with an attempt to define his terms. Right off the bat, Professor Mansfield asserted without any disclaimer that "John Wayne is still every American's idea of manliness."[34] He then proceeded with a detailed analysis of what makes John Wayne the epitome of manliness.

When I read that sentence—"John Wayne is still every American's idea of manliness"—I was startled. *Speak for yourself* was the first thought that came to my mind. Like any film aficionado, I know that "John Wayne" was born Marion Robert Morrison and that the real person, Mr. Morrison, bore little resemblance to the "John Wayne" character he played in the movies. Speaking personally, my idea of manliness is epitomized by men such as:

- Joshua Chamberlain, the Bowdoin professor of religion and rhetoric who commanded the 20th Maine Volunteer Infantry Regiment (we'll talk more about Chamberlain at the close of the next chapter);
- Dietrich Bonhoeffer, the German pastor who left a safe and comfortable home to return to Germany to organize resistance to the Nazis, and who was arrested and subsequently hanged at the Flossenburg concentration camp; and
- Yitzhak Rabin, the Israeli prime minister who had the courage to try to make peace with the Palestinians and was gunned down by a fellow Israeli Jew.

These men differ from John Wayne in many respects, most importantly in that they became famous for things they actually did. John Wayne was not a real man. He just played one in the movies. Moreover, Mansfield might be startled to learn that most young people today have no idea who "John Wayne" is.

Mansfield finally defines manliness as "confidence in the face of risk"[35]—an irrational bias "in favor of action over reflection."[36] In his estimation, boldly plunging forward into uncertainty is the very essence of manliness. He claims that "thinking is a challenge"[37] for real men—a claim that comes close to equating masculinity with stupidity.

Plunging forward boldly in the face of uncertainty, without thinking first, when other less risky options might be available, doesn't sound manly to me. It sounds dumb. But it also reflects the confusion surrounding our concepts of masculinity today. Indeed, if this Harvard professor is clueless about what real masculinity is about, how are our sons supposed to know better?

What Does It Mean to Be a Man?

I live not far from an all-boys school that I mentioned earlier in this chapter: the Georgetown Preparatory School (referred to later as "Prep") in Bethesda, Maryland. Each year the program sends crews of sixteen boys with four adult men to the highlands of the Dominican Republic for a five-week program called *Somos Amigos*, "We are friends." It's hot and humid. There's no air conditioning. The boys live with the peasants, eating what they eat, mostly rice and beans. They sleep on the floor, which is often nothing but mud and straw. There are rats. There's no electricity. There's no Internet.

Every one of the boys I've spoken with about this experience regards it among the most meaningful of their lives. And I think I know why. Those boys are learning through their sweat the answer to the question, "What does it mean to be a man?" The answer is: being a man means using your strength in the service of others. This school explicitly teaches that message. Every boy at Prep knows the school's motto: Men for Others. But didactic knowledge, *Wissenschaft*, is not sufficient. The leaders of the school, including headmaster Ed Kowalchick, understand that a boy must learn this truth by experience, *Kenntnis*. "You can preach all you like, but there's nothing like putting a shovel in a boy's hands to teach him some lessons," Mr. Kowalchick told me.

After one of the boys from Prep has spent five weeks working dawn to dusk to build an infirmary or a road or an aqueduct, and the job is done, and he returns home, he can watch NFL football on a Sunday afternoon and see a beer commercial that claims that real men drink Miller beer—and that boy can laugh. He knows that being a real man has nothing to do with drinking any particular brand of beer. It has to do with using your strength in the service of others.

That definition—giving all you have in the service of others—is an integral part of the Judeo-Christian tradition that has animated Western history for the past two millennia. It is not an original idea. "Greater love hath no man than this, that a man lay down his life for his friends" (John 15:13, KJV).

I am not suggesting that this definition of real manliness is the only one. I am well aware that the ancient Romans and Greeks had very different definitions; without doubt the Masai and the Samburu would also see the matter differently. But a culture is defined in part by how it answers the question "What defines a real man?" Every culture must make choices and value judgments. Indeed, one can almost define a culture by the choices its people make. We must choose, individually and collectively, how we are going to define masculinity. If we abstain from this choice, that failure to make a choice is itself a choice—and the marketplace will make the choice for us, as the Dartmouth panelists observed.

The end result of ignoring this question is not a generation of androgynous flower children. The result is, on the one hand, young men who have no motivation to work or to serve, young men who feel no shame in living indefinitely in their parents' homes, no shame in taking much and giving little in return. These young men—many of whom are white men living in the suburbs—don't have any concern about being seen as "real men." It's not important to them. Why should it be? Who wants to be Homer Simpson?

That's one outcome. On the other hand, we are beginning to reap a fearful harvest of young men who do care about being real men and who—receiving no guidance from the adult community about what that means—are turning instead to gang violence, or street racing, or drug abuse, for affirmation of their masculine identity and for their rites of passage. The devaluation and disintegration of the masculine ideal is the fifth factor driving the growing epidemic we've been investigating.

Affluence may have played some role in the decline of the masculine ideal in North America. Gilmore found that the more difficult it was to eke out survival in a particular time and place, the more strongly that culture celebrated traditional notions of manhood and masculinity. Remember the older Canadian man whom I quoted in the opening chapter? He said "When I was young, we had to walk three miles to school." Today, very few American children have to walk three miles to school. Few middle-class American children have to worry about whether there will be food on the table or a roof over their head. That may be part of the reason why "being a real man" matters less to some American boys than might have been the case a generation or two earlier.

What About Girls?

Boys are having more difficulty making the transition to manhood. That's the main point of this chapter and indeed of this book.

In making that point, I am not suggesting that girls have it any easier than boys. They don't. In February 2007, the American Psychological Association released a monograph, commissioned two years earlier, that documented just how difficult the transition to womanhood has become for American girls.[38] The culture of the marketplace teaches girls to value themselves in terms of how sexy they are, not in their own eyes but in the eyes of boys. Articles in magazines for young girls emphasize the value of exercise, for example, not in terms of health benefits but because exercise will (the articles assert) make the girl look sexier for the guys.[39] This way of valuing girls is not only destructive to girls' self-esteem—even supermodels are often dissatisfied with their appearance—but it is also wildly out of synch with the demands of the real world, the adult world. Unless she's an actress or a supermodel, a woman's success in the world is less a function of her appearance than it is of her competence. What you can do ultimately matters more than how you look. A woman might look like Angelina Jolie or Halle Berry—but if she shows up for work three hours late, doesn't answer her phone calls, and can't do the work she's assigned to do, then she won't be successful.

I hope we figure out what to do for girls before my daughter gets much older. But this book is about boys. We've considered the problem in some detail. We've examined five distinct factors that have derailed boys from reaching the goal of a healthy and productive manhood.

Now what can we do to get those goals back on track? That's the subject of the final chapter.

8

DETOX

We have already considered many strategies to counteract the five factors that are derailing so many boys and undermining the motivation of many young men. Now we're going to pull those strategies together.

The First Factor: Changes in Education

If you and I had the resources and the authority to remake American education, we could at least set a course that might assuage the harm being done to American boys and girls by twenty-first-century educational practices. The first thing we'd do would be to restore kindergarten as kindergarten, so that every child's first experience of schooling could be a positive experience. We'd push the emphasis on literacy and numeracy back to where it belongs, out of kindergarten and into first and second grade. We'd put *Kenntnis* and *Wissenschaft* back in balance, so that kids wouldn't be asked to learn about frogs and tadpoles until they've had some opportunity to play with real live frogs and tadpoles—not merely images on a computer screen. We'd give teachers more freedom to reintroduce competitive formats, preferably using team strategies, to engage children who flourish in those settings without disadvantaging kids who don't need that approach.

But you and I are not likely to have that authority or those resources any time soon. What can we do in the meantime? How can you do what's best in the world we're living in right now?

First: know what's going on in your school. If your school's kindergarten is like most kindergartens today, with an accelerated curriculum focusing on reading and math skills, you should seriously consider not enrolling your son until he is six. That one-year delay can make a world of difference. Visit the school before your son reaches kindergarten age. Talk to the principal. If possible, spend some time observing a classroom. Those activities should give you a good idea of the school's academic expectations and the strategies they employ to achieve them. If the teacher says, "We expect all our kindergarten children to be reading by February at the latest," that's a clue that your five-year-old son might not thrive at that school.

Look at the kids. Are they having fun? Is there a playful mood in the room? Do they have a chance to run around? Do they have some contact with nature, preferably outdoors, every day? Looking at goldfish through the glass pane of an aquarium does not count as "contact with nature" for this purpose. Remember that *Kenntnis* requires that a child touch, smell, and really experience the natural object. Just looking at nature through glass, or through the bars of a cage, isn't sufficient.

Second: Once your child is enrolled in school, if you see that the school is not providing a good learning experience for him, then team up with your fellow parents. Talk to your parent-teacher association (PTA), parent-teacher organization (PTO), parent-teacher-student association (PTSA), or whatever your school calls this group. Don't approach the principal or other school administrators by yourself. There's power in numbers. Recruit half a dozen like-minded parents and approach the principal as a group. One parent is just an annoyance. Six parents can't be ignored. Six parents acting together can change things. I've seen it happen. That's just as true at the high school level as it is at elementary school.

Find out how students are tested. If the only assessments that count are pencil-and-paper tests assessing *Wissenschaft,* then the leadership of that school may not understand the all-important balance between *Ken-*

ntnis and *Wissenschaft.* Does the school offer outlets for team competition within the school—not just athletically, but also academically? (Please reread chapter 2 if you're fuzzy on the rationale behind these recommendations.)

A few simple changes might accomplish a great deal. In Nebraska, for example, school leaders statewide have introduced testing formats that emphasize experiential learning, *Kenntnis,* rather than book learning, *Wissenschaft.* Elementary school students in Nebraska are now being tested on their knowledge of electricity not with a pencil-and-paper test, but by being given an electric circuit to assemble: if they assemble the circuit correctly, a small motor on the circuit board begins to whir, and a bell sounds. Nebraska educators are pleased with the results. Now other educators from as far away as California, Hawaii, and Vermont are coming to Nebraska to see how it works. "Any state can do [what Nebraska is doing]," says George Wood, director of the Forum for Education and Democracy, a nonprofit organization that supports the Nebraska initiative. "It's just a matter of whether they have the courage."[1] Unfortunately, the United States Department of Education prefers the pencil-and-paper tests. What's novel about the Nebraska initiative is that administrators are using the experiential tests *instead* of pencil-and-paper tests. There's already plenty of emphasis on pencil-and-paper tests throughout the curriculum. The Nebraska school administrators are trying to restore some balance between experiential methods and didactic methods, even—or rather, especially—in testing and assessment.

If your son is struggling at school, but your school seems to be doing a good job regarding the balance between *Kenntnis* and *Wissenschaft,* and the academic demands are not developmentally inappropriate, then you might also consider trying to establish a single-sex classroom for him. Single-sex education allows the school to create an alternative culture in which it's cool to study, in which team competition for academics is the most natural format imaginable, and in which restoring *Kenntnis* to its rightful place is likely to yield immediate positive results. Because of a recent change in federal regulations effected jointly by Senator Hillary Clinton (D-New York) and Senator Kay Bailey Hutchison (R-Texas), single-sex education is now fully legal in American public schools.² More information about the nuts and bolts of establishing a single-sex classroom—how to organize your fellow parents, how to approach the school leadership, what resources are available, and so forth—is available at www.BoysAdrift.com.

There's a lot at stake. I personally have been involved with schools that have made tremendous improvements in boys' engagement in school with relatively minor changes in school format. For example, at elementary schools in Waterloo, Iowa, and in Chicago, teachers have reported extraordinary gains in boys' achievement simply by making sitting optional. In these classrooms, some boys sit at their chairs; other boys stand; a few boys crouch on the floor. At the Midwestern conference of the National Association for Single Sex Public Education (NASSPE) in Chicago in October 2006, teachers Betsy Stahler and Jill Renn shared with us how the boys' performance at their Chicago school soared after they introduced this new policy—sitting is optional—along with adjustable-height desks, which can be lowered to a comfortable height for the boy who prefers to work on the floor, and raised above standard height for the boy who prefers to stand.³ At another school, in Waterloo, Iowa, boys from low-income families are on fire with enthusiasm for schoolwork—and their teacher, Jeff Ferguson, told me that a big reason for that enthusiasm is simply that the boys don't have to sit down if they don't want to. They can stand, or they can lie on the floor—whatever they like, as long as they are not bothering or distracting their neighbor.⁴ These classrooms are all single-sex, incidentally. A sitting-is-optional policy is typically more difficult to implement successfully in coed classrooms.

But please remember: If you are asking your school to make changes, avoid an adversarial approach. Remember that teachers and the administrators fundamentally want what you want: they want girls and boys to be excited about learning. Lend your principal this book. Buy your son's teacher Richard Louv's *Last Child in the Woods,* an excellent testament to the power of nature to enrich children's lives.

American parents are not alone in their concern about their boys' education. There's growing focus internationally on the disengagement of boys from schools. Parents in other countries have come up with imaginative strategies that are beginning to bear fruit—most of which are unknown to us in the United States. One particularly exciting innovation is the rapidly growing *Waldkindergarten* movement in German-speaking Europe: Germany, Austria, and northeastern Switzerland.

Waldkindergarten means literally "forest kindergarten." These are kindergartens* that have no building, no walls. The children meet the teacher in a local park or wooded area, every day, all year around. They may spend a day, or several days, just studying a dozen trees: sniffing each tree, playing in the leaves if it's autumn, learning about the seasonal cycles and life cycles of these trees, making a seesaw out of fallen limbs on an old stump.

The first questions American parents ask when they hear about *Waldkindergarten* is: "What do they do when the weather's bad? What if it snows? What if there's a heavy rain?" The answer the Germans give is always some variation of *Es gibt kein schlechtes Wetter, nur ungeeignete Kleidung*: "There's no such thing as bad weather, just unsuitable clothes."† If you watch these children playing in the snow, you realize how true that is. We parents don't like blizzards because bad weather slows us down. But five-year-olds love blizzards. With proper supervision, a five-year-old playing in snow is in no more jeopardy than a five-year-old on a playground in summertime.

Roland Gorges, a professor of education at Darmstadt College (just south of Frankfurt), assessed children in fourth grade, several years after they left the *Waldkindergarten*. He found that boys who start school in a *Waldkindergarten* are much less likely to be diagnosed with ADHD, and typically are more attentive in school in fourth grade, compared with boys from the same neighborhood who attended a conventional kindergarten.[5]

---

*Actually, *Waldkindergarten* is something of a misnomer, as many of these outdoor schools enroll children from pre–K through second grade.

†There is one exception to this rule: most *Waldkindergärten* do have a run-in shed or similar structure with lightning rods to provide a safe place for shelter in case of lightning.

The *Waldkindergarten* movement is one of the fastest-growing educa-tion trends in Europe right now.[6] American educators and parents would do well to learn about it. You can find out more about *Wald-kindergarten* (in English) and related initiatives at www.BoysAdrift.com.

The Second Factor: Video Games

In chapter 3, we considered four strategies to help your son reengage with the real world, so that he will have less need for the artificial world of video games. Any intervention is more likely to be effective if you pro-vide an alternative outlet for whatever boyish impulse you are trying to redirect. So if you are going to restrict your son's access to video games, you need to direct him to an alternative that is more exciting, more real, than anything video games can offer. Let me tell you about RaceLegal.

RaceLegal

In 2002, San Diego was experiencing a surge of deaths and injuries due to teenage boys racing their cars on city streets. That year, fourteen teenagers were killed and thirty-one were seriously injured in street rac-ing accidents. Stephen Bender, then a professor of epidemiology at San Diego State University, said that street racing had become an "epi-demic"—and as an epidemiologist he knew exactly what he was talking about when he used the word *epidemic*.

Professor Bender secured funding to launch a legal alternative to street racing, which he named RaceLegal. He obtained permission to use Qualcomm Stadium, the huge stadium owned by the San Diego Charg-ers football team, as a venue for legal races. Any teenager could race: all they needed was a valid driver's license and proof that they had the owner's permission to race the car. Initially, nobody showed up. Boys didn't see the point of paying to race at the stadium when they could race for free on city streets. So San Diego made the punishment for street racing more severe. Undercover cops began videotaping the races; then they would show up at racers' homes with a tow truck. "We hand-cuff them, put them in jail, impound the car for thirty days for $1,000, suspend their licenses for one year, fine them $1,500 and put two points on their license," said Sgt. Greg Sloan, who headed the unit. "If you get caught street racing for a second time, your car is forfeited forever—even if it's your parents' or a rental—and you get [more] jail time." The county prosecuted 290 cases under the law in 2001, 155 in 2002 and just sixty in 2003. The key was to create that "closed-loop system, including enforcement and a legal outlet," said Lydia DeNecochea, program director for RaceLegal. "We've had a real turnaround."[7]

As this book goes to press, we have final numbers from California through the end of 2005. In all of that year, there were no deaths related to illegal street racing in San Diego County, and only three serious injuries. "There is no doubt in my mind, nor among my colleagues, that the viable legal option of the RaceLegal program has contributed to the dramatic decline of illegal street racing," says Captain Glen Revell of the San Diego County Sheriff's Department. "And we see it as a decline in racing as well as deaths and injuries. We don't see the organized events we once did." Officer Scott Thompson of the San Diego Police Department agrees: "RaceLegal has been truly overwhelmingly effective in addressing the problem."[8]

Professor Bender's idea is catching on—slowly. In Noble, Oklahoma, teenage drivers pay fifteen dollars to race on Friday evenings at the Thunder Valley Raceway Park. "Beat the Heat" events on the second Friday of every month match high school kids racing their own cars against Noble's police officers driving police cruisers. Similar programs have begun in Atlanta, Las Vegas, and Muncie, Indiana.[9]

I have seen parents squirm uneasily in their chairs when I praise the RaceLegal program. Some parents are understandably less than enthusiastic about allowing teenage boys with no special training to race at speeds that reach 100 mph. I remind these parents that RaceLegal uses a straight track just one-eighth of a mile long, with no turns. Professor Bender's program has never had any driver seriously injured during a RaceLegal event. More to the point: Telling boys not to race on the street just isn't effective unless you provide a legal alternative.

What Does This Have to Do with Video Games?

Here's the connection: RaceLegal and programs like it are the best answer to the question, "What do I do after I've thrown my son's PlayStation and Xbox in the garbage?" If your son has been playing a motocross video game for hours, take him out to a motocross track, rent him a motorbike, and let him take some lessons doing the real thing. He may complain. He may say that he prefers the sanitized video game version over getting on an actual bike and going around an actual track. Challenge him. "Video games are just an imitation. Video games are just pretend," you might remind him. "This is the real thing. You're a big boy now. You can do this."

Boys who prefer the video game version over the real thing are making a choice very similar to boys who prefer online pornography to interacting with real girls. In fact, it's often the same boy: the boy who spends hours every day on his video game addiction is commonly, in my experience, at risk for preferring online pornography to real interactions with real girls.

If your son is addicted to first-person-shooter role-playing games such as *Grand Theft Auto*, you might think that this strategy can't be applied. After all, you can't very well let him loose on the streets and tell him to go carjack some late-model sports car and then murder police officers. But these boys usually have at least a smidgen of Nietzsche's will to power (see chapter 3), and often more than a smidgen. They don't shy away from physical confrontation—or at least they like to think they won't. Sign this boy up for a contact sport that involves real contact, such as football or rugby. Colliding at full speed with another boy, hitting him so hard "that the snot flew out of my nose and I couldn't breathe" (as one boy enthusiastically described it to me), goes a long way toward satisfying the same urge that otherwise might drive that boy to play *Grand Theft Auto*.

This point is counterintuitive to many parents, especially mothers. "Why would any boy, especially my son, want to collide with another boy so hard that snot flies out of his nose and he can't breathe?" The answer is: because some boys are like that, and he's that kind of boy.[10] Celebrate the fact. Co-opt that desire to hit hard and use it to help your son become an athlete, instead of a video game addict.

In *Why Gender Matters*, I quoted an experienced school counselor who said, "you can't change a bully into a flower child. But you can change him into a knight." I would adapt that insight in the context of video games. "You can't change a video game addict into a kid who loves chatting on the phone for hours. But you can change him into a competitive athlete."

The Third Factor: Medications for ADHD

In chapter 4, we saw how easy it is nowadays for a boy to acquire the label of "attention deficit." We saw how changes in education over the past three decades have contributed to a twenty-fold increase in the prescribing of medications for ADHD. Thirty years ago, elementary schools didn't expect a five- or a six-year-old boy to sit still and be quiet for hours at a stretch. Today they do. The result, as child psychiatrist Dr. Elizabeth Roberts recently observed, is that "Parents and teachers today seem to believe that any boy who wriggles in his seat and willfully defies his teacher's rules has ADHD."[11] Rather than question the wisdom of a curriculum that requires five-year-old boys to sit still and be quiet, it's easier just to prescribe the medication. After all, what's the harm?

We also saw the harm done by such an approach. We also learned why an empirical trial of medication for ADHD is a bad idea. The "try it, you'll like it" school of medicine is *not* a good choice when it comes to prescribing these medications for your son.

So what should you do when the school suggests that your son has ADHD? First of all, insist on a formal assessment by a qualified professional who is not biased in favor of diagnosing ADHD. In most cases that person should not be your child's primary care physician, because primary care physicians—pediatricians and family physicians—are not usually well-versed in the diagnostic subtleties involved in distinguishing ADHD from other explanations for why a boy might be inattentive or "hyper" in the classroom. Too often, primary care physicians—particularly in affluent suburban communities—may suggest a trial of medication "just to see if it works." Bad idea.

Many school districts employ psychologists specifically to do this type of assessment. Unfortunately, I have found that these psychologists are generally not a good choice. They usually have too many kids to evaluate and not enough time to evaluate them. More important: if the psychologist agrees that the boy has ADHD, then his or her job is done, that child's name can be crossed off the list of kids who need to be assessed, and everybody's happy, at least as far as the psychologist's colleagues in the school district are concerned.

If your son attends a private school, a similar process takes place. I have found that the psychologists recommended by private schools never find fault with the school; instead, they almost invariably agree with the teachers' assessment that the boy has ADHD.

If the psychologist disagrees with the teachers' assessment and questions the diagnosis of ADHD, that psychologist may quickly get into trouble. That's because very often, when a boy isn't paying attention, the problem is not with the boy but with the way he is being taught. You need a psychologist who has the courage and the independence to say to the school: "This boy doesn't have a problem. The school has a problem. The school is making developmentally inappropriate demands on this boy, and the school must change its ways." If a five- or six- or seven-year-old boy can't sit still and be quiet without fidgeting, he doesn't necessarily have ADHD. He shouldn't be put on medication just to keep him still. Instead, the school should recognize that expecting all young boys to sit still and be quiet simply isn't compatible with what we know about child development. If you move that child into a boy-friendly classroom (see chapter 2 for more detail about what that means), then that boy may do very well.

This statement is not conjecture. I have been involved with schools in Chicago; Waterloo, Iowa; Deland, Florida; and elsewhere, encompassing boys from many different socioeconomic and racial backgrounds, where boys previously labeled as "ADHD" have become high-achieving, academically proficient students—without medication—simply by changing a gender-blind classroom into a boy-friendly classroom. This transformation does not require any change in class size or per-pupil funding, just an improved awareness on the part of the faculty regarding what constitutes a boy-friendly classroom.

I used to stop right there. I used to say to parents, "Find a courageous psychologist to evaluate your child." If the parents couldn't find one, they were welcome to come to my office. Because I am both a medical doctor and a psychologist, I am qualified to do the formal assessment—

which may take four hours or more, over two visits—and I can also prescribe medication, if that should be necessary.

It's getting harder to find a psychologist willing to challenge the steamroller that's pushing so many kids onto medications. Medication is quick and easy—or so it seems to many parents. It's certainly easier than switching schools, and easier than trying to get your child's school to change its ways. Most important, the medication often "works," making the child is less fidgety and more attentive. What's not to like?

What's not to like, as we saw in chapter 4, is that these medications may damage a crucial area of the brain responsible for drive and motivation. What's not to like is that young children are being medicated to make the teacher's job easier—not because it's in the best interest of the child, but because it simplifies classroom management.

So if you're not convinced that your son needs to be on medication, and you can't find a courageous psychologist in your neighborhood, what can you do?

You may have to do some part of the assessment yourself. So let's call this next section:

A parent's guide to neurodevelopment assessment, with special attention to ADHD, for boys in elementary school (middle school and high school come next).

In assessing whether your child or any child has ADHD, you need to understand the five official criteria for diagnosing ADHD, adapted here from the official source, the American Psychiatric Association's *Diagnostic and Statistical Manual*, 4th Edition (*DSM-IV*). A child must meet all five criteria to be diagnosed as having ADHD.

1. **Hyperactivity/impulsivity or inattention.** This criterion is generally the easiest to meet. The key point I stress is that it is a necessary but not sufficient criterion for the diagnosis of ADHD. Many boys are hyperactive and/or impulsive and/or inattentive, but that finding alone does not justify the diagnosis of ADHD.
2. **Onset before seven years of age.** Problems severe enough to cause significant impairment must have been present before age seven.

3. **Multiple settings.** Impairment due to hyperactivity and/or impulsivity and/or inattention must be present in multiple settings, not just one or two. In young children, this criterion is key to determining which child truly has ADHD. All of us are inattentive from time to time. If you ask me to sit for an hour listening to a lecture about the history of needlepoint, I'll be inattentive. A boy who is only occasionally inattentive probably doesn't have ADHD. If your son's reading and language arts teacher says that he fidgets and doesn't pay attention, but his science teacher and gym teacher and math teacher all say he's doing fine, then it's unlikely that your son has ADHD. Even if most of the teachers report problems, but your son's Boy Scout troop leader and your son's soccer coach report no problems, I would still be hesitant about making a diagnosis of ADHD. Children who have problems only at school but not in other settings generally do not have ADHD. Moving that child to a different school—or changing the way the school teaches your son—may fix the problem.

4. **Significant impairment in social or academic functioning.** What constitutes significant impairment? One boy I saw recently is occasionally inattentive in school and out of school. He's in third grade, he has plenty of friends, and his grades are mostly B's with a few C's. This boy is not significantly impaired. Significant impairment doesn't mean getting B's instead of A's.

   The joke I hear in many affluent suburbs is that every child in town is either gifted, or learning-disabled, or both. Some parents just don't want to hear that the reason their child is getting B's and a few C's is because he's just not that smart. They would rather hear that their child has ADHD and needs medication rather than that their child is merely average, or God forbid, below average.

5. **Not attributable to another disorder.** Sometimes a child is inattentive, impulsive, and/or hyperactive for reasons that have nothing to do with ADHD. Family problems are a

common trigger. At one school I visited—Foley Intermediate School in Foley, Alabama—a teacher, William Bender, told me about a student, let's call him Damian, who
had been an OK student the previous year, in third grade,
but this year—fourth grade—he had become impossible.
Damian would act out, run around the classroom, defy
reasonable requests by teachers and staff, or just sit in his
chair like a lump ignoring everything that was said to him.
Damian had been assigned to Mr. Bender's all-boy classroom, where he found it easier to talk about why he was
acting out so much. "I figure if I'm bad enough, they'll call
my father to come whup me," he said with a smile.
Damian's father had abandoned the family the previous
summer. The father called once a month, or less.

Mr. Bender took Damian for a walk around the school
building.* "Let me tell you something, Damian," he said. "I
need you to hear this. Your daddy doesn't call very often.
When he calls, he wants to hear good news about you. He
wants to hear that you've been a good boy, that school's
going good, that everything's great. If all he hears is your
momma complaining about how bad you are, then I guarantee you that he's not going to want to come back. I'm
giving it to you straight, son." Mr. Bender knew that boys
this age don't want anything sugarcoated.

Damian shaped up. His "attention deficit disorder" vanished as quickly as it had appeared. But please don't take
this story as providing any sort of guidance in counseling
the children of divorced or separated parents. That's not

---

* Notice that Mr. Bender did not sit Damian down for a talk, face to face. Instead
he took Damian for a walk around the building, so they could talk shoulder to
shoulder. For more about the advisability of talking with boys shoulder to shoulder
rather than face to face, see *Why Gender Matters*, pp. 83–86. Or just remember this
rule of thumb: a good place to talk with your son is in your car, with you driving
and your son in the passenger seat: shoulder to shoulder, not face to face.

why I included it. Indeed, some professional counselors would take issue with Mr. Bender's comments to Damian. Some might be concerned that Mr. Bender was encouraging a false hope that Damian's father might return. I include Damian's story simply to emphasize that a hyperactive, impulsive boy may be hyperactive and impulsive for reasons that have nothing to do with ADHD.

I've seen similar cases involving childhood depression—which can mimic ADHD almost perfectly—as well as bipolar disorder. That's what the fifth criterion is all about: excluding other diagnoses. Before you take any action, remember that not all children who have a deficit of attention have attention deficit disorder!

Of course I'm not really suggesting that you can learn everything a professional needs to know about neurodevelopmental assessment by reading this book. But I think you should at least know some of the terminology and definitions provided here so that you can be a more informed and more capable guardian of your son's best interests.

Speaking of terminology and definitions, you will find other scales and other instruments to assess ADHD. In the United States, the Connors Rating Scale is a very popular instrument used to "diagnose" ADHD. I put "diagnose" in quotation marks because the Connors Scale doesn't diagnose anything. It is simply a checklist of characteristics sometimes associated with some aspects of ADHD. But even if a child scores across the board in the ADHD column on the Connors Scale, that child does not necessarily have ADHD. The diagnosis of ADHD is established only if the five criteria listed above are met. I'm not saying the Connors Scale has no role. I do find it of some use as a screening instrument. I'm just putting you on your guard: don't let anybody substitute their favorite screening instrument for the formal *DSM-IV* criteria.

Let's suppose that your son has been assessed and you're convinced that he does in fact meet all five criteria for ADHD. Once the diagnosis is confirmed, it is appropriate to consider medication as one facet in the program of treatment your consultant has prepared. If you and your consultant are convinced that medication is necessary, I generally recommend starting with one of the safer medications that have been proven effective in the treatment of ADHD in children, a medication such as Strattera or Wellbutrin. Avoid the use of the stimulant medications: Adderall, Ritalin, Concerta, Metadate, Focalin, Daytrana, and their generic equivalents, amphetamine and methylphenidate. If Strattera alone isn't effective, consider adding a low dose of Wellbutrin, or vice versa. Hold the stimulant medications in reserve. In my experience, the boy with true ADHD who needs 30 mg of Adderall every day to function well at school will often do just as well with 25 mg of Strattera and 5 mg of Adderall. The lower the dose of Adderall or other stimulant medications, the lower the risk of toxicity.

Many doctors are impatient with this approach. Most of the doctors treating children who have been diagnosed with ADHD start with the stimulant medications. Adderall is the most-prescribed medication for ADHD in the United States, followed by Concerta, Metadate, and generic Ritalin. But all these medications pose a risk to the brain that Strattera and Wellbutrin do not pose.

How Often Does a Teenage Boy "Develop" ADHD?

I was asked to evaluate another boy, who had been a star pupil in elementary school. This boy, let's call him Brad, had earned nearly straight A's and seemed genuinely to enjoy almost every subject. Then middle school began, and Brad started to disengage. He stopped raising his hand in class. His mother had to nag him to do homework, which she had never had to do before. Several teachers mentioned that Brad seemed to zone out in class. He just wasn't paying attention, wasn't concentrating, didn't seem to care.

"We read up about ADHD online, and he seems to fit the criteria," his mother said to me.

"Was he having problems like this earlier, a few years ago?" I asked.

"Absolutely not. He was always an honors student in elementary school. In every subject."

Then he doesn't fit the criteria, I wanted to say. Specifically, he doesn't meet criterion #2, "onset of impairment prior to seven years of age." But I didn't say that. Instead, I asked his mother, "What's going on with his social life?"

She gave me a strange look, as if to say: funny you should ask. "His social life has dried up since he started middle school. He used to have two or three good friends. Megan and Ashley were over all the time, Caitlyn would be over once or twice a month. Now—nobody. And the phone never rings."

"Are Megan and Ashley and Caitlyn at his middle school, in his grade?"

"Yes, that's what's strange about it. His best friends from elementary school are all in middle school with him, but they just don't seem to be friends anymore."

To make a long story short: Brad doesn't have ADHD. He's a gender-atypical boy, a boy who would rather read a book or write a poem rather than play football or tell fart jokes. Such boys often do very well in elementary school, where they often have at least several good friends—usually girls. In middle school, the girls realize that your popularity is largely determined by who you hang with, and the gender-atypical boys are rarely the cool kids. So the girls leave, and these boys are left alone. Sometimes the isolation motivates them to succeed academically, to "show everybody" how smart they are. Sometimes the isolation disengages them from school altogether, as happened with Brad.

After evaluating Brad myself, I concluded that he doesn't have ADHD. He's on the border between dysthymia (a mild form of depression) and full-blown clinical depression. He misses his friends. He feels devalued—because his peer group has devalued him. These are serious issues that need serious attention. Ironically, Brad improved substantially after another doctor prescribed Adderall, not because Brad had ADHD but (in my assessment) because of the antidepressant effects of Adderall. A better and safer choice, in terms of medication, would be Desyrel. Desyrel is just as effective as Adderall as an antidepressant, and Desyrel is many times safer than Adderall.

More important, however, Brad needs counseling—and his parents need some help—in developing a new life strategy. I addressed some of the challenges facing gender-atypical boys in chapter 9 of *Why Gender Matters*. The main point I want to make here is that when a previously successful boy is first "diagnosed" with ADHD after age ten, the correct diagnosis is seldom ADHD.

The Fourth Factor: Endocrine Disruptors

Cargill is a large multinational corporation, with roughly 150,000 employees in sixty-three countries around the world. In September 2005, I spoke to employees at their international headquarters just outside Minneapolis. I learned that Cargill has developed an alternative to plastic made from corn. This material is called PLA (polylactic acid). I drank spring water from a bottle made of Cargill's PLA. That bottle is indistinguishable from regular "plastic," except that you don't taste that subtle plastic taste you get from plastic bottles made from PET, polyethylene terephthalate. Most plastic bottles in the United States and Canada are made from PET.

I met at length with Ann Tucker, director of marketing for Nature-WorksPLA, the division of Cargill in charge of developing and promoting the new material. Ms. Tucker used to work for the plastics industry, but she came to Cargill because, as she said, "I want to be on the side of the good guys." Although she and her colleagues are well aware of the health risks of plastic bottles, they are reluctant to stress that point in their marketing because they don't want to offend potential megaclients such as Coke and Pepsi. Instead, they emphasize the fact that their material's cost is stable, whereas the price of PET is rising. PET is made from petroleum. Petroleum is expensive and its price is unstable. Corn is cheap. We rely on other countries for most of our petroleum. We can grow all the corn we need right here in North America. You can link to more information about Cargill's PLA at www.BoysAdrift.com.

Environmentalists are of course also concerned about the dangers of endocrine disruptors. Environmentalist Web sites such as www.ourstolen future.com and www.noharm.org emphasize the risks of environmental estrogens found in plastics and other commercial products. My concern about some of the environmental groups, however, is that they seem to regard big business as the enemy. I think that view is short-sighted. Cargill isn't the enemy here. Cargill is, as Ms. Tucker observed, on the good guys' side. Coke and Pepsi aren't the enemy either. They will introduce safer, more environmentally friendly PLA "plastic" bottles promptly—if enough people insist that they do so. There are some subtle differences between a bottle made from PET and a bottle made from the environmentally friendly PLA. For example, the PLA bottle should not be put into plastic recycling, because it's not plastic. A separate composting process needs to be available for the PLA bottle. That wouldn't be hard to establish in your community, or even in your backyard—but big companies are loath to invest the necessary time and effort to educate the consumer. You and I have to drive the conversion of the bottled water and soda industry from PET bottles to bottles made from PLA and similar corn-based products.

Stay informed. Visit *Boys Adrift*'s Web site, www.BoysAdrift.com, for the latest updates on environmental estrogens and links to sites with up-to-date recommendations.

The Fifth Factor: The Loss of Positive Role Models

Keep in mind J. R. Moehringer's key insight, which we discussed in the last chapter: "Manhood is mimesis." A boy is likely to become the kind of man he sees around him. A boy needs role models of healthy masculinity (just as girls need role models of healthy femininity). If you don't provide him with healthy role models, he may choose the unhealthy role models offered by the marketplace, from rap music or television or movies or even video games. The challenge is analogous to nutrition. Left to their own devices, not many boys will choose broccoli and Brussels sprouts over french fries and ice cream. That's why they need parents. It's the job of the parents to guide their son to make the right choice.

In 1997, as a "lame duck," California governor Pete Wilson proposed establishing single-sex academies within the public school system. The program was eliminated by his successor after just two years. The Ford Foundation awarded a grant to three scholars—Amanda Datnow, Lea

Hubbard, and Elisabeth Woody—to assess the effectiveness of the short-lived program.

As a general rule, when researchers evaluate the effectiveness of an educational program, they look at parameters such as grades, test scores, attendance, and discipline referrals. Did the program improve grades and test scores? Did more kids show up for class? Did they behave better in class? Datnow, Hubbard, and Woody asked none of those questions, although they did describe their eighty-six-page report as "comprehensive." Instead, they focused on whether or not the single-sex program strengthened or weakened gender stereotypes.

These three authors condemned the single-sex initiative on the grounds that it strengthened gender stereotypes. Teachers who failed to deconstruct sexist power relations for their students were criticized. One teacher who received particularly severe criticism was a man who had dared to speak to his students—all boys—about what it means to be a productive man. The teacher had said:

> We talked about strength, and we talked about self-control and being able to control your emotions and making sacrifices for others. You know we talked about if you have a family and you only have enough money for two cheeseburgers, you're not going to eat. ... You know you're going to feed your wife and your kids and you wait.[12]

Datnow, Hubbard, and Woody censured this teacher and castigated the tendency of other teachers to reinforce traditional gender stereotypes. They were disappointed that boys "... were told that they should learn to be strong men and take care of their wives. In most cases, traditional gender role stereotypes were reinforced, and gender was portrayed in an essentialist manner."[13]

This teacher was trying to provide the boys with a healthy image of what a man should be. He told them that the husband, the father, should wait to eat until he's taken care of his wife and kids. He was valiantly trying to give those boys some leadership, some guidance, some idea of what it means to be a man.

Not all traditional gender roles deserve to be condemned as gender stereotypes. There are life-affirming gender roles and there are gender stereotypes that are harmful and destructive. The "dumb blonde" is a negative and destructive gender stereotype, as is the "dumb jock." But no one should condemn as a gender stereotype the ideal of the husband and father who sacrifices himself for the sake of his wife and children. Instead, that ideal should be affirmed as a role model.

"Deconstructing" all images of the ideal husband and father is not likely to result in a father who insists on his wife sharing equally in all sacrifices. The result is far more likely to be a selfish young man who doesn't feel any strong obligation to the children he has fathered. In the United States, more than one in three babies is now born to an unmarried mother (35.7 percent to be exact). The growing trend away from married couples with children cuts across all racial and ethnic boundaries. As we discussed in chapter 6, married couples with one or more children now constitute only about one-quarter of households.[14]

To become a man, a boy must see a man. But that man doesn't have to be his father. In fact, ideally, it shouldn't be only his father. Even if your son has a strong father or father figure in his life, he also needs a community of men who together can provide him with varied models of what productive adult men do.

Restore the Bond Between Generations

We've seen that enduring cultures use gender-separate communities to pass the norms of that culture from one generation to the next. Women teach girls. Men teach boys. That doesn't exclude the possibility of men teaching girls and women teaching boys, of course. But there is no enduring culture where boys have been taught the rules of social behavior exclusively or even primarily by women. And there's something even more basic that should be stressed in that truth: enduring cultures have strong bonds across the generations. In contemporary American culture, we're seeing those bonds dissolving rapidly, in the span of a single lifetime. The *Washington Post* recently featured a series of interviews with men age sixty and over, which the writer notes is "the last generation of black men who share the memory of being deliberately taught how to walk in the world." For these men, "working hard is the basis for everything," it's "dignity and manhood." These men remember what the community was like just thirty years ago, when the young men would congregate at older men's houses. Prince Georges County (a middle-class, predominantly African-American suburb of Washington, DC) had many boys' clubs that were popular and well patronized back then. "The neighborhood was like another mama and daddy," says one of the older men. Nobody locked their doors.

Then in the 1970s the boys' clubs shut down. Things changed. The teenage boys didn't want to talk to the older men anymore. Drugs began making inroads into the community, followed closely by crime. Now these older men are disgusted by the lack of motivation they see in the teenage boys and young men. Some of these young men "wouldn't take a job as a pie taster in a pastry factory," complained one of the older men.

Certainly there were many more factors at play here than the closing of the boys' clubs. But when the boys' clubs shut their doors, there was no other convenient venue remaining where grandfathers, fathers, and teenage boys from different families could come together, shoot the breeze and share their experiences.[15] The typical American teenager doesn't hang out with middle-aged adults on the weekend anymore. The typical American teenager hangs out with other teenagers.

In the story I told in chapter 6—about the young Native Alaskan men who went off to hunt the sea lion, and wounded it but didn't kill it—the key point was the severing of the bonds between the generations. Cutting those bonds has an effect similar to cutting a boat loose from its anchor. The young men lose direction and purpose. They seek the pleasure of the moment. They avoid responsibility.

That's already starting to happen in our own culture. Parents have the power to stop it. If you belong to a church or synagogue, talk to your pastor or priest or rabbi about arranging an all-male retreat. Traditional Judaism, the various Christian denominations, as well as Islam, all have long traditions of gender-separate activities. All these traditions embrace the truth that children and teenagers must be taught by adults, not by one another.

If you're not comfortable with any faith community, contact your local chapter of the Boy Scouts. Or, as we discussed earlier, get your son involved in year-round competitive sports. Or sign him up for activities with the Izaak Walton League (www.iwla.org) or other outdoor nature conservancy organizations that have programs targeted at getting young people involved with the outdoors. Or if your son thinks he might like to hunt, help him to join a local skeet-shooting club where he can learn to shoot and (more important) make connections with a community of men of all ages with similar interests. Just enter the word "skeet" and the name of your state in Google and you'll find dozens of clubs to choose from, whether you live in New York or Idaho or Florida or Alaska.

Don't wait for your son to make this choice. If he's like most of the boys I work with, he may need a push. That's OK. Just choose an activity in which he can interact with grown men, where he can have opportunities to see how they live, how they relax, how they serve their families and their communities. In most cases, even a not-quite-perfect choice, perhaps even the wrong choice, will be better—will be more likely to engage your son in the real world—than no choice at all.

A Word of Warning

In the previous chapter, I said lots of favorable things about traditional cultures such as the Navajo and the Masai and Orthodox Jews. Now we must say something unkind, but true, about these cultures: they are sexist. A Navajo woman can never become a medicine man. An Orthodox Jewish woman can never become a rabbi or a cantor.

Many enduring cultures—cultures that have remained intact for hundreds of years—are sexist. That's unfortunate. Those traditional cultures often push girls and boys into pink and blue cubbyholes. We don't want that. But I don't think the solution is to ignore gender. Three decades of pretending that girls and boys are exactly the same, except for their genitalia, have not created a paradise of gender equity where boys respect and honor girls. They have given us, instead, Eminem and 50 Cent and Akon: musicians whose best-selling songs degrade and disparage women in ways that would have been unthinkable 30 years ago. Our cultural neglect of the significance of gender has—as the Dartmouth panelists correctly pointed out—resulted in a young adult culture that has veered off the deep end.

There has to be a third way. There has to be some alternative besides ignoring gender on the one hand, and pushing children into narrow and limiting gender roles, on the other.

This third way must begin by recognizing the importance of gender, by embracing and celebrating the gendered nature of the human experience. We must use this new understanding of gender not to reinforce old-fashioned *Leave It to Beaver* notions of gender roles but rather to broaden horizons for both girls and boys.

Joseph Campbell popularized the notion that cultures are defined in large part by the myths they tell.[16] I think there is considerable truth to that idea. If we're going to combat this fifth factor—if we're going to recreate an idea of "real men" that advantages boys without disadvantaging girls—then we must give careful thought to what stories we are going to tell boys and young men.

We must tell true stories that affirm real men and the value of real masculinity, without disrespecting women or devaluing women's accomplishments and importance.

Allow me to share one such story with you.

One Story

Joshua Lawrence Chamberlain was born in 1828, in the small town of Brewer, Maine. He entered Bowdoin College, about one hundred miles away, in 1848. Toward the end of his time at Bowdoin, he heard Harriet Beecher Stowe read aloud from the manuscript for the book that became *Uncle Tom's Cabin*. Although Chamberlain had never witnessed slavery first-hand, Stowe's book made a profound impression on him. He became convinced that slavery was an offense against God that it was the duty of Christians to abolish.

After graduating from Bowdoin in 1852, he returned home to study at Bangor Theological Seminary, just across the Penobscot River from his hometown of Brewer. In 1855, he finished his studies at the seminary and married Fannie Adams, the daughter of a local minister. Together they would have five children. That same year, Chamberlain accepted an offer to return to Bowdoin College as an instructor in rhetoric, religion, and languages. He was fluent in German, French, Latin, and Greek.

With the outbreak of the Civil War in 1861, Chamberlain wanted to join the war on the side of the Union and against slavery. Unlike most of his fellow Northerners, Chamberlain actually believed that white men should fight and die for the cause of freeing black slaves. He asked Bowdoin College for a year's leave to sign up. His request was denied. Instead, the college offered to provide him a year's travel with pay in Europe to study European languages, classical and modern. Chamberlain accepted the offer. He left the college—and promptly volunteered his services in the army.[17]

Fast forward to July 2, 1863, the second day of the battle of Gettysburg. We find Professor Chamberlain, now a full Colonel, leading the 20th Maine on the top of a small hill just south of Gettysburg: Little Round Top. The men of the 20th Maine were stationed at the extreme left flank of the Union lines. Colonel Chamberlain's knowledge of military tactics was drawn more from reading about the Peloponnesian Wars in the original Greek than from any contemporary manual of nineteenth-century military tactics, but he understood the significance of his regiment's position, securing the left flank and occupying the high ground. He realized that if the Confederates could displace his men and take up positions on Little Round Top, the Confederates would be perfectly positioned to cannonade the main body of the Union forces from the flank and the rear. In that event, the Union forces would most likely have to surrender. The Confederates would be able to take tens of thousands of Union prisoners, and there would be no Federal forces remaining between Lee's Confederate army and the District of Columbia. Many historians believe that the fate of the United States hinged critically on the outcome of the battle for Little Round Top.[18] If the Confederates could overwhelm the 20th Maine and take that hill, they would win the battle and perhaps the war.

Five times on that July day, the men of the 15th Alabama Regiment stormed up Little Round Top, and five times they were repulsed by the 20th Maine under Colonel Chamberlain's command.[19] After the fifth charge, Chamberlain learned that most of his men had run out of ammunition. "Every round was gone," Chamberlain was told. Each man had only been issued sixty rounds at the beginning of the fighting that morning, and the five Confederate charges had exhausted their supply.

What to do? Withdraw, and cede the high ground—and probably the battle, and perhaps the whole war—to the South? Or continue to fight?

Fight with what?

"Bayonets!" Chamberlain shouted. A single word, according to eyewitnesses, but every man understood what it meant: fix bayonets and charge.

It is a fearsome thing to order two hundred men with bayonets to charge more than five hundred men with rifles, but that was Chamberlain's order, and his men obeyed him. Not only did they obey, but they charged forward like madmen. The men "took up the shout and moved forward," wrote another eyewitness, "and [with] every man eager not to be left behind, the whole line flung itself down the slope through the fire and smoke and upon the enemy."[20] The Confederates, seeing wild men with bayonets screaming and charging down the hill, concluded that they were facing superior numbers (although they weren't)—so the men from Alabama retreated. "We ran like a herd of wild cattle," one Confederate later admitted.[21] And then night fell.

There is more to the battle of Gettysburg than the story of Little Round Top, of course, but Chamberlain's courage and audacity in that moment is still a meaningful story to tell boys today. Perhaps more important for our purposes than the story of Little Round Top, though, is another of Chamberlain's exploits, almost two years later at Appomattox.

General Grant had selected Chamberlain to accept the formal surrender of Confederate colors on April 12, 1865. As Confederate General John B. Gordon was leading the Confederates to surrender—disheartened, sick, many of the men wounded, and all of them wondering what awaited them at the hands of the victorious Union forces—Chamberlain, on his own initiative, gave this command to his men: "Attention! Carry-arms!"

Chamberlain's men snapped to attention and presented their arms as a show of respect to the defeated Confederates. General Gordon, in reply, wheeled his horse around and commanded his men to dip the Confederate colors in answer to Chamberlain's courtesy. There was "not a sound of trumpet or drum, not a cheer, nor a word nor motion . . . but awful stillness as if it were the passing of the dead."[22]

Chamberlain's salute was reported in Northern newspapers, inciting some controversy. Many on the Northern side felt that it was inappropriate for Chamberlain to have commanded his men to salute the defeated Confederates. Some apparently might have liked it better if Chamberlain's men had heckled or abused the rebels. But Chamberlain's education—rooted in the classics—led him to value the magnanimous gesture above the pettiness of revenge or spite. In chapter 7, we discussed the definition of a gentleman. Chamberlain's story adds one more line to the definition: A gentleman is magnanimous in victory.

There are many true stories of heroic men throughout American history. I like to tell the story of Joshua Chamberlain for several reasons. First, his story is not particularly well known. For most of the twentieth century, the story of Joshua Chamberlain was an obscure footnote familiar only to historians. There is no statue of Chamberlain at Gettysburg (although there is a small monument to the 20th Maine). He had to wait thirty years before he was finally awarded a medal for his bravery at Gettysburg, in 1893.

The second reason I like to tell this story is that Chamberlain was not a superhero. His deeds were modest in comparison to those of George Washington or Robert E. Lee or Abraham Lincoln or Theodore Roosevelt. And that makes it easier for boys and young men to relate to him. It's hard for a young man to imagine being George Washington or Abraham Lincoln. The demands on those men were so exceptional, the burdens so acute, that it strains the imagination to think, "How would I have acted in that situation?" Chamberlain's predicaments were simpler and easier to comprehend.

I remind boys that Chamberlain didn't have to fight at all. Bowdoin College wanted him to take a year off to go on an all-expenses-paid tour of Europe. He could have done so with no loss of honor. He chose to put himself in harm's way because he thought that it was the right thing to do, because he believed it to be the duty of Christian men to fight against slavery—even though many, perhaps most, of his fellow Christians at that time would not have agreed with him, and he knew it.

Another aspect of Chamberlain's story that I stress to boys and young men today is that Chamberlain was a great leader of men precisely because he was a scholar and a seminarian. He was not a professional warrior or tough guy. He wanted to join the fight not because he was big and strong—he wasn't—but because of his beliefs, which were grounded in his education. He knew what really mattered. And he didn't give orders for other men to fight while he remained safely at home. He himself went and fought.

Let me tell you another true story, one that is happening right now, a story whose ending has not yet been written.

John Nicolas was born with all the advantages. His parents were happily married, his father was a successful family doctor, they lived in a nice house in a comfortable suburban neighborhood. Nevertheless, John was not a good kid. He got in trouble a lot. He wasn't a good student. His parents and his teachers wondered why he couldn't seem to live up to the excellent example of his two older sisters, who always worked hard and earned good grades.

In eighth grade, things went from bad to worse. John set a new record for poor performance at the private school he attended, the Woodland Country Day School in Bridgeton, New Jersey. He failed every class. The school administrators politely suggested that John repeat eighth grade at the local public school. "The public schools have more resources for boys like John," they said.

John began using drugs heavily. "I was a pillhead," he told me. "Mostly Percocet, occasionally Vicodin or Darvon." He stole the drugs from his father's office. At first he only used them himself, then he also began selling some of the pills at the school. He was caught. That led to his first suspension from school. He was caught again, and suspended again. Then he was caught once more, this time red-handed in the act of selling pills, by a narcotics officer. He was charged with possession and distribution of a controlled dangerous substance. The school district initiated proceedings to have him expelled; he was, after all, failing all his eighth-grade classes. Again. He was told that his court hearing would be in ten days.

Seven days later, at about eight o'clock on the morning of January 15, 2004, two armed police officers arrived at John's house. They came to his room, handcuffed him, and drove him to the police station. There two Salem County sheriff's deputies were waiting to take him to the Salem County Courthouse. He was shackled, wrists and ankles, as he entered the courtroom. The hearing was going to take place three days early.

The judge was stern. Because there were earlier instances of drug offenses in John's school record, the judge did not consider this criminal charge to be a first offense. Instead, John learned that he was going to be sentenced to the juvenile detention center. The length of his sentence there would be determined at a subsequent hearing.

The next seven days John spent in a small cell with one cellmate. They shared one stainless steel toilet. No door. No privacy. "If you have to defecate, you defecate right there sitting on the toilet, with people walking by the cell and your cellmate looking at you," John told me. (Incidentally, John really did say *defecate*, not some other word. By the time I spoke with him, early in 2007, he had become a real gentleman.)

During that week, John's father spoke with the administrators at a boys' school, the Phelps School in Malvern, Pennsylvania (near Bryn Mawr and Haverford). Although Phelps is an elite college prep school, not a military school or reform school, Dr. Nicolas knew that the school had been successful in rehabilitating other boys like John: bright boys who had gone off track for one reason or another. The school administrators agreed at least to talk with John, to see whether he might be a suitable candidate for the school.

At the court hearing the following week, the judge offered John one last chance: if he would attend the boys' school, and behave perfectly, he would not be sent back to the juvenile detention center. But if he had even one unexcused absence, or the slightest breach of rules, he would go straight back to detention, very likely until his eighteenth birthday. Remember, this boy had been caught in the act of selling narcotics.

First, John had to persuade the school to take him. He met with the director of admissions, Mr. Chirieleison, who agreed to accept him as a student at Phelps. "My parents said it was a miracle. We're Greek Orthodox, and his name, *chirie eleison*, means 'Lord have mercy' in Greek. We recite that at every service."

"Do you agree with your parents? Do you think it was divine intervention?" I asked.

"No, I don't," John said. "I'm not that religious."

Religious or not, John was now enrolled at Phelps.

"I hated it," he told me. "I didn't know anybody. I was angry that I had to go to this school I'd never heard of. I blamed everybody except myself." He finished eighth grade at Phelps, earning B's and C's (a huge improvement over his previous three semesters).

Ninth grade went better. He began focusing on class more, and he started making friends. "I never had a brother. Now I began to realize I had lots of brothers. We were like all in it together, we did stuff together. I started to feel the camaraderie."

John began to take part in the life of the school, and told me:

At all the schools I'd been at before, I felt like I always had to put on a show for somebody. For the girls, I guess. And for me, the easiest way to impress the girls was to be a spaced-out pillhead. I know it sounds stupid. The girls probably weren't even that impressed. But at a coed school, you've got to wear a mask. You've got to be a jock or a skater dude or a pillhead or something like that. I was ashamed to just be who I was. I just felt that I always had to play the game of being somebody special, somebody interesting. But a few weeks into ninth grade, all that just started to fall away. I started to believe I could just be who I was. I didn't have to impress anybody.

"But couldn't that change have taken place at any good school?" I asked.

"I'd been to other good schools. Those schools near my home were fine. They're good schools. They're not to blame for me becoming a pillhead. For me, I think, any coed school would have been the wrong choice."

A few weeks into ninth grade, things were really going well for John. That was when he heard the news about Jimmy.*

---

*Jim's name has been changed for obvious reasons.

Jim had been a friend of John's since elementary school. They both hated school. They both got in trouble. But while John was popping pills, Jim was experimenting with more serious drug use, IV drug use, heroin. John remembers the day in ninth grade when he learned that Jim had committed suicide. "I never saw the note, but I heard from Jim's brother what was in it. Jim had written that he was a horrible person. He wrote that he was a piece of shit. He wrote that he hated his life. He told his parents he was sorry. He was hanging, dead, when they found him."

Jim's death paradoxically helped to push John along the right road. He began studying in earnest. His grades went way up. "I didn't have any distractions. There were no girls in the class. You don't have to impress the girls." I got the message that some of John's previous bad behavior had been a result of his trying to live up to the bad boy persona. And some of it, of course, was the drug addiction. But Phelps was different. "It's like having 150 brothers. They're looking out for you, you're looking out for them."

John started weight training. He lost fifty pounds. He weighs 185 pounds now—fifteen pounds less than he did in eighth grade—but he's four inches taller. He was elected class president, then he decided to skip eleventh grade so he could go straight from tenth grade into his senior year. That way he would graduate the same year that he would have if he had never flunked eighth grade.

"What do your sisters think of all this?" I asked.

"They're in shock and awe. They ask, 'What happened to you?' I just tell them that I went to Phelps and that made the difference."

"But why? How would things have been different if you had gone to a coed school?"

John's answer was immediate. "I have no doubt that if I'd gone to a coed school I would still be using drugs. I would probably be dead or in jail by now."

"Why?" I asked.

"Phelps has given me a sense of purpose. A sense of who I am. I don't have to be afraid of who I am. I can be proud. And like I said before. I didn't have to play the game, wear the mask."

John's story isn't over yet. He's doing well now, but the real test will come next year when he goes to college. He won't be under the close watch of his friends and his teachers. He'll have plenty of opportunities to buy the drugs he used to use.

John believes that his return to normalcy could not have happened at a coed school. I'm not totally persuaded on that point; I've visited some outstanding coed schools that have accomplished some amazing things with kids from very diverse backgrounds (Deerfield Academy in western Massachusetts comes to mind). But I think we have to respect John's opinion. After all, nobody knows his situation better than he does.

On a Tuesday evening in December 2006, I met with a group of parents in the auditorium of the Arlington Central Library in Arlington, Virginia. The place was packed (I felt flattered). The parents listened attentively as I described the five factors that I believe are disengaging boys from school—and in a broader sense, from life, from the real world of striving and achievement and loss. I outlined how we might turn the situation around, encouraging more boys to succeed or at least to try harder, without disadvantaging girls—because, after all, it's in the interest of young women as well as young men that we change the course we are now on. Young women need good men, reliable and hard-working men, not bullies or slacker dudes.

Now it was time for the questions, which I knew from experience are always more challenging than the formal part of the presentation.

"Dr. Sax, my son is intelligent, and curious, but he says school is a waste of time. He says only girls care about doing well in school. What can I do to change that?"

I responded with some stories about public schools that have adopted the single-sex format. I described how the single-sex format—particularly at schools that use team competition—has led to a surge in boys' motivation to achieve.

Another parent had doubts. "Dr. Sax, you're really pushing this thing with single-sex education. But the real world is coed. School should prepare kids for the real world. Single-sex education just isn't the real world." That's a reasonable objection, I acknowledged, but the research suggests a different reality. In most coed schools, the focus is on who's cute and who likes whom. In a single-sex school, it's easier to focus on academics. At a single-sex school, being cute isn't as important—either for girls or for boys.[23] In that sense, the single-sex format is actually better preparation for the real world than the coed format is.

"I'm persuaded by what you said about video games," another parent said. "But what about my son's friends? He goes over to their house and plays all the video games you've been warning us about."

"You can't do this by yourself," I said again. "Call up the parents of your son's friends. Ask what video games their boys are playing. Work with your school to create a community of parents who share your concerns about video games. Ask the parent-teacher association to host a forum to educate other parents about the hazards of video games. Get the word out."

"Dr. Sax, I have to admit I'm kinda freaked out by what you said about Adderall," one woman said. "My son was on Adderall for three years, when he was ten until he was thirteen. We stopped the medication when he started ninth grade. But I'm nagging him so much now. I nag him to do his homework. I nag him to go outside and get some exercise. I even nag him to call his friends. If I didn't push him, I think he might just stay in his room all the time with his computer and his video games and his television."

"Let me share two thoughts with you," I answered. "First, consider moving his computer and his television out of his room and into a public area, like the kitchen or the dining room. When he's alone in his room with the door closed, surfing the Net, you really don't know what's going on. But if he's in a public place, then it's easier for you to keep an eye on what he's doing. Don't be coy. Tell him that you have a responsibility to know what he's doing all the time that he's online, and the easiest way for you to honor that responsibility is for him to be in a public area of the house."

"But is my son's brain damaged forever because he took Adderall for three years?" the mother asked.

"We don't know. All we know is that young laboratory animals who took these medications were lazy when they grew up. We don't know for sure how that finding translates into our species at all. We don't know what dose of these medications is safe, if any. We don't know how long a boy can take the medication before some damage occurs."

"That's not very reassuring," she said.

"But remember, Dr. Carlezon didn't try to rehabilitate those laboratory animals," I added. "He didn't take them bike riding or take them on hikes in the mountains or encourage them to read good books. Speaking of books, there's a book coming out in a few weeks that you will definitely want to read. It's by a science writer named Sharon Begley. She presents some very interesting research suggesting that the brain can heal itself, even in adulthood.[24] The brain has more power to grow and to change than we previously imagined. Get your son away from the video games and get him outdoors. That's a good first step."

"He used to love mountain biking," she said. "My husband still goes mountain biking, but my son hasn't gone with him for a long time. Maybe he and his father could start doing that again."

I nodded. It was hard to know what else to say.

"I was stunned by what you said about plastic bottles," another woman said. "I thought it was so healthy to drink bottled water. What am I supposed to do about that—for my children, and for me?"

"We're fortunate, here in the Washington area," I said. "Just walk into any Whole Foods Market in the area. You'll find water in glass bottles. They've got every beverage you can imagine in glass bottles. The people who buy for the Whole Foods chain are well aware of these concerns and they've provided plenty of safe, environmentally friendly alternatives—not just beverages but also prepared foods, poultry, fish, meat, produce— everything that you eat or drink."*

It was getting late. Many parents had to get home to relieve the babysitter and put their kids to bed. I stayed and chatted with a group of parents until the janitor came to kick us out around ten p.m.

I'm encouraged. We don't have all the answers. Far from it. But I think we're at least asking the right questions. Parents who are adopting

---

*You can find a listing of local Whole Foods Market at this link: http://www.wholefoodsmarket.com/stores/index.html. There are now over two hundred Whole Foods Markets throughout the United States, Canada, and the United Kingdom, with more in the pipeline. You can read an extended interview with Whole Foods founder John Mackey, broadcast February 26, 2007, at this link: http://marketplace.publicradio.org/shows/2007/02/26/PM200702266.html.

these strategies are sending me success stories from every corner of the country, from every demographic group, involving young boys, tweens, teenagers, and young men. Many parents have already figured out one or more of these factors on their own, before they hear me speak, but they welcome the research. "I knew video games were bad for my son, but I couldn't convince anybody else. It's good to have these studies, hard data, to share with other parents," one father told me.

If you've stayed with me this far, you know that we have a lot of work to do. No one person is going to be able to do this alone. We have to work together.

So please let's get in touch with one another. I'm doing about fifty public events a year right now, an average of about one event per week, talking with teachers and meeting with parents all around the United States, Canada, Mexico, and Australia. I hope you'll consider coming to one of my events. You'll find my full itinerary at www.BoysAdrift .com. Let's meet. Let's talk. You can also send an e-mail to me at leonard-sax@prodigy.net.

We all want the same thing: a healthy world for our children and our grandchildren. We all realize that "healthy" means more than just having enough food to eat and clothes to wear. It means our daughters and our sons living lives that are meaningful and fulfilled.

So let's stay in touch.

ACKNOWLEDGMENTS

My first debt is, of course, to boys and young men such as John Nicolas, who were willing to share their stories with me. I am also grateful to all the parents who have spent so many hours talking with me about this topic, as well as to all the people who sent thoughtful and provocative e-mails to me. Although I was able to use only a few of those e-mails, I read every message and I appreciate the time people took to write. I would also like to thank my associate, Dr. Amar Duggirala, for teaching me some basic facts about India that were relevant.

Christopher Wadsworth, former executive director of the International Boys' Schools Coalition (www.boysschoolscoalition.org), has been a faithful friend and advisor throughout the years that went into this book. Bradley Adams, Christopher's successor as head of the IBSC, has been equally supportive; without his help, I would never have met John Nicolas. I also thank Chris Chirieleison for making that meeting possible.

Professor Judith Kleinfeld has arguably done more than any other person to bring the issue of Boys Adrift to public attention, not with inflammatory press events but with patient and thorough scholarship. In founding and directing the Boys' Project (www.boysproject.net), she has labored mightily to bring together scholars, educators, parents, and others from every corner of North America and even outside of North

America. Her guidance and insight have been invaluable. I am also grateful for her helpful suggestions regarding early drafts of some chapters.

Dr. Shanna Swan was kind enough to review a draft of chapter 5 and to suggest some important corrections and clarifications.

Professor David Gilmore's reply was certainly the most unexpected of all the responses I received to any draft of this manuscript. I appreciate his honesty, his candor, and his encouragement.

Regarding the trades: carpentry, plumbing, electrical, and so on. Because I know so little about these vocations, I am especially indebted to Neal Brown, Jeff Donohoe, and Myles Gladstone for their instruction. I also thank my father-in-law, Bill Kautz, retired excavator and all-around handyman, for teaching me the relevant vocabulary—and for fixing our shower.

If I had based this book only on my experience in my office, combined with my reading of the scholarly papers, this book would have been much narrower in its focus and probably would be less useful to people outside the mid-Atlantic states. It's been a great privilege to visit schools around the United States, Canada, and Australia, and to meet with girls and boys there as well as with their teachers and parents. I am particularly indebted to the following schools, and to the boys and the teachers and administrators who make them such fine institutions (listed in alphabetical order):

- Avon Old Farms, Avon, Connecticut
- Brighton Grammar, Melbourne, Australia
- Clear Water Academy, Calgary, Alberta
- Cunningham School for Excellence, Waterloo, Iowa
- Foley Intermediate School, Baldwin County, Alabama
- Georgetown Preparatory School, Bethesda, Maryland
- Haverford School, Haverford, Pennsylvania
- Phelps School, Malvern, Pennsylvania
- San Antonio Academy, San Antonio, Texas
- Stuart Hall for Boys, San Francisco, California
- Woodward Avenue Elementary, Deland, Florida

I benefited greatly from the advice and good judgment of my agent, Felicia Eth, from the inception of this project. Jo Ann Miller, my editor at Basic Books, provided an extraordinarily detailed critique of the first draft of this book, improving it immeasurably. The second draft led to an extended back-and-forth line-by-line dialogue and debate between author and editor. Throughout the process, Jo Ann struggled mightily to keep me on track, patiently explaining to me why I should not include long digressions about my daughter, or about the evils of (some) rap music, or about side effects of medications irrelevant to this topic. Her encouragement at every stage, beginning with our first meeting, has been greatly appreciated. Without her, this book might well have been a "failure to launch." Any flaws that remain are solely my responsibility.

About 180 years ago, an old poet wrote that "the eternal feminine draws us onward" ("*das Ewig-Weibliche zieht uns hinan*"). For me, the eternal feminine is my wife, Katie, and my daughter, Sarah. But they don't draw me onward. They draw me Home—for which I am eternally grateful.

NOTES

Chapter 1

1. All stories in this book are factual. In many cases I have changed names and identifying details to protect the individual's privacy. E-mail addresses, where given, are provided with the express permission of the e-mail correspondent.

2. See for example Tamar Lewin's lengthy feature for the *New York Times*, "At College, Women Are Leaving Men in the Dust," July 9, 2006, pp. A1, A18, A19.

3. Again, please see Tamar Lewin's article for the *New York Times*, "At College, Women Are Leaving Men in the Dust," July 9, 2006, pp. A1, A18, A19. See also:

- "Class Divide: As girls dominate at school, educators fight back," *The Weekend Australian*, April 8–9, 2006.
- Andrew Sum, Neeta Fogg, Paul Harrington, and associates, *The Growing Gender Gaps in College Enrollment and Degree Attainment in the U.S.* Washington, DC: Business Roundtable, 2003.
- For documentation of a similar problem in the U.K., see Kevin Schofield, "University Gender Gap Is Even Wider but No-one Knows Why," *The Scotsman*, September 14, 2004.
- In Canadian universities, the female/male ratio is 59/41 and trending upward, i.e., heading toward 60/40 and beyond. See the daily report from Statistics Canada for November 23, 2006, "Gender

Differences in University Participation," online at http://www.stat-can.ca/Daily/English/061123/d061123f.htm; see also "The Gender Imbalance in Participation in Canadian Universities," by Louis Christofides, Michael Hoy, and Ling Yang, full text available online at http://www.utoronto.ca/rdc/files/papers/L_Yang_Gender.pdf.

- Michelle Conlin, "The New Gender Gap: From kindergarten to grad school, boys are becoming the second sex," *Business Week,* May 26, 2003. Available online at www.businessweek.com/print /magazine/content/03_21/b3834001_mz001.htm?mz.

4. Again, read Tamar Lewin's feature for the *New York Times,* "At College, Women Are Leaving Men in the Dust," July 9, 2006, pp. A1, A18, A19. See also "Postsecondary Participation Rates by Sex and Race/Ethnicity: 1974–2003," National Center for Education Statistics, 2005, available online at http://nces.ed .gov/pubs2005/2005028.pdf.

5. These figures are drawn from "The State of American Manhood," by Tom Mortenson, writing for the September 2006 edition of *Postsecondary Education Opportunity,* www.postsecondary.org.

6. I am grateful to Tom Mortenson for pointing this out. In 1976–77, 494,424 American men earned a bachelor's degree, compared with just 423,476 American women. In the latest year for which the government has provided figures, 2002–2003, 573,079 men earned a bachelor's degree, compared with 775,424 American women. In the twenty-six-year span between 1977 and 2003, the number of women earning bachelor's degrees increased by 83 percent, while the number of men earning bachelor's degrees increased by only 16 percent. Here's the link to the data from the National Center for Educational Statistics: http://nces.ed.gov/programs/digest/d04/tables/dt04_262.asp. More analysis of these data is available at Tom Mortenson's Web site, www.postsecondary.org.

7. My paper was entitled "Reclaiming Kindergarten: Making kindergarten less harmful to boys," published in *Psychology of Men and Masculinity,* volume 2, pp. 3–12, 2001. You can read the full text at no charge at www.BoysAdrift.com. But you don't need to, because everything in that paper, and much more, is in this book.

8. I address declining male sperm counts in American men at greater length in chapter 6. Here are a few of the key studies:

- R. Slama and associates, "Epidemiology of Male Reproductive Function," *Revue d'Epidémiologie et de Santé Publique* [Review of Epidemiology and Public Health], volume 52, pp. 221–242, 2004.
- Jane Fisher, "Environmental Anti-androgens and Male Reproductive Health," *Reproduction,* volume 127, pp. 305–315, 2004.
- S. Pflieger-Bruss, H. C. Schuppe, W. B. Schill, "The Male Reproductive System and Its Susceptibility to Endocrine Disrupting Chemicals," *Andrologia,* volume 36, pp. 337–345, 2004.
- W. G. Foster, "Environmental Toxicants and Human Fertility," *Minerva Ginecologica,* volume 55, pp. 451–457, 2003.
- Shanna Swan, E. P. Elkin, L. Fenster, "The Question of Declining Sperm Density Revisited: An analysis of 101 studies published 1934–1996," *Environmental Health Perspectives,* volume 108, pp. 961–966, 2000.

9. The sexualization of girls' preteen years has finally begun to receive attention both in the media and from scholars. See for example Stacy Weiner's article in the *Washington Post,* February 20, 2007, "Goodbye to Girlhood," pp. F1 and F4. See also *The Report of the APA Task Force on the Sexualization of Girls,* published in February 2007, available at http://www.apa.org/pi/wpo/sexualization.html.

Chapter 2

1. Jerry D. Weast, Superintendent of Schools for Montgomery County, Maryland, "Why We Need Rigorous, Full-Day Kindergarten," from the May 2001 issue of *Principal Magazine.*

2. This extraordinary study is still accepting new patients. If you have a child age five through eighteen whom you would like to enroll, and you can travel to Bethesda, Maryland, go to http://intramural.nimh.nih.gov/chp/brainimaging /index.html for more information about enrolling in the study.

3. Jay Giedd, Liv Clasen, Rhoshel Lenroot, and associates (fifteen authors in total), "Puberty-Related Influences on Brain Development," *Molecular and Cellular Endocrinology,* volume 254, pp. 154–162, 2006.

4. Harriet Hanlon, Robert Thatcher, and Marvin Cline, "Gender Differences in the Development of EEG Coherence in Normal Children," *Developmental Neuropsychology,* volume 16, pp. 479–506, 1999. Similar results were reported in

a smaller study, by A. P. Anokhin and associates, "Complexity of Electrocortical Dynamics in Children: Developmental aspects," *Developmental Psychobiology*, volume 36, pp. 9–22, 2000.

5. For additional references and information on the relevance of these brain differences to education, please see chapter 5 of my book *Why Gender Matters*, New York: Broadway, 2006.

6. The comments in this section are based on my own longitudinal observations of more than one thousand children in my practice in Montgomery County, Maryland, over seventeen years (1990–2006), as well as a series of papers by Deborah Stipek and her associates. See:

- Deborah Stipek and associates, "Good Beginnings: What difference does the program make in preparing young children for school?" in the *Journal of Applied Developmental Psychology*, volume 19, pp. 41–66, 1998.
- Deborah Stipek, "Pathways to Constructive Lives: The importance of early school success." in the book *Constructive & Destructive Behavior: Implications for family, school, & society*, published by the American Psychological Association, pp. 291–315, 2001.
- Tricia Valeski and Deborah Stipek, "Young Children's Feelings about School," *Child Development*, volume 72, pp. 1198–1213, 2001. In this review, Valeski and Stipek observe that children who fail to do well in kindergarten develop "negative perceptions of competence," and those negative perceptions may be "difficult to reverse as children progress through school" (p. 1199).

7. The international test is the PISA—the Programme for International Student Assessment. One of the critics I have in mind is John Stossel, who stresses the poor performance of American children in comparison with the children of other nations in his critique of American education. See Stossel's book *Myths, Lies, and Downright Stupidity*, chapter 5, "Stupid Schools," especially pages 108–111 (New York: Hyperion, 2006).

8. If you'd like some documentation of this fact, and/or you'd like to learn more about the Finnish system of education, go to the relevant page of the

Finnish National Board of Education, which is http://www.edu.fi/english
/page.asp?path=500,4699,4847.

9. These data come from the PISA international Web site, http://pisacountry
.acer.edu.au/. PISA is the abbreviation for the Programme for International
Student Assessment.

10. See for example Nara Schoenberg's article, first published April 25, 2006
in the *Chicago Tribune* and subsequently reprinted in many newspapers nationwide, "Boys Ahead of the Game When They're Held Behind."

11. The quotes from Betsy Newell and from Dana Haddad both come from
Elissa Gootman's front-page article for the *New York Times*, "Preschoolers Grow
Older as Parents Seek an Edge," October 19, 2006.

12. See my paper "Reclaiming kindergarten: Making kindergarten less harmful to boys," *Psychology of Men & Masculinity*, volume 2, pp. 3–12, 2001. You can
read the full text of this article at no charge by going to www.BoysAdrift.com.

13. Elizabeth V. Lonsdorf, Lynn E. Eberly, and Anne E. Pusey, "Sex Differences
in Learning in Chimpanzees," *Nature*, volume 428, pp. 715–716, 2004.

14. Erica Check, "The X Factor," *Nature*, volume 434, pp. 266–267, 2005; and
more definitively, the article by Mark Ross, Darren Grafham, Alison Coffey, and
110 other associates, "The DNA Sequence of the Human X Chromosome," *Nature*, volume 434, pp. 325–337, 2005.

15. See for example: Genome Sequencing and Analysis Project, "Initial sequence of the Chimpanzee Genome and Comparison with the Human
Genome," *Nature*, volume 437, pp. 69–87, 2005; and also D. E. Wildman and associates, "Implications of Natural Selection in Shaping 99.4 Percent Nonsyn-
onymous DNAIdentity between Humans and Chimpanzees," *Proceedings of the
National Academy of Sciences*, 100:7181–7188, 2003.

16. See pages 11–28 of my book *Why Gender Matters*, New York: Broadway,
2006.

17. For a useful introduction to the topic of sex differences among nonhuman primates, read *Behavioral Sex Differences in Nonhuman Primates*, edited by
G. Mitchell, New York: Von Nostrand Reinhold, 1979.

18. Regarding the tendency of young male monkeys, and humans, to engage
in rough-and-tumble play more than females do, see the following:

- G. Eaton, D. F. Johns, B. B. Glick, J. M. Worlein, "Development
  in Japanese Macaques (*Macaca fuscata*): Sexually dimorphic

behavior during the first year of life," *Primates,* volume 26, pp. 238–248, 1985.

- A. Hinde and Y. Spencer-Booth, "The Behaviour of Socially Living Rhesus Monkeys in Their First Two and a Half Years," *Animal Behaviour,* volume 15, pp. 169–196, 1967.
- D. Symons, *Play and Aggression: A study of rhesus monkeys,* New York: Columbia University Press, 1978.
- For more information on sex differences in playfighting among primates, please go to www.genderdifferences.org/playfighting .htm.

19. We teach all girls and all boys the rule that young people under twenty-one should not drink alcohol. One consequence of this phenomenon—whereby ignoring the rules raises your status in the eyes of the boys—is that girls attending coed high schools, and women who attend coed colleges, are much more likely to get drunk or to have problems with alcohol compared with girls from the same communities who attend girls' schools or women who attend women's colleges. See Avshalom Caspi, Donald Lynam, Terrie Moffitt, and Phil Silva, "Unraveling Girls' Delinquency: Biological, dispositional, and contextual contributions to adolescent misbehavior." *Developmental Psychology,* volume 29, pp. 19–30, 1993. Regarding women at women's colleges compared with women at comparable coed colleges, see George Dowdall, Mary Crawford, and Henry Wechsler, "Binge Drinking among American College Women: A comparison of single-sex and coeducational institutions," *Psychology of Women Quarterly,* volume 22, pp. 705–715, 1998.

20. Marianne Hurst, "Girls Seen to Help Avert Violence," *Education Week,* May 18, 2005, p. 12.

21. Although many researchers have noted the greater propensity of women to ask for directions, the author best known for highlighting this difference between the sexes is Deborah Tannen; see her book *You Just Don't Understand: Men and Women in Conversation,* New York: HarperCollins, 2001 (revised edition).

22. Michael E. Pereira and Lynn A. Fairbanks, *Juvenile Primates: Life history, development, and behavior,* New York: Oxford University Press, 2002, Part II, "Growing into Different Worlds," p. 75.

23. Karen B. Strier, "Growing Up in a Patrifocal Society: Sex differences in the spatial relations of immature muriquis," in Michael E. Pereira and Lynn A.

Fairbanks, *Juvenile Primates: Life history, development, and behavior,* New York: Oxford University Press, 2002, pp. 138–147.

24. Lisbeth B. Lindahl and Mikael Heimann, "Social Proximity in Early Mother-Infant Interactions: Implications for gender differences?" *Early Development and Parenting,* volume 6, pp. 83–88, 1997.

25. See for example the recent paper by Jianzhong Xu of Mississippi State University, "Gender and Homework Management Reported by High School Students," *Educational Psychology,* volume 26, pp. 73–91, 2006.

26. See for example the study by Wei-Cheng Mau and Richard Lynn, "Gender Differences in Homework and Test Scores in Mathematics, Reading and Science at Tenth and Twelfth Grade," *Psychology, Evolution, and Gender,* volume 2, pp. 119–125, 2000.

27. See for example the recent study by Lynne Rogers and Sue Hallam, "Gender Differences in Approaches to Studying among High-Achieving Pupils," *Educational Studies,* volume 32, pp. 59–71, 2006.

28. Angela Lee Duckworth and Martin E. P. Seligman, "Self-Discipline Gives Girls the Edge: Gender in self-discipline, grades, and achievement test scores," *Journal of Educational Psychology,* volume 98, pp. 198–208, 2006.

29. Tricia Valeski and Deborah Stipek, "Young Children's Feelings about School," *Child Development,* 72: 1198–1213, 2001.

30. Eva Pomerantz, Ellen Altermatt, and Jill Saxon, "Making the Grade but Feeling Distressed: Gender differences in academic performance and internal distress." *Journal of Educational Psychology,* 94:396–404, 2002.

31. Angela Lee Duckworth and Martin E. P. Seligman, "Self-Discipline Gives Girls the Edge: Gender in self-discipline, grades, and achievement test scores," *Journal of Educational Psychology,* volume 98, pp. 198–208, 2006.

32. René A. Spitz, "Hospitalism: An enquiry into the genesis of psychiatric conditions in early childhood," *Psychoanalytic Study of the Child,* volume 1, pp. 53–74, 1945.

33. Richard Louv, *Last Child in the Woods: Saving our children from nature-deficit disorder,* Chapel Hill: Algonquin Books, 2005.

34. Louv, p. 57.

35. Louv, pp. 63, 67.

36. Quoted in Louv, p. 66.

37. Quoted in Louv p. 104.

38. See for example Andrea Faber Taylor, Frances E. Kuo, and William C. Sullivan, "Coping with ADD: The surprising connection to green play settings," *Environment and Behavior,* volume 33, pp. 54–77, 2001; and also (by the same authors) "Views of Nature and Self-Discipline: Evidence from inner city children," *Journal of Environmental Psychology,* February 2002, pp. 46–63.

39. Helen Schneider and Daniel Eisenberg, "Who Receives a Diagnosis of Attention-Deficit / Hyperactivity Disorder in the United States Elementary School Population?" *Pediatrics,* volume 117, pp. 601–609, 2006.

40. Quoted in Richard Louv's book *Last Child in the Woods: saving our children from nature-deficit disorder,* Chapel Hill: Algonquin Books, 2005, p. 47.

41. This simple definition is drawn from Ulric Neisser's more elaborate definition. Neisser was the first to coin the term "cognitive psychology" (in 1967). Here is his definition of cognition:

> . . . the term "cognition" refers to all processes by which the sensory input is transformed, reduced, elaborated, stored, recovered, and used. It is concerned with these processes even when they operate in the absence of relevant stimulation, as in images and hallucinations. . . . Given such a sweeping definition, it is apparent that cognition is involved in everything a human being might possibly do; that *every psychological phenomenon is a cognitive phenomenon.*

(Ulric Neisser, *Cognitive Psychology,* New York: Appleton-Century-Crofts, 1967, p. 4; emphasis added.)

42. Helen Schneider and Daniel Eisenberg, "Who Receives a Diagnosis of Attention-Deficit / Hyperactivity Disorder in the United States Elementary School Population?" *Pediatrics,* volume 117, pp. 601–609, 2006.

43. Why are white children more likely to be diagnosed with ADHD than black or Hispanic children? To understand the answer, you must understand that establishing the diagnosis of ADHD requires that the evaluating professional demonstrate a disparity between *ability* and *achievement.* If we see a boy who is getting C's and D's, but we know that he's capable of being a straight-A student, then we might reasonably suspect ADHD. However, if that boy is not capable of earning better grades than the grades he is getting, then the diagnosis of ADHD is less likely to be considered. Unfortunately, America remains in many ways a racist society. Teachers still tend to have higher expectations for

white boys than for black or Hispanic boys. If a white boy is not doing well in school, teachers—including African-American teachers—are more likely to suspect that the white boy "isn't working up to his potential." If an African-American boy is not doing well in school, the unfortunate fact is that teachers are less likely to suspect that the boy has hidden talents and abilities. Ironically, the end result of this racist assessment is that many more white boys than black boys are taking medication which they probably should not be taking. See for example the paper I wrote jointly with Kathleen Kautz, "Who First Suggests the Diagnosis of Attention-Deficit / Hyperactivity Disorder?" *Annals of Family Medicine,* volume 1, pp. 171–174, 2003. See also Helen Schneider and Daniel Eisenberg, "Who Receives a Diagnosis of Attention-Deficit / Hyperactivity Disorder in the United States Elementary School Population?" *Pediatrics,* volume 117, pp. 601–609, 2006.

44. Gretchen LeFever, Keila Dawson, and Ardythe Morrow, "The Extent of Drug Therapy for Attention Deficit-Hyperactivity Disorder among Children in Public Schools," *American Journal of Public Health,* volume 89, pp. 1359–1364, 1999.

45. Mr. Mathews' article was entitled "Study Casts Doubt on the Boy Crisis: Improving test scores cut into girls' lead," published on the front page of the *Washington Post,* June 26, 2006, full text at www.washingtonpost.com/wp-dyn/content/article/2006/06/25/AR2006062501047.html.

46. Here are the latest data, released by the U.S. Department of Education in February 2007, for twelfth graders tested in reading, nationwide:

1992, girls: 297	1992, boys: 287
2005, girls: 292	2005, boys: 279

The girls' score in 2005 dropped five points relative to the 1992 score, but the boys dropped eight points, widening the gap to thirteen points. This gap is roughly equivalent to one grade level. See "Female Students Outperform Male Students by a Wider Margin in 2005 than in 1992," published by the National Center for Education Statistics, available online at http://nces.ed.gov/nationsreportcard/pdf/main2005/2007468_2.pdf, February 22, 2007.

47. Professor Judith Kleinfeld presented this analysis of the NAEP data at the White House Conference on Helping America's Youth, June 6, 2006. You can read the full text of her analysis at this link: www.singlesexschools.org/Kleinfeld.htm.

48. Judy Willis, "The Gully in the 'Brain Glitch' Theory," *Educational Leadership*, volume 64, pp. 68–73, 2007. The quotation comes from page 72.

49. Mark Bauerlein and Sandra Stotsky, "Why Johnny Won't Read," *Washington Post*, January 25, 2005, p. A15.

50. Steven Johnson, *Everything Bad Is Good for You*, New York: Riverhead, 2005.

51. Here are the statistics from the CDC:

> Percentage of boys who were overweight in 1965: 4.0
> Percentage of boys who were overweight in 2000: 16.0
> (Source: www.cdc.gov/nchs/data/hus/tables/2003/03hus069.pdf.)

52. You can read Mathews's online column at http://www.washington post.com/wpdyn/content/article/2006/06/27/AR2006062700638.html?nav=rss_opinion/columns. Mathews quotes me on page 3 of this column. You can go directly to page 3 at this link: http://www.washingtonpost.com/wp-dyn/content/article/2006/06/27/AR2006062700638_3.html?nav=rss_opinion/columns.

53. See my book *Why Gender Matters* (Broadway, 2006), pp. 29–30. The sources I cited in my book were:

- William Killgore, Mika Oki, and Deborah Yurgelun-Todd, "Sex-Specific Developmental Changes in Amygdala Responses to Affective Faces," *NeuroReport*, volume 12, pp. 427–433, 2001; and
- William Killgore and Deborah Yurgelun-Todd, "Sex Differences in Amygdala Activation during the Perception of Facial Affect," *NeuroReport*, volume 12, pp. 2543–2547, 2001.
- A more recent study by the same team, published after *Why Gender Matters* went to press, has confirmed substantially different developmental trajectories in the localization of brain activity associated with negative affect. See the paper by William Killgore and Deborah Yurgelun-Todd, "Sex-Related Developmental Differences in the Lateralized Activation of the Prefrontal Cortex and Amygdala during Perception of Facial Affect," *Perceptual and Motor Skills*, volume 99, pp. 371–391, 2004.

54. De Lench continues:

> Under a system of full inclusion, teams would be added as neces-
> sary to meet the demand, even if it meant fielding, say, two or three
> junior varsity basketball teams. Every athlete would practice, but
> only those with good academic standing, good attendance records
> and no disciplinary problems would suit up for games. To ensure
> that schools would field the most competitive teams, the most
> skilled players would still get the bulk of the playing time at the var-
> sity level. But no one would be cut.
>
> The extra teams could be at least partially funded through addi-
> tional user fees, with money raised by booster clubs, by donations
> from local businesses and by the parents of the athletes themselves,
> some of whom could be recruited as volunteer coaches.
>
> It makes no sense from a public health standpoint to continue a
> policy that contributes to an overall decline in physical fitness
> among adolescents and young adults and does nothing to combat
> drug use by keeping teens busy in after-school programs such as
> sports.

See her article "Let Everybody Play," *Washington Post,* December 10, 2006, p. B7.

55. Margaret Shih, Todd Pittinsky, and Nalini Ambady, "Stereotype Susceptibility: Identity salience and shifts in quantitative performance," *Psychological
Science,* volume 10, pp. 80–83, 1999.

56. Princeton psychologists Joel Cooper and Kimberlee Weaver, in their book
Gender and Computers: Understanding the digital divide (Mahwah, New Jersey:
Lawrence Erlbaum, 2003), describe many studies demonstrating that young girls
and teenage girls underperform on tests of math and science ability *particularly
when they are reminded of the gender stereotype.* See particularly their chapter 3,
"The Social Context of Computing," and chapter 5, "A Threat in the Air." These
authors also describe studies showing how much better girls do, on average, in
single-sex classrooms, perhaps in part because the stereotype threat is not present: see chapter 7, "Solutions: Single-sex schools and classrooms?"

57. Roy Baumeister, Jennifer Campbell, Joachim Krueger, and Kathleen Vohs.
"Does High Self-Esteem Cause Better Performance, Interpersonal Success,

Happiness, or Healthier Lifestyles?" *Psychological Science in the Public Interest,* volume 4, pp. 1–44, 2003.

58. The exception is the boy who writes a story threatening a classmate. If Jonathan writes a story describing how he is going to murder Emily, the girl who sits next to him in English, and he has previously made threatening remarks to or about Emily, then that story is itself a provocative threat and an act of violence. But if Brett writes a story about a World War II prison escape, that story is not a threat and not an act of violence. "Zero tolerance" policies often deliberately ignore such distinctions.

59. The classic scholarly paper on this topic is "The Classroom Avenger" by Dr. James McGee and Dr. Caren DeBernardo, originally published in *The Forensic Examiner,* volume 8, May–June 1999. Both authors were employed by Sheppard Pratt (a psychiatric hospital) at the time that they wrote this article. Their article is available online at no charge from Sheppard Pratt at this link: http://www.sheppardpratt.org/Documents/classavenger.pdf.

60. This example is from Jonathan Turley's article, "My Boys Like Shootouts. What's wrong with that?" *Washington Post,* February 25, 2007, p. B1.

61. These three examples—New Jersey, Alabama, and Louisiana—come from the article "Zero Tolerance for Common Sense," by Paul Rosenzweig and Trent England, available online at http://www.heritage.org/Press/Commentary /ed080504a.cfm.

62. The original Latin is *Naturam expellas furca, tamen usque recurret,* from the *Epistles* of Horace, volume 1, §10, line 24.

Chapter 3

1. The global *Halo* competition I am referring to here took place in May 2005. Although the organizers requested that participants be at least eighteen years of age, no serious mechanism was in place to ensure compliance with this rule. More information about the competition is available at http://www.xbox.com /en-US/community/news/2005/0427-halo2globaltournament.htm.

2. I still find some Americans who regard Nietzsche as "the Nazi philosopher." The notion that Nietzsche's philosophy was concordant with German National Socialism, aka "Nazism", was an idea that the Nazis themselves vigorously promoted—but a notion that we now know to be false. After all, Friedrich Nietzsche is the man who consistently liked to say things such as "I despise the

Germans. Just being around Germans gives me a tummy ache." Nietzsche even invented a (fake) Polish ancestry for himself, insisting that his family name was actually Nietzky rather than Nietzsche, solely to dissociate himself from German culture. When his sister announced her engagement to a leader of the anti-Semitic movement in Germany, Nietzsche replied that he would never attend their wedding. When a friend urged him to reconsider, he replied, "*Zwischen einer rachsüchtigen antisemitische Gans und mir, gibt es keine Versöhnung*" ("Between me and that revenge-seeking anti-Semitic bitch, there can be no reconciliation"). For more information on the general misunderstanding of Nietzsche in English-speaking countries, please see my paper on Nietzsche published in *The Journal of Medical Biography*, Royal Society of Medicine, 2003, especially pages 50–53 (you can download it at no charge at www.BoysAdrift.com).

3. John S. Watson, "Memory and 'Contingency Analysis' in Infant Learning." *Merrill-Palmer Quarterly*, volume 13, pp. 55–76, 1967.

4. Henry Gleitman, *Psychology*, New York: W. W. Norton, 1980, p. 147.

5. This quote is the closing line of section 349 of Nietzsche's *The Will to Power*, translated by Walter Kaufmann and R. J. Hollingdale, New York: Vintage Books, 1968, p. 191.

6. Two recent studies have carefully investigated the question of how many hours per week girls and boys are playing video games. Both studies found that boys are playing thirteen or more hours a week *on average*, while girls are playing at least five hours per week on average. See:

- Craig Anderson, Douglas Gentile, and Katherine Buckley, "Study 3: Longitudinal study with elementary school students," in the authors' book *Violent Video Game Effects on Children and Adolescents*, New York: Oxford University Press, 2007, pp. 95–119. These authors conducted a study of 430 third-, fourth-, and fifth-graders from five different elementary schools (four public schools, one private school). The boys played video games, on average, 13.4 hours per week; the girls played on average 5.9 hours per week.
- Douglas Gentile, Paul Lynch, Jennifer Ruh Linder, and David Walsh, "The Effects of Violent Video Game Habits on Adolescent Hostility, Aggressive Behaviors, and School Performance,"

Journal of Adolescence, volume 27, pp. 5–22, 2004. These authors studied 607 eighth- and ninth-graders from four different schools (three public schools, one private school). The boys played video games, on average, thirteen hours per week, while the girls played on average five hours per week.

7. These examples come from Mike Musgrove's article for the *Washington Post,* "Family Game Night, version 2.0," March 4, 2007, pp. F1, F4.

8. Steven Johnson, *Everything Bad Is Good for You: How today's popular culture is actually making us smarter,* New York: Riverhead, 2005.

9. Greg Toppo, "Games Take On Books: An educator's experiment supports teaching potential," *USA Today,* November 30, 2006, p. 10D. On the very same page, right next to this article extolling the virtues of video games, is another article by the same journalist, Greg Toppo, "Violent Play Rewires Brain," reporting yet another study documenting the hazards of video games. You have to give *USA Today* some credit for having the courage to juxtapose these two stories.

10. James Paul Gee, *What Video Games Have to Teach Us about Learning and Literacy,* New York: Palgrave Macmillan, 2004; and David Williamson Shaffer, *How Computer Games Help Children Learn,* New York: Palgrave Macmillan, 2006.

11. James Paul Gee, *What Video Games Have to Teach Us about Learning and Literacy,* New York: Palgrave Macmillan, 2004, p. 142.

12. Professor Gee will be the principal investigator on two projects to bring video games into the classrooms. The MacArthur Foundation gave Professor Gee and his people $1.8 million for one project and $1.2 million for a second project. For more information, see the University of Wisconsin's press release announcing the grant, "MacArthur Foundation Provides $3 million for Digital Learning Initiatives," at this link: http://www.news.wisc.edu/13057.html.

13. David Williamson Shaffer, *How Computer Games Help Children Learn,* New York: Palgrave Macmillan, 2006, pp. 5–6.

14. Shaffer, p. 6 and *passim.*

15. For a recent survey of some of this literature, see Sadie Dingfelder's article for *Monitor on Psychology* (a monthly magazine that is mailed to all 150,000-plus members of the American Psychological Association), "Your Brain on Video Games," February 2007, pp. 20–21, available online at http://www.apa.org/monitor/feb07/yourbrain.html.

16. A significant negative correlation between academic performance and amount of time playing video games has been documented in the following studies:

- **Elementary school students:** Craig Anderson, Douglas Gentile, and Katherine Buckley, "Study 3: Longitudinal study with elementary school students," in the authors' book *Violent Video Game Effects on Children and Adolescents,* New York: Oxford University Press, 2007, pp. 95–119.

- **Eighth- and ninth-grade students:** Douglas Gentile, Paul Lynch, Jennifer Ruh Linder, and David Walsh, "The Effects of Violent Video Game Habits on Adolescent Hostility, Aggressive Behaviors, and School Performance," *Journal of Adolescence,* volume 27, pp. 5–22, 2004.

- **High school students:** Craig Anderson, Douglas Gentile, and Katherine Buckley, "Study 2: Correlational study with high school students," in the authors' book *Violent Video Game Effects on Children and Adolescents,* New York: Oxford University Press, 2007, pp. 78–94.

- **College students:** Craig Anderson and Karen Dill, "Video Games and Aggressive Thoughts, Feelings, and Behavior in the Laboratory and in Life," *Journal of Personality and Social Psychology,* volume 78, pp. 772–790, 2000.

See also Peter Richards's article "Computers Widen Gender Gap for Boys," *The Guardian,* August 29, 2005. Richards is describing a study by the Department for Education and Skills, conducted by researchers from Leeds University and Sheffield University. You can link to a free download of the complete report, or a summary (your choice) at: www.dfes.gov.uk/research/programmeofresearch/projectinformation.cfm?projectid=14522&resultspage=1. Repeated searches of the PsychINFO and Medline/PubMed databases, through April 2007, generated no study reporting a contrary finding, i.e., a positive correlation between academic performance and time spent playing video games.

17. All quotes in this paragraph come from Patrick Welsh's article for the *Washington Post,* "It's No Contest; Boys will be men, and they'll still choose video games," December 5, 2004, p. B1.

18. "Children Are Less Able than They Used to Be," John Crace, *Guardian*, January 24, 2006, p. 3.

19. "Smart as We Can Get? Gains on certain tests of intelligence are ending in some places," David Schneider, *American Scientist*, August 2006.

20. "Children Are Less Able than They Used to Be," John Crace, *Guardian*, January 24, 2006, p. 3. Emphasis added.

21. Jon Martin Sundet, Dag Barlaugh, and Tore Torjussen, "The End of the Flynn Effect? A study of secular trends in mean intelligence test scores of Norwegian conscripts during half a century," *Intelligence*, volume 32, pp. 349–362, 2004.

22. Thomas Teasdale and David Owen, "A Long-Term Rise and Recent Decline in Intelligence Test Performance: The Flynn effect in reverse," *Personality and Individual Differences*, volume 39, pp. 837–843, 2005.

23. The study is "Exposure to Violent Video Games Increases Automatic Aggressiveness," by Eric Uhlmann and Jane Swanson, *Journal of Adolescence*, volume 27, pp. 41–52, 2004.

24. Craig Anderson, "An Update on the Effects of Playing Violent Video Games," *Journal of Adolescence*, volume 27, pp. 113–122, 2004.

25. N. L. Carnagey and Craig Anderson, "Violent Video Game Exposure and Aggression: A literature review," *Minerva Psichiatrica*, volume 45, pp. 1–18, 2004.

26. Jeroen Jansz, "The Emotional Appeal of Violent Video Games for Adolescent Males," *Communication Theory*, volume 15, pp. 219–241, 2005.

27. See Craig Anderson, "Violent Video Games: Myths, facts, and unanswered questions," *Psychological Science Agenda*, volume 16, October 2003; full text available online at http://www.apa.org/science/psa/sb-anderson.html.

28. You can read Professor Anderson's guidelines in full at this link: http://www.psychology.iastate.edu/faculty/caa/VG_recommendations.html

29. "Are Kids Too Wired for Their Own Good?" *Time* magazine cover story, lead journalist Claudia Wallis, March 27, 2006.

30. Patrick Welsh, *Washington Post*, "It's No Contest; Boys will be men, and they'll still choose video games," December 5, 2004, p. B1.

31. Tamar Lewin, "At Colleges, Women Are Leaving Men in the Dust," *New York Times*, July 9, 2006, pp. A1, A18, A19. Emphasis added.

32. Tamar Lewin, "At Colleges, Women Are Leaving Men in the Dust," *New York Times*, pp. A1, A18, A19, July 9, 2006. Emphasis added.

33. Craig Anderson, Douglas Gentile, and Katherine Buckley, *Violent Video Game Effects on Children and Adolescents,* New York: Oxford University Press, 2007, p. 66.

34. This story is available online at this link: www.sjsa.ab.ca/outdoor /testimonial.htm.

Chapter 4

1. "National Institute of Mental Health Multimodal Treatment Study of ADHD Follow-up: Changes in effectiveness and growth after the end of treatment," *Pediatrics,* 113:762–769, 2004.

2. Dr. Peter Breggin is one writer who has argued that ADHD was invented by the pharmaceutical industry in order to sell drugs. See his books *Talking Back to Ritalin: What doctors aren't telling you about stimulants for children,* Common Courage Press, 1998; and also *The Ritalin Fact Book: What your doctor won't tell you,* Perseus, 2002.

3. American Psychiatric Association, *Diagnostic and Statistical Manual of Mental Disorders,* 4th Edition, Washington, DC: APA, 1994, pp. 78–84.

4. See Linda Johnson's article for the Associated Press, "Adult Use of Drugs for ADHD Doubles," September 15, 2005. See also my article, "Ritalin: Better living through chemistry?" published in *The World and I,* November 2000, pp. 287–299, and available online at www.whygendermatters.com.

5. The phrase "medicate young minds" is borrowed from Elizabeth Roberts's article, "A Rush to Medicate Young Minds," *Washington Post,* October 8, 2006, p. B7.

6. *DSM-IV* criteria for oppositional-defiant disorder (313.81) include

- often argues with adults;
- often actively defies or refuses to comply with adults' requests;
- often deliberately annoys people;

and so forth. The full citation is American Psychiatric Association, *Diagnostic and Statistical Manual of Mental Disorders,* 4th Edition, Washington, DC: APA, 1994, pp. 91–94.

7. Jennifer Harris, February 2006 *Psychotherapy Networker,* quoted in Elizabeth Roberts's article, "A Rush to Medicate Young Minds," *Washington Post,* October 8, 2006, p. B7.

8. The first and in many ways still most important article calling attention to the growing tendency to prescribe medication for preschool kids was written by Julie Magno Zito, Daniel J. Safer, Susan dosReis, James F. Gardner, Myde Boles, and Frances Lynch, "Trends in the Prescribing of Psychotropic Medications for Preschoolers," *Journal of the American Medical Association,* volume 283, pp. 1025–1030, 2000.

9. Julie M. Zito and associates, "Antidepressant Medications for Youths: A multi-national comparison," *Pharmacoepidemiological Drug Safety,* volume 15, pp. 793–798, 2006.

10. Julie M. Zito, Daniel J. Safer, Susan DosReis, "Concomitant Psychotropic Medication for Youths," *American Journal of Psychiatry*, volume 160, pp. 438–49, 2003. The full text of this article is available at no charge at http://ajp.psychiatryonline.org/cgi/reprint/160/3/438. You can also link to the full text at no charge at www.BoysAdrift.com.

11. Leonard Sax and Kathleen Kautz, "Who First Suggests the Diagnosis of Attention-Deficit Hyperactivity Disorder? A survey of primary-care pediatricians, family physicians, and child psychiatrists," *Annals of Family Medicine*, volume 1, pp. 171–174, 2003.

12. Dr. Gabrieli's presentation was entitled "Educating the Brain." You can purchase an audio CD of his presentation at this link: www.fltwood.com /onsite/brain/2006–04/.

13. See William A. Carlezon and C. Konradi, "Understanding the Neurobiological Consequences of Early Exposure to Psychotropic Drugs: Linking behavior with molecules," *Neuropharmacology,* volume 47, Supplement 1, pp. 47–60, 2004. See also another article from Dr. Carlezon's lab, "Early Developmental Exposure to Methylphenidate [Ritalin] Reduces Cocaine-Induced Potentiation of Brain Stimulation Reward in Rats," *Biological Psychiatry,* volume 57, pp. 120–125, 2005.

14. **University of Michigan:** T. E. Robinson and B. Kolb, "Structural Plasticity Associated with Exposure to Drugs of Abuse," *Neuropharmacology,* volume 47, Supplement 1, pp. 33–46, 2004.

Medical University of South Carolina: P. W. Kalivas, N. Volkow, and J. Seamans, "Unmanageable Motivation in Addiction: A pathology in prefrontal-accumbens glutamate transmission," *Neuron,* volume 45, pp. 647–650, 2005.

University of Pittsburgh: S. P. Onn and A. A. Grace, "Amphetamine Withdrawal Alters Bistable States and Cellular Coupling in Rat Prefrontal Cortex and Nucleus Accumbens Neurons Recorded in Vivo." *Journal of Neuroscience,* volume 20, pp. 2332–2345, 2000.

Brown University: Y. Li and J. A. Kauer, "Repeated Exposure to Amphetamine Disrupts Dopaminergic Modulation of Excitatory Synaptic Plasticity and Neurotransmission in Nucleus Accumbens," *Synapse,* volume 51, pp. 1–10, 2004.

Sweden: R. Diaz-Heijtz, B. Kolb, and H. Forssberg. "Can a Therapeutic Dose of Amphetamine during Pre-Adolescence Modify the Pattern of Synaptic Organization in the Brain?" *European Journal of Neuroscience,* volume 18, pp. 3394–3399, 2003.

Italy: G. Di Chiara, V. Bassareo, S. Fenu, M. A. De Luca, and associates, "Dopamine and Drug Addiction: The nucleus accumbens shell connection," *Neuropharmacology,* volume 47 supplement 1, pp. 227–241, 2004.

Netherlands: Louk J. Vanderschuren, E. Donné Schmidt, T. J. De Vries, and associates, "A Single Exposure to Amphetamine Is Sufficient to Induce Long-term Behavioral, Neuroendocrine, and Neurochemical Sensitization in Rats," *Journal of Neuroscience,* volume 19, pp. 9579–9586, 1999.

15. For an overview of sex differences in the neurological substrate of ADHD, please see my paper, "The Diagnosis and Treatment of ADHD in Women," *The Female Patient,* volume 29, pp. 29–34, November 2004. The full text is available online at no charge at www.BoysAdrift.com.

16. Robert Paul, Adam Brickman, Bradford Navia, and associates (nine authors altogether), "Apathy Is Associated with Volume of the Nucleus Accumbens in Patients Infected with HIV," *Journal of Neuropsychiatry and Clinical Neuroscience,* volume 17, pp. 167–171, 2005.

17. Goh Matsuda and Kazuo Hiraki, "Sustained Decrease in Oxygenated Hemoglobin During Video Games in the Dorsal Prefrontal Cortex: A NIRS study of children," *Neuroimage,* volume 29, pp. 706–711, 2006.

18. Steven Johnson, *Everything Bad Is Good for You,* New York: Riverhead, 2005, pp. 34 and 39.

19. The book Andrew recommended—and which I subsequently purchased and read—was *Unearthing Atlantis,* by Charles Pellegrino, New York: Random House, 1994.

20. Goh Matsuda and Kazuo Hiraki, "Sustained Decrease in Oxygenated Hemoglobin During Video Games in the Dorsal Prefrontal Cortex: A NIRS study of children," *Neuroimage,* volume 29, pp. 706–711, 2006.

21. Leonard Sax, "The Feminization of American Culture: How modern chemicals may be changing American biology," *The World & I,* October 2001, pp. 243–261, available online at http://www.worldandi.com/public/2001 /October/sax.html. If you read this article, please keep in mind that my views have changed substantially since 2001 in light of subsequent investigations.

Chapter 5

1. David Fahrenthold, "Male Bass across Region Found to Be Bearing Eggs: Pollution concerns arise in drinking-water source," *Washington Post,* September 6, 2006, pp. A1, A8.

2. This quote is taken from David Fahrenthold's September 6, 2006, article in the *Washington Post* cited in note 1 above. For recent updates on this story, go to www.potomacriverkeeper.org.

3. Laura Sessions Stepp, "Cupid's Broken Arrow: Performance anxiety and substance abuse figure into the increase in reports of impotence on campus," *Washington Post,* May 7, 2006.

4. **Washington and Idaho:** James Nagler and his associates made a similar discovery in tributaries of the Columbia River in Washington and Idaho: many of the female-appearing fish they found were actually genetically male. These fish were completely feminized: they looked female, they made eggs instead of sperm, but they were genetically male. See: James J. Nagler, Jerry Bouma, Gary H. Thorgaard, and Dennis D. Daub, "High Incidence of a Male-Specific Genetic Marker in Phenotypic Female Chinook Salmon from the Columbia River." *Environmental Health Perspectives,* volume 109, pp. 67–69, 2001.

Florida: In central Florida, Dr. Louis Guillette and associates with the United States Fish and Wildlife Service found male alligators with shriveled testicles. These alligators also have abnormally low male hormone levels and abnormally high female hormone levels. Likewise, male panthers living in the wildlife preserves around Lake Apopka, not far from Orlando, are going extinct, at least in part because the male panthers are no longer capable of making sperm. The emasculation of male panthers has been linked to plastic derivatives such as various phthalates and bisphenol A, in the watershed. See:

- Louis J. Guillette Jr., Timothy S. Gross, Greg R. Masson, John M. Matter, H. Franklin Percival, and Allan R. Woodward, "Developmental Abnormalities of the Gonad and Abnormal Sex Hormone Concentrations in Juvenile Alligators from Contaminated and Control Lakes in Florida," *Environmental Health Perspectives,* volume 102, pp. 680–688, 1994.
- Charles F. Facemire, Timothy S. Gross, and Louis J. Guillette Jr., "Reproductive Impairment in the Florida Panther," *Environmental Health Perspectives,* volume 103, supplement 4, pp. 79–86, 1995. Full text available online at no charge at this URL: http://www.ehponline.org/members/1995/Suppl–4/facemire-full.html.

For an accessible and reader-friendly introduction to these developments in central Florida, see Janet Raloff's article "The Gender Benders: Are environmental hormones emasculating wildlife?" *Science News,* January 8, 1994, available at no charge online at http://www.sciencenews.org/pages/sn_edpik/ls_7.htm.

Great Lakes: Theo Colborn, Frederick vom Saal, and Ana Soto, "Developmental Effects of Endocrine-DIsrupting Chemicals in Wildlife and Humans," *Environmental Health Perspectives,* volume 101, pp. 378–384, 1993.

Alaska: Kurunthachalam Kannan, Se Hun Yun, and Thomas J. Evans, "Chlorinated, Brominated, and Perfluorinated Contaminants in Livers of Polar Bears from Alaska," *Environmental Science and Technology,* volume 39, pp. 9057–9063, 2005.

England: Susan Jobling, Monique Nolan, Charles R. Tyler, Geoff Brighty, and John P. Sumpter, "Widespread Sexual Disruption in Wild Fish," *Environmental Science and Technology,* volume 32, pp. 2498–2506, 1998.

Greenland: Christian Sonne, Pall Leifsson, Rune Dietz, Erik Born, and associates, "Xenoendocrine Pollutants May Reduce Size of Sexual Organs in East Greenland Polar Bars (*Ursus maritimus*)," *Environmental Science and Technology,* volume 40, pp. 5668–5674, 2006.

5. C. A. Sáenz, A. M. Bondiovanni, and L. Conde, "An Epidemic of Precocious Development in Puerto Rican Children," *Journal of Pediatrics,* volume 107, pp. 393–396, 1985.

6. L. W. Freni-Titulaer, J. Cordero, L. Haddock, G. Lebrón, R. Martínez, and J. Mills, "Premature Thelarche in Puerto Rico: A search for environmental factors," *American Journal of Diseases of Childhood,* volume 140, pp. 1263–1267, 1986.

7. See: Louis J. Guillette Jr., Timothy S. Gross, Greg R. Masson, John M. Matter, H. Franklin Percival, and Allan R. Woodward, "Developmental abnormalities of the gonad and abnormal sex hormone concentrations in juvenile alligators from contaminated and control lakes in Florida," *Environmental Health Perspectives*, volume 102, pp. 680–688, 1994. See also Charles F. Facemire, Timothy S. Gross, and Louis J. Guillette Jr, "Reproductive impairment in the Florida panther," *Environmental Health Perspectives*, volume 103, supplement 4, pp. 79–86, 1995. Full text available online at no charge at this link: http://www.ehponline.org/members/1995/Suppl–4/facemire-full.html.

8. Ivelisse Colón, Doris Caro, Carlos J. Bourdony, and Osvaldo Rosario, "Identification of phthalate esters in the serum of young Puerto Rican girls with premature breast development," *Environmental Health Perspectives*, volume 108, pp. 895–900, 2000.

9. See for example P. D. Barbre, "Environmental Estrogens and Breast Cancer," *Best Practice & Research Clinical Endocrinology & Metabolism*, volume 20, pp. 121–143, 2006.

10. Paul Kaplowitz and associates, "Reexamination of the Age Limit for Defining when Puberty Is Precocious in Girls in the United States: Implications for evaluation and treatment," *Pediatrics*, volume 104, pp. 936–941, 1999.

11. See for example E. Den Hond and G. Schoeters, "Endocrine Disruptors and Human Puberty," *International Journal of Andrology*, volume 29, pp. 264–271, 2006. Full text available at no charge online at http://www.blackwell-synergy.com/doi/abs/10.1111/j.1365–2605.2005.00561.x (click on "PDF").

12. See for example Kate Ramsayer, "Slowing Puberty? Pesticide may hinder development in boys," *Science News*, volume 164, p. 372, 2003. This article is based in part by a study published by Habibullah Saiyed and colleagues, "Effect of endosulfan on male reproductive development," *Environmental Health Perspectives*, volume 111, pp. 1958–1962, 2003.

13. See "Chemical Used in Food Containers Disrupts Brain Development," no byline, *Science Daily*, December 3, 2005. This article is based on two articles published in December 2005 by Dr. Scott Belcher and associates: 1) "Ontogeny of Rapid Estrogen-Mediated Extracellular Signal-Regulated Kinase Signaling in the Rat Cerebellar Cortex: Potent nongenomic agonist and endocrine disrupting activity of the xenoestrogen bisphenol A," *Endocrinology*, volume 146, pp. 5388–5396, 2005; and 2) "Rapid Estrogenic Regulation of Extracellular Signal-regulated Kinase 1/2 Signaling in Cerebellar Granule Cells Involves a G Protein-

and Protein Kinase A-Dependent Mechanism and Intracellular Activation of Protein Phosphatase 2A," *Endocrinology,* volume 146, pp. 5397–5406, 2005.

14. K. Nguon, B. Ladd, M. G. Baxter, and E. M. Sajdel-Sulkowska, "Sexual Dimorphism in Cerebellar Structure, Function, and Response to Environmental Perturbations," *Progress in Brain Research,* volume 148, pp. 343–351, 2005. The quotation is from page 343; emphasis added.

15. Walter Adriani, Daniele Della Seta, Francesco Dessi-Fulgheri, Francesca Farabollini, and Giovanni Laviola, "Altered Profiles of Spontaneous Novelty Seeking, Impulsive Behavior, and Response to D-Amphetamine in Rats Perinatally Exposed to Bisphenol A," *Environmental Health Perspectives,* volume 111, pp. 395–401, 2003.

16. Giovanni Laviola, Laura Gioiasa, Walter Adriani, and Paola Palanza, "D-Amphetamine-Related Reinforcing Effects Are Reduced in Mice Exposed Prenatally to Estrogenic Endocrine Disruptors," *Brain Research Bulletin,* volume 65, pp. 235–240, 2005.

17. A. M. Geller, W. M. Oshiro, N. Haykal-Coates, P. Kodavanti, and P. J. Bushnesll, "Gender-Dependent Behavioral and Sensory Effects of a Commercial Mixture of Polychlorinated Biphenyls (Aroclor 1254)," *Toxicological Science,* volume 59, pp. 268–277, 2001. See also R. Hojo, S. Stern, G. Zareba, V. Markowski, C. Cox, J. Kost, and Bernard Weiss, "Sexually Dimorphic Behavioral Responses to Prenatal Dioxin Exposure," *Environmental Health Perspectives,* volume 110, pp. 247–254, 2002.

18. C. S. Roegge, B. W. Seo, K. Croton, and S. L. Schantz, "Gestational-Lactational Exposure to Aroclor 1254 Impairs Radial-Arm Maze Performance in Male Rats," *Toxicological Science,* volume 57, pp. 121–130, 2000. See also Bernard Weiss, "Sexually Dimorphic Nonreproductive Behaviors as Indicators of Endocrine Disruption," volume 110, pp. 387–391, 2002.

19. Yoshinori Masuo, Masatoshi Morita, Syuichi Oka, and Masami Ishido, "Motor Hyperactivity Caused by a Deficit in Dopaminergic Neurons and the Effects of Endocrine Disruptors: A study inspired by the physiological roles of PACAP in the brain," *Regulatory Peptides,* volume 123, pp. 225–234, 2004. Available online at www.sciencedirect.com. See also Masami Ishido, Yoshinori Masuo, J. Savato-Suzuki, S. Oka, E. Niki, and Masatoshi Morita, "Dicyclohexylphthalate causes Hyperactivity in the Rat Concomitantly with Impairment of Tyrosine Hydroxylase Immunoreactivity," *Journal of Neurochemistry,* volume 91, pp. 69–76, 2004.

20. For more about differences in the rate of diagnosis of ADHD in different countries, see my article "Ritalin: Better living through chemistry," originally published in *The World & I*, November 2000, available online at http://www.worldandi.com/public/2000/november/sax.html.

21. Dr. Amar Duggirala, personal communication, June 2006.

22. This paragraph summarizes a large body of work. More than one hundred studies over the past twenty years have demonstrated the association between testosterone and "drive" in men, and the relative lack of such association in women. Here are some representative studies, in chronological order:

- Alan Booth and associates, "Testosterone and Winning and Losing in Human Competition," *Hormones and Behavior,* volume 23, pp. 556–571, 1989.
- B. Gladue, M. Boechler, and K. McCaul, "Hormonal Response to Competition in Human Males," *Aggressive Behavior,* volume 15, pp. 409–422, 1989.
- K. D. McCaul, B. Gladue, and M. Joppa, "Winning, Losing, Mood, and Testosterone," *Hormones and Behavior,* volume 26, pp. 486–504, 1992.
- A. Mazur, E. J. Susman, and S. Edelbrock, "Sex Differences in Testosterone Response to a Video Game Contest," *Evolution and Human Behavior,* volume 18, pp. 317–326, 1997.
- A. Mazur and Alan Booth, "Testosterone and Dominance in Men," *Behavioral and Brain Sciences,* volume 21, pp. 353–363, 1998.
- E. Cashdan, "Are Men More Competitive than Women?" *British Journal of Social Psychology,* volume 34, pp. 213–229, 1998.
- David Geary and M. V. Flinn, "Sex Differences in Behavioral and Hormonal Response to Social Threat," *Psychological Review,* volume 109, pp. 745–750, 2002.
- H. S. Bateup, Alan Booth, and associates, "Testosterone, Cortisol, and Women's Competition," *Evolution and Human Behavior,* volume 23, pp. 181–192, 2002.
- Katie Kivlighan, Douglas Granger, and Alan Booth, "Gender Differences in Testosterone and Cortisol Response to Competition," *Psychoneuroendocrinology,* volume 30, pp. 58–71, 2005.

23. Bruce McEwen, "Steroid Hormones and Brain Development: Some guidelines for understanding actions of pseudo-hormones and other toxic agents," *Environmental Health Perspectives,* volume 74, pp. 177–184, 1987.

24. See Neil MacLusky, Tibor Hajszan, and Csaba Leranth, "The Environmental Estrogen Bisphenol A Inhibits Estradiol-Induced Hippocampal Synaptogenesis," *Environmental Health Perspectives,* volume 113, pp. 675–679, 2005. See also Yale University's press release, "Chemical Present in Clear Plastics Can Impair Learning and Cause Disease," March 28 2005, available online at www.yale.edu/opa/newsr/05–30–28–02.all.html.

25. Lise Aksglaede, Anders Juul, Henrik Leffers, Niels Skakkebæk, and Anna-Maria Andersson, "The Sensitivity of the Child to Sex Steroids: Possible impact of exogenous estrogens," *Human Reproduction Update,* volume 12, pp. 341–349, 2006. See also G. C. Panzica, C. Viglietti-Panzica, and M. A. Ottinger, "Neurobiological Impact of Environmental Estrogens," *Brain Research Bulletin,* volume 65, pp. 187–191, 2005.

26. According to the CDC, 4.0 percent of boys were overweight in 1963–1970; in 1999–2002, 16.9 percent of boys were overweight. In 1971–1974, only 3.6 percent of girls were overweight; in 1999–2002, 14.7 percent of girls were overweight. See NCHS (National Center for Health Statistics) Data on Child Health, updated February 2005, available at www.cdc.gov/nchs/data/factsheets/childhlth.pdf.

27. For example: in 1971, 294,015 girls participated in high school sports; in 1999, the number was 2,675,874, according to Girls Inc.: http://www.girls-inc.org/ic/content/GirlsAndTheirBodies.pdf.

28. Nathaniel Mead, "Origins of Obesity: Chemical exposures," *Environmental Health Perspectives,* volume 112, number 6, May 2004, p. A344.

29. Nathaniel Mead, "Origins of Obesity: Chemical exposures," *Environmental Health Perspectives,* volume 112, number 6, May 2004, p. A344.

30. Joyce M. Lee, Danielle Appugliese, Niko Kaciroti, Robert F. Corwyn, Robert H. Bradley, and Julie C. Lumeng, "Weight Status in Young Girls and the Onset of Puberty," *Pediatrics,* volume 119, pp. 624–630, 2007.

31. Ines Sedlmeyer and Mark Palmert, "Delayed Puberty: Analysis of a large case series from an academic center," *Journal of Clinical Endocrinology and Metabolism,* volume 87, pp. 1613–1620, 2002.

32. L. A. Landin published data demonstrating that "over the years, more and more fractures were caused by slight trauma whereas the more severe

trauma contributed a smaller fraction of the injuries," Kids today break their bones more easily than they used to. And kids are less active, so the risk of severe trauma is lower. Landin's article is "Fracture Patterns in Children: Analysis of 8,682 fractures with special reference to incidence, etiology and secular changes in a Swedish urban population 1950–1979," *Acta Orthopaedica Scandinavica Supplementum*, volume 202, pp. 1–109, 1983.

33. R. A. Lyons, A. M. Delahunty, D. Kraus, and associates, "Children's Fractures: A population-based study," *Injury Prevention*, volume 5, pp. 129–132, 1999.

34. A. Johansen, R. J. Evans, M. Stone, and associates, "Fracture Incidence in England and Wales: A study based on the population of Cardiff," *Injury*, volume 28, pp. 655–660, 1997.

35. For an overview of the literature demonstrating how cola beverages adversely affect bone mineralization in children, see my chapter "Dietary Phosphorus as a Nutritional Toxin: The influence of age and sex," in *Annual Reviews in Food & Nutrition* (Victor Preedy, editor), London: Taylor & Francis, pp. 158–168, 2003.

36. See for example the article published in November 2006 by Guowei Pan, Tomoyuki Hanaoka, Mariko Yoshimura, and associates, "Decreased Serum Free Testosterone in Workers Exposed to High Levels of Di-n-butyl phthalate (DBP) and di–2-ethylhexyl phthalate (DEHP)," *Environmental Health Perspectives*, volume 114, pp. 1643–1648, 2006. Available at http://www.ehponline.org/docs/2006/9016/abstract.html (click on "PDF" for full text at no charge).

37. See for example:

- Mari Golub, Casey Hogrefe, Stacey Germann, and Christopher Jerome, "Endocrine Disruption in Adolescence: Immunologic, hematologic, and bone effects in monkeys," *Toxicological Sciences*, volume 82, pp. 598–607, 2004.
- Monica Lind, Matthew Milnes, Rebecca Lundberg, Diedrich Bermudez, Jan Örberg, and Louis Guillette, "Abnormal Bone Composition in Female Juvenile American Alligators from a Pesticide-Polluted Lake (Lake Apopka, Florida)," *Environmental Health Perspectives*, volume 112, pp. 359–362, 2004.

38. For a review of hardwired sex differences in young children, I would ask that you read my book, *Why Gender Matters: What parents and teachers*

need to know about the emerging science of sex differences, New York: Broadway, 2006.

39. A. K. Hotchkiss, J. S. Ostby, J. Vandenbergh, and L. Gray, "Androgens and Environmental Antiandrogens Affect Reproductive Development and Play Behavior in the Sprague-Dawley Rat," *Environmental Health Perspectives,* volume 110, supplement 3, pp. 435–439, 2002.

40. Beverly Rubin, Jenny Lenkowski, Cheryl Schaeberle, Laura Vandenberg, Paul Ronsheim, and Ana Soto, "Evidence of Altered Brain Sexual Differentiation in Mice Exposed Perinatally to Low, Environmentally Relevant Levels of Bisphenol A," *Endocrinology,* volume 147, pp. 3681–3691, 2006. See also Frederick vom Saal, "Bisphenol A Eliminates Brain and Behavior Sex Dimorphisms in Mice: How low can you go?" *Endocrinology,* volume 147, pp. 3679–3680, 2006.

41. Thomas Travison, Andre Araujo, Amy O'Donnell, Varant Kupelian, and John McKinlay, "A Population-Level Decline in Serum Testosterone Levels in American Men," *Journal of Clinical Endocrinology and Metabolism,* volume 92, pp. 196–202, 2007.

42. For a recent review of the purported relationship between environmental estrogens and a surge in male infertility over the past three decades, see Julia Barrett's article, "Fertile Grounds for Inquiry: Environmental effects on human reproduction," *Environmental Health Perspectives,* volume 114, pp. A644–649, 2006, available online at no charge at this link: http://www.ehponline.org /members/2006/114–11/focus.html.

Forty years ago, infertility was a woman's problem. When I was in medical school at the University of Pennsylvania, infertility was taught as part of the OB/GYN rotation—and that's still the way it's taught at most medical schools. Infertility experts today are almost always gynecologists, very seldom urologists—even though in our era, the twenty-first century, physicians agree that when a couple is infertile, the problem lies with the man just as often as it lies with the woman.

Was that always the case? It's hard to say. Forty years ago, it was not unusual for physicians to go so far as to operate on a woman to reopen her (supposedly) blocked fallopian tubes, only to find that the woman was normal. Then, belatedly, the physician would test the husband and discover that the husband's semen contains no sperm. For further discussion of historical trends in the diagnosis of infertility, see the monograph by Margaret Marsh and Wanda Ronner, *The Empty Cradle: Infertility in America from colonial times to the present,* Baltimore: Johns Hopkins University Press, 1996, especially pp. 198–202 and 223–229.

43. Nils Skakkebæk, E. Rajpert-De Meyts, and Katharina Main, "Testicular Dysgenesis Syndrome: An increasingly common developmental disorder with environmental aspects," *Human Reproduction,* volume 16, pp. 972–978, 2001. The quotations are from page 977.

44. Shanna H. Swan, Katharina M. Main, Fan Liu, Sara L. Stewart, Robin L. Kruse, Antonia M. Calafat, and associates, "Decrease in Anogenital Distance Among Male Infants with Prenatal Phthalate Exposure," *Environmental Health Perspectives,* volume 113, pp. 1056–1061, 2005.

45. This exact phrase comes from Dr. Swan's e-mail to me, February 7, 2007.

46. See for example:

- N. Barlow, B. McIntyre, and P. Foster, "Male Reproductive Tract Lesions at Six, Twelve, and Eighteen Months of Age Following in Utero Exposure to di(n-butyl) Phthalate," *Toxicology and Pathology,* volume 32, pp. 79–90, 2004.

- S. M. Duty, Antonia Calafat, M. J. Silva, L. Ryan, and R. Hauser, "Phthalate Exposure and Reproductive Hormones in Adult Men," *Human Reproduction,* volume 20, pp. 604–610, 2005.

- M. Ema and E. Miyawaki, "Adverse Effects on Development of the Reproductive System in Male Offspring of Rats Given Monobutyl Phthalate, a Metabolite of Dibutyl Phthalate, during Late Pregnancy," *Reproductive Toxicology,* volume 15, pp. 189–194, 2001.

- M. Ema, E. Miyawaki, A. Hirose, and E. Kamata, "Decreased Anogenital Distance and Increased Incidence of Undescended Testes in Fetuses of Rats Given Monobenzyl Phthalate, a Major Metabolite of Butyl Benzyl Phthalate," *Reproductive Toxicology,* volume 17, pp. 407–412, 2003.

47. Shanna Swan, E. P. Elkin, and L. Fenster, "The Question of Declining Sperm Density Revisited: An analysis of 101 studies published 1934–1996," *Environmental Health Perspectives,* volume 108, pp. 961–966. See also Professor Swan's more recent review article, "Does Our Environment Affect Our Fertility? Some examples to help reframe the question," *Seminars in Reproductive Medicine,* 24:142–146, 2006.

48. Shanna Swan, Fan Liu, and associates, "Geographic Differences in Semen Quality of Fertile U.S. Males," *Environmental Health Perspectives,* volume 111, pp. 414–420, 2003.

49. S. M. Duty, M. J. Silva, and associates, "Phthalate Exposure and Human Semen Parameters," *Epidemiology,* volume 14, pp. 269–277, 2003.

50. Jane Fisher, "Environmental Anti-androgens and Male Reproductive Health: Focus on phthalates and testicular dysgenesis syndrome," *Reproduction,* volume 127, pp. 305–315, 2004. See also Lise Aksglaede, Anders Juul, Henrik Leffers, Niels Skakkebæk, and Anna-Maria Andersson, "The Sensitivity of the Child to Sex Steroids: Possible impact of exogenous estrogens," *Human Reproduction Update,* volume 12, pp. 341–349, 2006.

51. Shanna Swan, "Parents Needn't Wait for Legislation to Shield Kids from Toxins in Products," *San Francisco Chronicle,* January 9, 2006.

Chapter 6

1. I am indebted to Walt Prichard for this anecdote—which he insists is a true story.

2. I hosted a symposium at the annual convention of the American Psychological Association in August 2005 on the topic of sex differences in hearing, vision, and smell. Among the presenters at my symposium was Dr. Pamela Dalton of the Monell Chemical Senses Center in Philadelphia. Dr. Dalton has conducted research showing that for many odors, women have a sense of smell that is one hundred thousand times more sensitive than any man's. She has published two articles on this topic:

1. Pamela Dalton and associates, "Gender-Specific Induction of Enhanced Sensitivity to Odors," *Nature Neuroscience,* volume 5, pp. 199–200, March 2002;

2. Jeanmarie Diamond, Pamela Dalton, Nadine Doolittle, and Paul A.S. Breslin, "Gender-Specific Olfactory Sensitization: Hormonal and cognitive influences," *Chemical Senses,* volume 30, supplement 1, pp. 224–225, 2005.

3. According to Miller & Long's web site, www.millerandlong.com, Miller & Long is "the largest concrete contractor in the United States."

4. Charles Murray, *Wall Street Journal,* January 17, 2007, "What's Wrong with Vocational School?" The full text of this article is available online at no charge at this link: http://www.aei.org/publications/filter.all,pubID.25464 /pub_detail.asp.

5. All quotes from Dr. Murray in this paragraph are from his essay for the *Wall Street Journal,* January 17, 2007, "What's Wrong with Vocational School?"

6. E-mail from Professor Judith Kleinfeld, January 19, 2007.

7. The analysis was "The State of American Manhood," by Tom Mortenson, writing for the September 2006 edition of *Postsecondary Education Opportunity,* www.postsecondary.org.

8. Louis Uchitelle, David Leonhardt, and Amanda Cox, "Men Not Working, and Not Wanting Just Any Job," *New York Times,* July 31, 2006, pp. A1, A18, A19.

9. There are such men; I can think of three in my practice here in Maryland—three full-time stay-at-home fathers, in a practice of seven thousand patients. Admirably, these men are beginning to organize and promote their cause. Check out www.DadStaysHome.com, www.rebeldad.com, and www.slowlane.com. I especially like http://www.slowlane.com/articles/mcclain /mr_mom_dont.html, with its "Ten Things Not to Say" to a full-timedad. My favorite on the list: don't call a full-time dad "Mr. Mom," The kids already have a mom. Try calling him "Mr. Dad."

10. Laura Sessions Stepp, *Unhooked: How young women pursue sex, delay love and lose at both,* New York: Riverhead/Penguin, 2007, p. 8.

11. Tom Roberts, "To Be Married Means to Be Outnumbered," *New York Times,* October 15, 2006.

12. Eduardo Porter and Michelle O'Donnell, "Facing Middle Age with No Degree, and No Wife," *New York Times,* August 6, 2006.

13. Blaine Harden, "Numbers Drop for the Married with Children," *Washington Post,* March 4, 2007.

14. Eduardo Porter and Michelle O'Donnell, "Facing Middle Age with No Degree, and No Wife," *New York Times,* August 6, 2006, p. A18.

15. Leonard Sax, "What's Happening to Boys?" *Washington Post,* March 31, 2006. Available online at no charge at www.BoysAdrift.com.

16. Eduardo Porter and Michelle O'Donnell, "Facing Middle Age With No Degree, and No Wife," *New York Times,* August 6, 2006.

17. Sam Roberts, Ariel Sabar, Brenda Goodman, and Maureen Balleza, "51 Percent of Women Are Now Living without Spouse," *New York Times,* January 16, 2007.

18. There is no recent, comprehensive, demographically reliable survey addressing the frequency of masturbation among young adults in the United States. However, studies of young people in disparate developed countries such as Hong Kong and Australia suggest that young people in developed countries today are engaging in similar sexual practices with similar frequency, whether they are Asian or Western. For example, compare the report by Mohsen Janghorbani and Tai Lam, "Sexual Media Use by Young Adults in Hong Kong: Prevalence and associated factors," *Archives of Sexual Behavior,* volume 32, pp. 545–553, 2003, with the report by Richters, Grulich, deVisser and associates, "Sex in Australia: Autoerotic, esoteric and other sexual practices engaged in by a representative sample of adults," *Australia and New Zealand Journal of Public Health,* volume 27, pp. 180–190, 2003. The high frequency of masturbation among young men suggested in these studies is certainly in agreement with a nonscientific study conducted by *NOW,* a Toronto lifestyle magazine. Their results are posted online at http://www.nowtoronto.com/minisites/loveandsex /2006/survey.cfm. However, this survey is subject to all the problems of a nonscientific sample. In particular, we have no way of knowing whether respondents to this survey or others like it are a representative sample of young adults.

19. See for example Jennifer Schneider's paper, "A Qualitative Study of Cybersex Participants: Gender differences, recovery issues, and implications for therapists," *Sexual Addiction and Compulsivity,* volume 7, pp. 249–278, 2000. Schneider found many men who had experienced an "escalating pattern of compulsive cybersex use after they discovered Internet sex."

20. Martin Kafka and John Hennen, "The Paraphilia-Related Disorders: An empirical investigation of nonparaphilic hypersexuality disorders in outpatient males," *Journal of Sex and Marital Therapy,* volume 25, pp. 305–319, 1999.

21. Najah S. Musacchio, Molly Hartrich, and Robert Garofalo, "Erectile Dysfunction and Viagra Use: What's up with college-age males?" *Journal of Adolescent Health,* volume 39, pp. 452–454, 2006. These authors surveyed sexually active males age eighteen to twenty-five years. Thirty-five percent overall reported erectile dysfunction: 25 percent only with condom use (which might well discourage those men from future condom use); 13 percent in other circumstances; 9 percent both with condom use and in other circumstances.

22. The article I wrote was "What's Happening to Boys?" published in the *Washington Post,* March 31, 2006. The e-mail I quoted was written not directly in response to the article, but in follow up to the online real-time chat hosted by

the *Washington Post*, based on my article. You can read the full transcript of the online chat at www.BoysAdrift.com.

23. The monograph in question is *Net.seXXX: Readings on sex, pornography, and the Internet*, edited by Dennis Waskul, New York: Peter Lang Publishing, 2004. The quote is from Andreas Philaretou's review of this monograph, which appeared in the *Journal of Sex Research*, volume 42, p. 180, 2005.

24. Andreas Philaretou, "Sexuality and the Internet," *Journal of Sex Research*, volume 42, p. 181, 2005.

25. The most astute of these critiques is, in my opinion, Ariel Levy's *Female Chauvinist Pigs: Women and the rise of raunch culture*, New York: Free Press, 2005. A less incisive but still useful book on the same topic is Pamela Paul's *Pornified: How pornography is transforming our lives, our relationships, and our families*, New York: Times Books, 2004.

26. For a lengthy survey of this phenomenon, see the cover story of *Newsweek*, February 12, 2007, "Girls Gone Bad," by Kathleen Deveny with Raina Kelley, available online at http://www.msnbc.msn.com/id/16961761 /site/newsweek/.

27. You can read the full transcript of the *Washington Post* chat and my original op-ed for no charge at www.BoysAdrift.com.

28. You can read this man's comment and my reply in full at www .BoysAdrift.com.

29. You can link to streaming audio of the "On Point" interview at www .BoysAdrift.com.

30. NPR correspondent Sylvia Poggioli noted in February 2007 that one-half of Italian men between the ages of 25 and 35 are still living at home with their mothers. You can link to streaming audio of her story at www.BoysAdrift.com. The CBS newsmagazine *60 Minutes* did a story on the growing proportion of Italian men who are remaining unmarried, remaining home with their parents. The story aired on March 4, 2001. You can find out more, and purchase the video, at this link: http://store.cbs.com/item.php?id=1062&sid=581.

31. For a detailed and scholarly overview of the *hikkikomori*, see Michael Zielenziger's book *Shutting Out the Sun: How Japan created its own lost generation*, New York: Nan A. Talese, 2006.

Chapter 7

1. I am grateful to my former patient Anders Eklof for suggesting this title.

2. J. R. Moehringer, *The Tender Bar*, New York: Hyperion, 2005.

3. Moehringer, p. 39.

4. David Brooks, "Virtues and Victims," *New York Times*, April 9, 2006.

5. David Gilmore, *Manhood in the Making: Cultural concepts of masculinity*, New Haven: Yale University Press, 1990, pp. 14–15.

6. Gilmore, p. 25.

7. "Florida Searches for Root of Surge in Violent Crime; Orlando, other areas see big jumps in a year," *USA Today*, November 1, 2006.

8. "Head-on Response to Gangs: Police confront growing threat," Steven Rosenberg, *Boston Globe*, November 9, 2006.

9. Andy Paras, "Rural Areas Sprout Gangs; More than half of agencies in South Carolina law enforcement survey report gang activity," *The Post and Courier*, September 30, 2006.

10. Elisabeth Griffith, PhD, personal communication, November 6, 2003.

11. Thorkil Vanggaard, *Phallos: A symbol and its history in the male world*, New York: International Universities Press, 1972. For more about the status of homosexuality among the Spartans and other ancient Greeks, see chapter 3, "Phallic Worship in Ancient Greece," pp. 59–70.

12. Actually there are, or were, two cultures on record that break these rules: two cultures in which brave men were not esteemed above cowards, in which hardworking men were not celebrated: Tahiti and Semai. You will find a detailed discussion of these two exceptions at www.BoysAdrift.com.

13. I am referring of course to the Kinaaldá ceremony. For a lightweight but wonderfully photographed introduction to the Kinaaldá ceremony, I recommend Monty Roessel's photographic essay, *Kinaaldá: A Navajo girl grows up*, Minneapolis: Lerner, 1993.

14. Peggy Drexler, *Raising Boys without Men: How maverick moms are creating the next generation of exceptional men*, Emmaus, PA: Rodale, 2006, p. 92.

15. David Gilmore, *Manhood in the Making: Cultural concepts of masculinity*, New Haven: Yale University Press, 1990, p. 11.

16. Gilmore, p. 150.

17. Gilmore, p. 95.

18. Jeffrey P. Hantover, "The Boy Scouts and the Validation of Masculinity," *Journal of Social Issues*, volume 34, pp. 184–195, 1978. See also Julia Grant's article "A 'Real Boy' and Not a Sissy: Gender, childhood, and masculinity, 1890–1940," *Journal of Social History*, volume 37, Summer 2004,

available online at http://www.findarticles.com/p/articles/mi_m2005/is_4_37
/ai_n6137399/pg_1.

19. Alfred Habegger, *Gender, Fantasy, and Realism in American Literature*,
New York: Columbia University Press, 1982, pp. 199–200.

20. David Gilmore, *Manhood in the Making: Cultural concepts of masculinity*,
New Haven: Yale University Press, 1990, p. 108.

21. Gilmore, p. 136.

22. Gilmore, p. 141.

23. Gilmore, p. 145.

24. Gilmore, p. 39.

25. Dr. Kline gave her panel the name "The Commission on Children at
Risk"—arguably a misnomer, since the panel commissioned itself. The group
met face-to-face at Dartmouth Medical School, then proceeded to write eighteen scholarly papers culminating in the monograph *Hardwired to Connect: The
new scientific case for authoritative communities*. In addition to Dartmouth
Medical School, principal sponsors of the panel's activities included the Institute for American Values and YMCA of America. The panel does not have a
Web site, but more information about its activities is available at hardwiredto
connect@dartmouth.edu. Copies of the monograph *Hardwired to Connect* are
most easily obtained from the Institute for American Values, 1841 Broadway,
Suite 211, New York, NY 10023. Copies can be ordered online at the IAV Web
site, http://www.americanvalues.org/html/hardwired.html.

26. As of February 2007, the most recent reports available from the CDC were
for calendar year 2003. See "Deaths: Final Data for 2003," *National Vital Statistics
Reports*, volume 54, Hyattsville, MD: National Center for Health Statistics, 2006.
Online at http://www.cdc.gov/nchs/data/nvsr/nvsr54/nvsr54_13.pdf.

27. "The State of American Manhood," by Tom Mortenson, writing for the
September 2006 edition of *Postsecondary Education Opportunity*, www.postsec
ondary.org, p. 20.

28. *Hardwired to Connect* (see reference 25 above), p. 10.

29. Sherry Benton and associates, "Changes in Counseling Center Client
Problems across 13 Years," *Professional Psychology: Research and practice*, volume 34, p. 69, 2003.

30. *Hardwired to Connect* (see reference 25 above), p. 10.

31. Alison Cooper, "One Mazda, Two Mishaps, and a Couple of Lessons in
Parenting," *Washington Post*, November 19, 2006, p. B8.

32. On March 31, 2006, CNN anchor Lou Dobbs referred to Mexican immigrants as an "army of invaders" intent on reannexing parts of the southwestern United States to Mexico. On November 19, 2003, Dobbs asserted that "illegal alien smugglers and drug traffickers are on the verge of ruining some of our national treasures," and on April 14, 2005, Dobbs stated that "the invasion of illegal aliens is threatening the health of many Americans," These quotes are excerpted from the Web page "CNN's Immigration Problem: Is Dobbs the exception—or the rule?" at www.fair.org/index.php?page=2867.

33. *Hardwired to Connect* (see note 25), pp. 23, 24.

34. Harvey Mansfield, *Manliness,* New Haven: Yale University Press, 2006, p. 17.

35. Mansfield, p. 23.

36. Mansfield, p. 20.

37. Mansfield, p. 20.

38. You can read the entire APA report, or just a summary, at no charge, at this link: http://www.apa.org/pi/wpo/sexualization.html.

39. American Psychological Association, Task Force on the Sexualization of Girls, *Report of the APA Task Force on the Sexualization of Girls,* Washington, DC: American Psychological Association, 2007, pp. 8–9.

Chapter 8

1. Rhea Borja, "Nebraska Swims Hard against Testing's Tides," *Education Week,* February 21, 2007, pp. 32, 33, 34.

2. More information about the change in federal regulations legalizing single-sex education in public schools is available at www.singlesexschools .org/html; click on "Policy."

3. Betsy Stahler and Jill Renn spoke at the NASSPE Midwest Regional Conference in Lisle, Illinois, on October 14, 2006. As this book goes to press, both Ms. Stahler and Ms. Renn have agreed to give an updated presentation on this topic at the NASSPE National Conference in Lincolnshire, Illinois, October 6th and 7th, 2007. More information about both conferences is available at www.singlesexschools.org.

4. *NEA Today,* the monthly newsmagazine of the National Education Association, published a feature article in 2006 about the success of Jeff Ferguson's all-boys classroom. It's a great article—except for the title, which is "No Girls Allowed." You can read the online version of the article at this link: http://www .nea.org/neatoday/0604/singlesex.html.

5. Roland Gorges, "Der Waldkindergarten," *Unsere Jugend,* Spring 2000, pp. 275–281.

6. In 1997, there were fewer than two dozen *Waldkindergärten* in Germany. As of December 2006, one online directory lists 517 *Waldkindergärten* (go to www.es-info.de/waldkindergarten/db-start.htm).

7. All quotes in these two paragraphs come from George P. Blumberg's article for the *New York Times,* "Full Throttle and Fully Legal," September 17, 2004.

Another footnote: in 2005, Professor Bender and I submitted a proposal to the American Psychological Society (since renamed the Association for Psychological Science) to present a symposium at their annual meeting. Dr. Bender and I wanted to bring the news about RaceLegal and similar programs to a wider audience of psychologists and counselors. The APS declined our proposal: instead, they hosted a series of symposia on the benefits of applying cognitive psychology in the classroom. If you read chapter 2 of this book, you'll appreciate the irony of that choice.

8. Bill Center, "RaceLegal Praised for Contributing to Decline in Street Racing," *San Diego Union-Tribune,* December 22, 2005.

9. See my op-ed article "Teens Will Speed; Let's watch them do it," *Washington Post,* November 28, 2004, p. B8.

10. A more accurate answer would make reference to the recent discovery of significant sex differences in the wiring of the autonomic nervous system. For most girls, and some boys, the *parasympathetic* division of the autonomic nervous system predominates. For gender-typical boys like this boy, however, the *sympathetic* division of the autonomic nervous system has greater control. These boys typically prefer cooler room temperatures (69° F rather than 75° F) and they may very well enjoy hitting and being hit. References to the relevant literature are provided in my 2006 review, "Six Degrees of Separation: What teachers need to know about the emerging science of sex differences," *Educational Horizons,* Spring 2006, pp. 190–200, available online at www.BoysAdrift.com.

11. Elizabeth Roberts, "A Rush to Medicate Young Minds," *Washington Post,* October 8, 2006, p. B7.

12. Amanda Datnow, Lea Hubbard, and Elisabeth Woody, *Is Single Gender Schooling Viable in the Public Sector?* Ford Foundation, 2001. Available online via http://www.oise.utoronto.ca/depts/tps/adatnow/final.pdf.

13. Datnow, Hubbard, and Woody, p. 7.

14. See Blaine Harden's article "Numbers Drop for the Married with Children," *Washington Post*, March 4, 2007. See also Neely Tucker, "Dad, Redefined; He's not there in the house, will he be there for his son?" *Washington Post*, December 17, 2006, pp. A1, A24.

15. All quotes in these two paragraphs come from Lonnae O'Neal Parker's article for the *Washington Post*, December 29, 2006, pp. A1, A10.

16. For an introduction to Campbell's ideas, there is no better choice than the book he cowrote with Bill Moyers (based on the PBS television series they did together), *The Power of Myth*, New York: Anchor, 1991.

17. These biographical details are based on Alice Rains Trulock's biography, *In the Hands of Providence: Joshua L. Chamberlain and the American Civil War*, Chapel Hill: University of North Carolina Press, 1992. See also Edward Longacre's *Joshua Chamberlain: The Soldier and the man*, Da Capo Press (reprint edition), 2003.

18. Glenn LaFantasie has challenged the conventional view regarding the strategic significance of the events on Little Round Top, in particular with regard to the bayonet charge. He asserts that the 15th Alabama was not preparing a sixth charge up the hill and may in fact have been preparing to retreat—which might explain their hasty surrender in response to the bayonet charge. See his book *Twilight at Little Round Top: July 2, 1863—the tide turns at Gettysburg*, Hoboken, NJ: John Wiley & Sons, 2005. For the more traditional view, see for example Michael Shaara's Pulitzer Prize–Winning *The Killer Angels*, on which the movie *Gettysburg* was based. Shaara made Chamberlain a major character in his account of the battle, which is drawn from letters and diary entries of the combatants. See also Stephen W. Sears, *Gettysburg*, New York: Houghton Mifflin, 2003.

19. Glenn LaFantasie, *Twilight at Little Round Top: July 2, 1863—the tide turns at Gettysburg*, Hoboken, NJ: John Wiley & Sons, 2005, p. 172.

20. Glenn LaFantasie, *Twilight at Little Round Top: July 2, 1863—the tide turns at Gettysburg*, Hoboken, NJ: John Wiley & Sons, 2005, p. 189.

21. Stephen W. Sears, *Gettysburg*, New York: Houghton Mifflin, 2003, p. 296.

22. Innumerable eyewitness records document this account and historians are agreed on its veracity. See for example Alice Rains Trulock, *In the Hands of Providence: Joshua L. Chamberlain and the American Civil War*, Chapel Hill: University of North Carolina Press, 1992, pp. 304–306.

23. This book is not the appropriate forum for a detailed discussion of the case for single-sex education. You'll find more relevant information online at the web site of the National Association for Single Sex Public Education (NASSPE), www.singlesexschools.org. Even better, you might consider attending one of NASSPE's conferences or workshops.

24. Sharon Begley's book—published January 2, 2007—is titled *Train Your Mind, Change Your Brain: How a new science reveals our extraordinary potential to transform ourselves,* New York: Ballantine Books, 2007. See especially chapter 6, "Mind over Matter: Mental activity changes the brain."

INDEX